Urban Play

Urban Play

Make-Believe, Technology, and Space

Fábio Duarte and Ricardo Álvarez

The MIT Press
Cambridge, Massachusetts
London, England

This book was set in Stone Serif and Stone Sans by Westchester Publishing Services. Printed and bound in the United States of America.

Library of Congress Cataloging-in-Publication Data

Names: Duarte, Fábio, 1970- author. | Álvarez, Ricardo , 1974- author.
Title: Urban play : make-believe, technology, and space / Fábio Duarte and
    Ricardo Álvarez.
Description: Cambridge, Massachusetts ; London, England : The MIT Press,
    [2021] | Includes bibliographical references and index.
Identifiers: LCCN 2020047250 | ISBN 9780262045346 (Paperback)
Subjects: LCSH: Public spaces--Psychological aspects. | Play environments. |
    Augmented reality. | Digital media--Psychological aspects.
Classification: LCC NA9053.S6 D85 2021 | DDC 711/.558--dc23
LC record available at https://lccn.loc.gov/2020047250

10 9 8 7 6 5 4 3 2 1

To Mona, Emiliano, Maria José, Mateo, Mom, and Dad
To Vanessa and Valentina
This is for you

Contents

Introduction: Playfulness and Technology

Never underestimate the power of play.

Human history can be told in many ways. One way is to use technological breakthroughs as landmarks, organizing our narratives around key moments in history when particular technologies lead to a radical reorganization of society. We don't need to go as far back as the prehistoric wheel or even the more recent discovery of electricity or the invention of the Internet to get an idea of the societal transformations technology can bring about. At each step technology changes our understanding of the world, how we relate to each other, how we transform nature, and how new concepts are conceived and spread across large territories and different cultures. It influences how we create—how we express our values, concepts, and sentiments. Technology also transforms the way we envision and build the future. In this sense, technology can be understood as a medium, as a way of expressing and shaping worldviews. Often new ideas and experiences emerge, are socially molded and spread through technology.

This book focuses on how playful technology influences spatial design and can be used to create resonant spaces, that is, spaces that go beyond mere functionalism and achieve an emotional response from people using them. We are interested in the critical moments when technology is seminal in reshaping how we experience and design spaces. At these transformational moments, design reaches its full potential as an intellectual tool for exploring uncharted terrains of creativity. When we are engulfed in such transformational moments, it is not yet certain if an idea will work or not; if it will be accepted or rejected by society; if it is the result of a whim that will

soon fade into a background of myriad gadgets and technological experimentations, all with different degrees of success; or, more occasionally, if it
will be the idea that will reshape how we experience spaces. Uncertainty is
the baseline of transformational moments.

When technology becomes central to the mainstream process of spatial
design, when it becomes well established among practitioners and society,
its value tends to lie more in its functionalities, and risk-taking and new
explorations fade away. In its mainstream phase, the technology has already
proven its value, it works as expected under a given set of circumstances,
and it enables certain procedures; the results, as varied as they might seem,
are still within a circumscribed range of what can be expected from the
technology.

Of course, technology should not be confused with an artifact or the
material components that are arranged together in a particular way. The
windmill is an artifact, as is the computer or a piece of software; but accompanying any well-established technological artifact is a set of principles,
rules, languages, and behaviors that are shared by a community that has
integrated this technology into its social fabric. Established technologies
play functional roles within certain groups in particular and within society in general. Such technologies are powerful because of, or despite, their
predictability. While we can count on their outcomes, and we organize part
of society and arrange our lives around them, we often absorb their use in
surprising ways.

However, in the early stages of its development, any technology is messy
and uncertain. Experiments fail multiple times, machines produce unforeseeable outputs, or things simply don't work. But technologies, in their nascent
phases, also open up multiple possibilities. In many areas—particularly in
those that involve creativity, such as spatial design—emergent technologies
bring with them possibilities of imagining, proposing, and experiencing
spaces in unexpected and novel ways.

Thinking about the future of emergent technologies is an exciting pros-
pect. On the one hand, the future is fundamentally unpredictable: we cannot be certain how it will happen, or even if it will occur at all. But on the
other hand, the future is pretty predictable, or highly probable: if no major
event happens, we can be fairly confident what our tomorrow will be,
minor occurrences aside. The same happens with spatial design. Take any
city in which a set of building regulations exist: each new building needs

to be designed within this regulatory framework and needs to go through a usually lengthy process of approvals by a series of authorities and boards as if each of the proposed buildings were unique. But how often does a building actually surprise you? How often does a building really change how people experience space? In Italo Calvino's *Invisible Cities* (1978), Marco Polo amazes Kublai Khan with his descriptions of all the fantastic cities he has visited in the vast Mongol empire; however, at a certain point Khan interrupts Polo and himself describes a city in all its details, a city he has never visited. Asked how he is able do that, Khan says that by finding patterns in Polo's descriptions of so many cities he can also describe a city in minute detail, even if he hasn't set foot there; and even if this city does not exist, it is credible enough. When Khan asks Polo to describe his hometown of Venice, Polo replies that with every city he mentions, he is always saying something about Venice. Patterns and reference models constitute a mental framework we use to make sense and create spaces.

This predictability relies on established norms, behaviors, and technologies. With nascent technologies, however, these norms and behaviors are not yet consolidated, which makes the results unpredictable. And this is exciting! Many of our attempts to imagine and build technologies and the future they promise will turn out to be fundamentally flawed. But some technologies will be transformational. Thus, the central argument of this book is that technology is powerful not when it becomes optimally functional but when it is essentially playful—when imagining and tinkering with technology equals imagining and tinkering with possible futures. This is particularly important today. Take a look at scholarly journals and technical magazines dedicated to urban issues, and one particular term will stand out: "smart cities." The concept of smart cities has increasingly been guiding academic research, private investment, and real estate development. Regardless of the different emphasis that marketing departments or academic gurus may place on particular aspects of this concept, the general goal of smart cities is to make cities more efficient—and what easier way is there to be more efficient than by enhancing predictability? However, accompanying any prevalent narrative there is a counterdiscourse constituted of the same basic substance. Gabriel Mugar and Eric Gordon (2020) propose the concept of "meaningful inefficiencies" as a civic design strategy that privileges less efficient means to achieve some goals, but with the advantage of building trust among participants along the way. Civic design becomes stronger and gets social support by embracing meaningful inefficiencies, which is inherent to the voluntary nature of play (players can leave the playing field at any time), which, in turn, allows players to reflect on the rules and limitations around which play is defined.

Programmable City is a project led by Rob Kitchin at the National University of Ireland, Maynooth, that investigates the role of digital technologies, the translation of urban phenomena into data and code, and how an understanding of these processes can inform infrastructure management and city governance.[1] Kitchin is a critic of smart cities, conscious that by codifying the world into rules, algorithms, and databases, the ultimate goal is to make cities highly predictable with optimized processes—or as he puts it, programmable. However, within the smart cities discourse, technology (and software in particular, in Kitchin's argument) is seen as immaterial and neutral, as if it should be shielded from criticism, whereas his approach is to unveil and discuss the complex and mutable set of economic and discursive relations that create and empower such technologies (Kitchin, 2011). And yet, Kitchin's Programmable City initiatives in the city of Dublin revolve around urban management dashboards (if the whole smart cities movement could be reduced to one iconic element, the epitome of efficiency, it would be the urban management dashboard).

Playable City goes in the opposite direction.[2] Started in Bristol, England, this project acknowledges that cities are permeated by digital technologies, but rather than using these technologies to improve urban management, it promotes interactive installations that bring citizens together through technology to engage in and enjoy collectively often unexpected urban experiences. In 2014 Jonathan Chomko and Matthew Rosier received the Playable City Award for their project Shadowing, which plays with a staple artifact in many smart cities: streetlights that react to people's presence, dimming to save energy when there is nobody in the vicinity.[3] For the Shadowing project, when an augmented streetlight detects a pedestrian it not only lights up but also projects on the sidewalk the shadows of other people who passed the streetlight earlier. When pedestrians realize these tricks, they often begin to play with the shadows, promoting imaginary encounters between unknown people who shared the same space at different times. Combining high tech with public engagement and frequently satirical criticism of smart cities, Playable City projects look for bugs and challenge the prescriptive narratives usually employed in smart cities initiatives (Nijholt, 2017).

Different versions of the Playable City project can be found in Melbourne, Tokyo, Tel Aviv, London, São Paulo, and Austin, Texas.

Artificial intelligence and new techniques that did not exist or were in a very rudimentary phase less than ten years ago, such as convolutional neural networks and machine learning, are allowing us to tackle problems that were thought to be outside the realm of existing computational knowledge. Artificial intelligence has beaten the world chess and Go champions and is powering vehicles that can drive autonomously in congested urban areas. These initiatives have been attracting the attention not only of specialists but also of the general public, sometimes in unexpected ways. Augmented reality, the merging of synthetic images with the physical world around us, which is now the object of considerable attention among technologists and designers, was a niche area of research until 2016, when Niantic launched *Pokémon Go* and brought augmented reality to the general public. With the launch of the game, millions of people around the world began to use their mobile devices to chase Pokémon virtually embedded in real cities. These virtual creatures can appear in specific locations, sometimes triggered by physical features of the space but usually because the mobile device is at a specific geolocation. In the field of video games, immersive and massively collaborative games such as *Fortnite*, *Minecraft*, and *Destiny* show new ways of connecting people through creative technologies.

The merely functional aspects of technology can work against technology itself. They may actually undermine its transformational power. Take the Rio de Janeiro Operations Center (COR) in Brazil. Praised by countless smart-cities advocates and gurus, but also strongly criticized by scholars and civic organizations, it brings together representatives from thirty different municipal authorities to a central physical location and collects data from multiple locations around the city in an Orwellian control room. Created in 2010, the technology used at the COR (again, considered as a set of artifacts, principles, norms, and behaviors) soon became outdated. While the mayor and technocrats were still praising the Dr. Strangelove approach to a central control room, in the streets of Rio de Janeiro people were chasing Pokémon: digital technologies were already enmeshed in the urban fabric in ways that the dozens of cameras deployed by the city to monitor the streets, beaches, and favelas would never catch.

Technology is powerful when it is playful, when fiction, fantasy, and shameless failures are allowed into the creative process of technological development and deployment. Technology has a transformational impact on spatial design when designers are simultaneously *tinkerers* and *dreamers*, when they are experimenting with technological possibilities across space, time, and social scenarios. It is fundamentally the realm of flexible and impermanent design that feeds and transforms the ways we experience and enjoy space. These experiments can lead to more consolidated approaches to spatial design, but this is another story that comes later in the creative process. Here we want to explore the argument that playfulness is an essential part of technology, particularly when this technology may drive profound transformations in spatial design.

In the 1960s Marshall McLuhan, originally a professor of literature in Canada, wrote several groundbreaking books on the transformational power of technology. McLuhan was not the first scholar to focus on the fundamental role of technology in human history, but his emphasis on popular media was not common. And, importantly, his focus was on the media itself, not its content. In the sixteenth century, printed books were subversive not because of their content but because they allowed the written word to circulate faster and without intermediaries. No more scribes manually copying religious manuscripts (sometimes altering and censoring passages) in monasteries secluded from the external world. On the contrary, the printing press allowed the same text to be printed thousands of times. One copy of a certain book was exactly the same as any other. More books in circulation meant more laypeople interested in learning to read and having direct access to religious canons without members of religious orders and congregations as intermediaries; and, equally radical, these texts, including the Catholic Bible, were translated into and printed in modern languages, not Latin, allowing laypeople to read them and make sense of them in their own way. McLuhan (1962) advanced the idea of the Gutenberg press as mass media, having a similar transformational social role as newspapers, radio, television, and the Internet centuries later.

One of McLuhan's most famous maxims, "the medium is the message," could go hand in hand with the idea that humans and nonhumans influence each other and in fact form an assemblage, in which characteristics of both influence the very properties of each element. There is no human existence in isolation from our surroundings, which include the nonhuman (e.g., nature), the inhuman (e.g., images and imaginaries), and human-made devices. Thus, technology is not a separate entity but part of the human ecosystem, and it defines our very existence. Humans are technological creatures in the sense that virtually all our relations with the world are mediated by technological artifacts—from ancient stone tools for killing animals for food to computers that process abstracts ideas in codified nota-tion and outperform humans in speed and complexity. But as Bruno Latour (1996) points out, we should avoid the subject-object distinction between humans and nonhumans, just as we should avoid projecting subjectivi-ties onto things or treating humans as objects. Whenever technology is referred to in this book, we mean the mediated relations that occur between humans and nonhumans.

In fact, Vilem Flusser (1995) notes that the words *machine* and *mechanics* come from the Greek *mechos*, a device meant to aid in deception; that the origin of the word *technique* is *technos*, or art, which points to the mutation of one thing into another; and that both words, *mechos* and *technos*, are linked to the notion of design, which can mean "to shape" or "to simulate." In this sense, design and technology point toward the transformation of something into something else while keeping the original substance. As when a sculptor carves marble: we marvel at the muscular bodies of Roman marble sculptures, the clothes and foliage blowing in an imaginary wind. All of this is design because what is actually there before our eyes, for our hands to touch, is only a piece of rock. Flusser is right to say that in all design there is an element of self-deception, an idea we will return to later.

At some point technologies and design achieve a certain stability, allow-ing them to become common ground for larger social groups. But creativity emerges in moments of instability, when a new technology overthrows a well-established one, or from within, when internal, often minute changes slowly move a technology so far from what it once was that it becomes a completely different technology. These periods of experimentation and instability favor playfulness over efficiency. Going off the beaten track might make the journey longer, lead to an impassable cliff, or be dangerous, but it is only by playing that we explore new territories, create new devices and languages, and transform ourselves. We must never underestimate the power of play.

In this book we combine theoretical reflections on the role of play in spatial design triggered by technological transformations with discussions of precedents, current immersive technologies, and architectural and urban experimentations in which playfulness has transformed spatial experiences and design. We pay special attention to contemporary technologies that have the potential to change how designers imagine spaces and how people experience spaces. We end the book by briefly discussing the challenges of forming new generations of designers who will embrace the notion that creativity will come from playing with new technologies in uncharted ways. Such endeavors will not always be more efficient, but they may lead to technological breakthroughs and unprecedented spatial concepts and experiences.

*   *   *

The book begins with a discussion of the importance of the act of play, in the chapter "Orchestrating Serendipity." As is probably clear by now, when we mention "play" we are not interested in the objective of play—as when we are playing sports, in which goals are defined beforehand. This is only one use of the verb *play*, a use that entails specific goals constrained by rules and expected behaviors. By contrast, here play is explored in its essential meaning of acting for one's own enjoyment rather than to achieve any exogenous purpose. To be sure, professional players enjoy themselves when playing, even if the goal is to score points or defeat an opponent. But in these situations as well, we highlight the playfulness within the play—that is, within the rules of the game. More importantly, we make the case that play has human importance (social, intellectual, and psychological) far beyond the objectives of the play itself. The conceptual basis of the chapter is Johan Huizinga's *Homo Ludens*, originally published in 1938, the main thesis of which is precisely that play is an act with intrinsic purposes, not dependent on previous motivations or expected intentions. Play is what happens in creative processes, which are full of serendipitous moments when the unexpected and unforeseeable take control of the situation and change the path one was following, sometimes leading to novel results that will change accepted paradigms and the rules of the game.

Playing often entails consciously entering states of self-deception. When children play, they know that none of them is a ghost or vampire or butterfly; but only by entering this world of make-believe can they experience the enjoyment of play. This is similar to what happens when actors are impersonating characters. The lead actors in *Romeo and Juliet* are not actually Romeo and Juliet, and the troupe and audience know that; but impersonating the characters, believing in the impersonation and entering this self-deceptive state are what allow us to project ourselves onto the play and understand ourselves as individuals and society in all our nuances, accepting fears, passions, and prejudices that we would otherwise ignore, put aside, or not admit openly. In self-deception, we accept an experience as truthful even though we are aware that it is not. Sometimes it is as if there were a switch and we were constantly aware that at any moment we could flick the switch and the state of self-deception would end; but other times we don't have any psychological or physiological control over self-deception. As we discuss in the chapter "Artifices of Self-Deception," self-deception plays a fundamental role in the construction of human subjectivity and our ability to build interpersonal ties. Self-deception is also of vital importance in expanding our perception and understanding of space—from the architecture of Disney World to video games and virtual reality, all of which play with our imagination, our social interaction, and our physiological perception of space, combining self-deception with immersive experiences.

These chapters in which we discuss fundamental concepts of the book are followed by examples that aim to test our argument that technology has a transformational impact on spatial design when it is playful. If make-believe is an important aspect of play, and play is powerful in transforming spatial design, we may ask: Is it possible, and is it worth it, to materialize make-believe worlds? In the chapter "Embodying Fantasies," we discuss examples in which fantasies were built into the physical world and how these projects have been extending their influence to other aspects of spatial design. The iconic example of an embodied fantasy is Disney World.

Disney opened its first park, Disneyland, in California in 1955. After ten years, one-quarter of the US population had visited the park (King, 1981). In 1971 Disney World opened in Florida. Technology has played an important role in creating and keeping this fantasy space alive since its inception. Less than one year after the park opened, *New York Times* critic Paul Goldberger (1972) reported that architects and planners were fascinated by Disney World, particularly the technological achievements it incorporated, most of which were behind the scenes: separate levels for services, vacuum tubes to collect waste crisscrossing the park, and the monorail moving visitors. Added to this infrastructure was the sense of amazement and welcoming that enchanted millions of visitors—and in cases like the Main Street or EPCOT, the embodying of visitors' fantasies of what urban spaces ought to be like. It is true that Disney World is a controlled environment, but as Margaret King (1981) puts it, the park encapsulates American myths, and the experimental approaches to the humanizing of technology that it adopted influenced design and forms of social interaction outside the entertainment world. The designer and architectural theorist Robert Venturi was an admirer of Disney World, saying it had given people what architects had been unable to give them for a long time (Goldberger, 1972). Fast-forward to 2020, and Disney World continues to be at the forefront of technological experimentation, creating mixed reality experiences that seamlessly combine virtual reality with tangible artifacts to promote spatial experiences that might soon be present in cities.

Examples of the embodiment of fantasies can be found in many real cities. An influential example is Las Vegas, and of particular importance is the analysis of the city by Robert Venturi, Denise Scott Brown, and Steven Izenour (1977), who showed how an iconic city could emerge out of a nondescript urban strip in the middle of the Nevada desert and influence contemporary urbanism. More recently, Dubai, in the United Arab Emirates, has been using leading-edge technology to create large parks that are green throughout the year, artificial islands in the shape of the world map, indoor ski slopes in the desert, and highly curated architectural follies. Dubai represents a "bingo urbanism" (82), "a post-polycentric urban pattern," (83) (Jensen, 2013) with thematic enclaves that break down any historical continuity or spatial references other than buildings designed to become immediate references in the global urban imagery. At the same time, media coverage has sought to shape the internal and external perception of the city. Efforts to unveil the "real Dubai" (Elsheshtawy, 2009) cannot escape the realization that Dubai's urbanism is indeed the true face of Dubai: it embodies multifaceted fantasies that combine leading-edge technology and globetrotter imagery, and it has been emulated all over the world.

In line with these experiments, designers are proposing projects in which the users' behavior, mediated by technology, is directly responsible for creating spatialities. These projects are usually on a smaller scale than the projects discussed in "Embodying Fantasies," are mainly built for temporary use, and are explicitly experimental—the ultimate goal is not to produce a permanent construction but to create architectural and spatial experiences powered by technological experimentation. Whereas all the elements in the projects discussed in "Embodying Fantasies" combine to direct—either explicitly or tacitly—users' enjoyment in spaces that are manufactured and often manicured to guide their experience, in the chapter "Tinkering with Spatialities" we discuss projects that come into existence only in response to the user's behavior. Here, playfulness is not only part of the project concept but also essential to its performance. In general, these projects are based on a combination of sensors and actuators in what has been called responsive architecture, a term stemming from the work of Nicholas Negroponte (1970), one of the founders of the Media Lab at the Massachusetts Institute of Technology (MIT).

Works discussed in this chapter include Carlo Ratti's Digital Water Pavilion, built for Expo 2008 in Zaragoza, Spain, and Guto Requena's Dancing Pavilion, created for the 2016 Olympic Games in Rio de Janeiro, Brazil. Sensors and actuators responding to environmental conditions and people's presence and behavior can be as trivial as doors that open automatically, heaters that adjust the ambient temperature according to thermostats, or lights that dim based on the number of occupants in a room. These are gadgets added to space in a purely functional way. Sometimes responses mediated by human–machine interaction go awry, as Jacques Tati showed in his movie *Mon Oncle* (1958), in which Monsieur Hulot explores his relatives' modern house full of automatic gadgets. In Tati's humorous critique, humans need to adapt their behavior to machines to make them work, leaving no room for spontaneity.

In both cases, from trivial automatic doors to the paraphernalia that has now taken over our houses, the basic features of the buildings do not change. However, in "Tinkering with Spatialities" we discuss examples in which it is the human-machine interaction that creates architecture. Both Ratti and Requena use technology not to add functionalities to buildings but to enhance people's experience of these spaces. This type of technological exploration can be found at the level of the building materials, such as the programmable textiles or fluid lattices produced by MIT's Self-Assembly Lab, as well as at the city scale, as with projects by the UK-based Blast Theory group that combine role-playing games based on locative media and communication technologies using the city as a playground. It is through the user's interaction with technology that unexpected spatialities are created. If people did not experiment with the technologies, the space itself could not even exist (as in the Digital Water Pavilion), or the architecture would be an empty box and would not transform the surroundings (as in the Dancing Pavilion).

Next we explore recent media that are slowly resonating among scholars and practitioners of spatial design. Video games and interactive media, such as virtual reality (VR) and augmented reality (AR), have learned extensively from architecture, urbanism, and other disciplines in their pursuit of the synthesis of place. Over the years, these media have led to the development of cultural values, design practices, and tools with an increasing focus on user experience and spatial sensory characteristics that go beyond those commonly used by urban designers and architects. This has been accomplished by infusing the design process with interactivity and participatory dynamics and leaving the resulting spaces open to variations depending on the users' behavior. Spatial design and placemaking can learn from the video game and interactive-media development process by incorporating features ranging from storytelling and multiple viewpoints to a collective engagement in self-deception, participatory practices, and flexible design.

We focus first on video games, which combine storytelling, shared narratives in multiplayer games, and spatial configurations that change depending on how players interact with each other and with the game environment. The change in spatial configurations is triggered by a concentration of visual and auditory stimuli in relatively contained spaces, which James Ash (2013, p. 31) calls "intense spaces." In "Orchestrating Serendipity," we argue that spatial design and video game development are much more closely related than would appear to be the case at first glance. Indeed, both share the creation of large-scale artificial environments for human interaction as their fundamental raison d'être. There is a rich literature on video game design, psychology, and sociology, which we discuss here. More specifically related to video game spaces are experimental works by multimedia artists that involve video games with enhanced spatial characteristics, as well as other works that try to show what might happen if video game spaces could spill out of the consoles into physical spaces. Although we mention some of these works, in the chapter "Learning from Video Games" we use a series of commercially available video games, from *Pac-Man* (1980) and *Super Mario Bros.* (1985) to *L.A. Noire* (2011), and *Assassin's Creed Odyssey* (2018) as well as interviews with game developers and designers who are integrating game engines into their design process, to discuss how the evolution of video games and current video game developments have the potential to inform the creative process underlying spatial design.

While video games have the power to change how we conceive and design spaces, other recent technologies might also radically transform how we experience space—in fact, they have already proven their power, influencing our spatial perception at a physiological level in a way no other technology has been able to. In the chapter "Virtual Reality, Empathy, and Design," we focus on virtual reality (VR) and augmented reality (AR) as technologies that create immersive experiences. While earlier VR technologies create a cocoon effect, as if we were entering a capsule within ordinary spaces, modern VR and AR systems can simulate the sensation of being present in synthetic worlds that stimulate us simultaneously at the cognitive and emotional levels. And as these technologies keep progressing, the power of the immersion is creating a mixed reality (MR) medium. In this chapter we explore what happens when such immersive technologies are enmeshed in space and generate mixed realities.

Moving beyond traditional two-dimensional surfaces, which require a certain degree of abstraction for communication purposes, VR conveys information in a more visceral way, allowing it to be absorbed directly through our senses—an example of how self-deception can be an intellectual tool to advance knowledge and try out novel approaches to spatial design. We look at the evolution of VR technologies, from their origins through the current state of the art to the foreseeable future, in order to critically analyze their potential implications for spatial-design practices. Equally exciting is the blending of the real and the virtual into a seamless hybrid reality, a possibility that AR systems have been exploring. With technologies such as onboard graphics processing, location sensors, and broadband telecommunications leaving the laboratories and becoming affordable, AR allows designers to create and experience a range of realities that hybridize the physical with the synthetic world in real time.

Drawing on interviews with VR and AR developers and practitioners, we reflect on the possibilities for design methods and languages afforded by the medium while exploring the way different studios and designers are shaping the new frontiers of experiential design. In this hypermediatized future of hybrid realities, how will we ultimately experience space? The answer to this question lies in imagining how our human condition will be challenged and enhanced by these new media forms.

In all these examples we see the emergence of characteristics that might change how we imagine, design, and experience spaces. Spatial narratives

shared across cultures, fostered by the use of artificial intelligence techniques adopted by designers to explore new forms of spatialities in which
humans, nonhumans, nature, and technology interact and influence each
other. Although these technologies have a transformational impact on spatial design that has rarely been equaled in the history of design, we argue
that they all share one feature: playfulness. They are not ready yet, and
because of that, they are open to experimentation, imagination, and multiple narratives. Technologists and designers are playing with these new
technologies freely, as if we were in a technology and design playground.

1 Orchestrating Serendipity

Playing Spaces

Picture this scene: a rainy summer day at a farmhouse, late afternoon. Two mango trees and a few shrubs on a dirt terrain by a creek. Children sit on the front porch. A placid scene. The rain stops. One of the children says, "Let's play!" It is all it takes to have them climbing the trees, jumping from branch to branch, splashing water, playing hide-and-seek around the shrubs, building towers with mud. Mango trees, shrubs, dirt, and water become a playground, each element signifying something else. Reality and imagination mingle together. This is not a backyard; it's the alien environment of planet LV-582, where the human soldiers of the Sol Alliance fought the hordes of the Yerxhz League in a legendary battle. Each child incorporates a specific role (the space marine? an extraterrestrial warrior?); trees and mud and creek create imaginary lands (a jungle? a bottomless pit? an ocean of steaming acid?); sticks become laser rifles or light sabers; mangoes turn into anti-grav grenades. (If you are not playing with them, it is impossible to be sure.) All this rich make-believe is foreign to the immediate scene in which you, as an outsider of the children's fantasy place, can see and touch. "Popcorn is ready!"—shout the adults in charge. Soldiers and aliens immediately become children again; the canyons of LV-582 return to their previous state as trees and shrubs. Play is over.

Play is a transformative act—an act of shared complicity that overlays multiple and changing layers of meaning onto objects, people, actions, and places. Play might also peel layers of socially accepted meaning from objects, people, and actions. In both cases, play creates new possibilities, along with unintended, suppressed, or unexpected scenarios of interaction.

In its pure, distilled form, play is a continuous ballet of ever-changing actions and meanings—in essence, a ballet of emergent design.

This is because play acts by dislocation: if something is supposed to have a definitive position or meaning, play moves this element to another context in which its original interpretation does not make sense, and in which it may thus acquire novel uses and dynamics. Play frequently takes elements out of their state of equilibrium and creates chain reactions among them and their surroundings in unexpected ways. It takes us away from our comfort zone, away from the ordinary rhythms, habits, and meanings that mark the way we relate with the world. By doing so, play transforms our relations with the world and, in its radical form, transforms the world altogether.

These concepts can be demonstrated with two examples from the arts in which elements of playfulness were used to foster radical art expressions and disruptions.

In 1917 Marcel Duchamp changed the art world when he picked up a urinal produced by J. L. Mott Iron Works, turned it upside down, signed it as "R. Mutt," and submitted the art piece, titled *Fountain*, to the annual exhibition of the Society of Independent Artists. The work was rejected, but a photograph of it was published the same year in the art magazine *The Blind Man* and became a landmark of modern art. Duchamp was playing with the art world, which, even within the community of independent artists, was deeply attached to the aura of the art object; an object would be considered artistic only if produced by an artist. With the urinal Duchamp seemed to be saying: Art is an intellectual process, a radical concept or approach to aesthetics, not a final product; but if you need an object signed by an artist, here you go—a signed urinal. The urinal is an object of loaded meaning that borders on the absurd; disconnected from the plumbing system and turned upside down, it loses its original meaning and intent as a urinal, and it becomes an art piece because an artist, R. Mutt, says it is.

A few decades later, Merce Cunningham and John Cage transformed dance. Choreography had long been created as a response to music. Although dance and music are two different languages, choreography usually followed the music, almost note by note, through a mimetic interpretation of the content of the music (picture, for instance, the classical choreography of Tchaikovsky's *Swan Lake*). Cunningham and Cage wanted to question preconceived notions of what dance ought to be and proposed a different approach. They jointly decided on a few structural points, such as time lengths and starting and ending points of sections, and then worked separately. Choreography and music would be created independently, with each artist exploring his art form's language freely. Dancers rehearsed in silence, in order to keep an element of surprise in the results, since the choreographer and dancers could get used to the composer's style. And then, on opening night, music and dance met on stage to perform for the first time, creating unexpected yet exhilarating results of expression. The Merce Cunningham Dance Company, founded in 1953, has worked over the years with dozens of different composers, following the principle that serendipity happens when there is room for chance to generate unexpected results.

Art is a particularly fertile area for play, which can be part of the process of creating art and at the same time transformative to the field. Play is fundamentally an activity based on establishing relationships. It is often an act of self-discovery, of exploring the world and positioning oneself in it while creating interpersonal and social bonds. Play is found among many animals—think of newborn cubs playing with each other—as a determinant behavior that helps them to create bonds, establish ranks, and find mates. Psychologists and educators have long studied the role of play in the formation of a child's personality, behavior, and social life. When a child is immersed in play, she is in an "area of experiencing, to which inner reality and external life both contribute" (Winnicott, 1971/2005, p. 3). Often, a playful external environment is only the fruit of the child's imagination, as when a child starts to play by herself in an empty room, not requiring any external stimuli. When children play among themselves in the same sparse room with few or no external stimuli, they are exercising social skills and creating their own behavioral norms. Building relationships between the external world (objectively perceived) and the inner self (subjectively conceived) starts from birth, and it happens in an intermediate area between reality testing and imagination that Donald Winnicott (1971/2005) calls the "play area" (p. 18).

Winnicott draws attention to two important aspects of play as the act that bridges the external and the inner worlds: transitional objects and transitional phenomena. He stresses that the focus should be not on the objects or phenomena but on the transitional role they serve. From the moment a child starts playing with her own thumb or her mother's breasts, and continuing when she moves on to a teddy bear or play figurines, she is engaging in a process in which she slowly recognizes a reality that is external to her own body.

Through these objects the child transitions from a self that seems indivisible from the external world (the world as an extension of the child) to an understanding of the world as a constant negotiation between herself and the otherness that exists in spite of herself—an otherness that will eventually constitute her own self understood as a composite of the inner and external worlds. As Miguel Sicart (2014) puts it, transitional objects such as toys are "alterity machines" (p. 43).

Also, by using an object to represent a different object (for instance, using a cardboard box in the middle of the living room to represent a boat in the sea), children develop abstract thinking. In fact, although in recent years the majority of best-selling toys have electronic components, Singer and Singer (2005) report that open-ended and make-believe toys such as teddy bears and Lego bricks are still among children's favorites in Great Britain.

Similar to transitional objects, transitional phenomena help the child model her identity. Imagination is the realm of transitional phenomena by which the external world stimulates but also resists the child's desires and illusion. In this process, transitional phenomena confirm the external reality as something that the child relates to but that is not a product of her own volition. Transitional phenomena can include interactions with parents and teachers as well as with fictional characters and electronic media (Singer & Singer, 2005).

The terms used by Winnicott (transitional objects, transitional phenomena, and intermediate area) stem from the work of Johan Huizinga, who published a landmark book on play, *Homo Ludens*, in 1938. In Huizinga's definition, "play is a voluntary activity or occupation executed within certain fixed limits of time and place, according to rules freely accepted but absolutely binding, having its aim in itself and accompanied by a feeling of tension, joy, and the consciousness that it is 'different' from 'ordinary life'" (Huizinga, 1938/1950, p. 28).

Huizinga's definition of "play" can be split into six parts:

1. "a voluntary activity"
2. "executed within certain fixed limits of time and place"
3. "according to rules freely accepted but absolutely binding"

4. "having its aim in itself"

5. "accompanied by a feeling of tension [and] joy"

6. "consciousness that it is 'different' from 'ordinary life'"

Caillois (1961) also labeled the six characteristics of play as free, separate, uncertain, unproductive, governed by rules, and make-believe.

Combining these characteristics, authors tend to divide play into two broad groups: play and games, which are etymologically derived from the Latin words *ludus* and *jocus*. Huizinga (1938/1950) argues that *ludus* is the general term for play, which encompasses recreation and contests as well as theatrical representations, whereas *jocus*, which means joking or jesting, eventually became the most used term in several languages with Latin roots, such as *jogo* and *jogar* in Portuguese or *joc* and *juca* in Romanian. Eventually *jocus* became more commonly related to structured plays (or games), organized by rules that are reflected in time, space, and the player's behavior with well-defined goals, whereas *ludus* became related to play for the sole enjoyment of play without extrinsic goals. Caillois (1961) goes one step further and classifies play in four main rubrics: agôn (competitive games, in which all players have equal chances within defined rules), alea (chance games, in which the outcomes do not depend on the player's dexterity), mimicry (make-believe games, in which players, play space, and conventions belong to an imaginary world), and ilinx (in which the pursuit of vertigo is the ultimate goal). The problem with Caillois's classification is that we can imagine several combinations using these rubrics—and Caillois himself spends a good portion of his book proposing them, discussing which goes well with the other (for instance, *ludus* is compatible with mimicry but not with ilinx, because achieving a specific goal demands self-control and order, which would go against the pursuit of vertigo).

In the context of this book, we use three of Huizinga's characteristics of play to propose that play has an important role in creating new possibilities of designing and enjoying space. Let us start with Huizinga's words by saying that "play is a voluntary activity . . . having its aim in itself . . . and accompanied by a feeling of tension [and] joy" (Huizinga, 1938/1950, p. 28). What remains of his definition are the three elements that structure this book's argument that play is "'different' from 'ordinary life,'" is based on "rules freely accepted but absolutely binding," and happens within "fixed limits of time and place." We do not necessarily agree with

Huizinga's approach in its entirety, especially with the impression that play always happens within a spatiotemporal sphere apart from the world; but the relevance of his work for the study of play makes it instrumental for a critical discussion of play and space.

Make-Believe: Playing with the Player

Make-believe and play are intimately related. Make-believe is not deception or self-deception. Make-believe requires that all parties involved are engaged in an illusory world. As we discuss in the chapter, Artifices of Self-Deception, deception and self-deception imply that one believes p is true when it is known that p is not. Make-believe is a shared illusion. All parties involved know p is not true, but they momentarily agree on pretending that p is true for the purpose of play, because they enjoy and profit from being temporarily deluded by p. The words *illusion* and *delusion* both come from *illudere*, which comes from *ludus* (play).

William Shakespeare's *Hamlet* is centered on Prince Hamlet's quest for revenge against his uncle Claudius, who murdered his father, the king of Denmark, and married Hamlet's mother. Deemed mad and suspicious of everyone, in Act 2 Hamlet engages a troupe of actors to perform *The Murder of Gonzago*, a play about a king's assassination that is similar to what happened to King Hamlet. Hamlet's goal is to determine whether Claudius is guilty or innocent based on his reaction to the plot—or, rather, to expose Claudius before the court, since Hamlet is certain of his guilt. Claudius indeed stops the play when poison is poured into the king's ear, but he does not confess to any wrongdoing.

Illusion and reality are intertwined throughout *Hamlet*, moreover, because "reality," in this case, is the main play itself—another illusion toward the audience. In a monologue that takes place after Hamlet welcomes the players, he seems fascinated and disturbed by this duality:

> Is it not monstrous that this player here,
> But in a fiction, in a dream of passion,
> Could force his soul so to his own conceit
> (Shakespeare, *Hamlet*, 2.2.551–564)

The Murder of Gonzago is an act of make-believe performed with the intent of influencing its immediate reality (the court of Denmark), but the immediate reality inside the play is yet another illusion: Shakespeare's play itself, performed before another reality, the audience in the theater, which is engaged in the make-believe. In both cases, the play is a transitional phenomenon that allows the audience (the court of Denmark, or the audience in the theater) to reflect about its own reality while engaged in and enjoying an illusory world.

In fact, throughout the play Hamlet arrogantly declares himself the only person able to distinguish between seeming and being, in a world in which the truth is "cloaked in ambivalence and contradictory signs" (Demastes, 2005, p. 31). In his journey full of certainties (Claudius killed his father) and doubts (his love for Ophelia), Hamlet uses illusion as a strategy, appearing to be mad when sane, and sane when mad—and it has been suggested that he might be using this shifting disguise to establish control over both his personal and his political situations (Dawson, 1978). Also, for Hamlet, make-believe serves as a transitional phenomenon to model and force his character upon his immediate social context.

The strategic illusion created by Hamlet has equally powerful and transformative roles in our daily plays, with make-believe helping us transition from the personal to the social sphere, expand our presence in space and time, and negotiate moral values and political stances. Huizinga (1938/1950) points out that make-believe is at the basis of our initiation to how we experience the world. Illusion is the interface between what is objectively perceived and what is subjectively conceived. Illusion expands throughout our lives, from storytelling and playing in childhood to arts and religion in adulthood. The structure of the Catholic Mass culminates with the eucharist, when the community shares the bread and wine, which are the body and blood of Christ. While there exists no rational way to demonstrate this is so, the bread, made of many grains, and the wine, made of many grapes, represent the ensemble of individuals that constitutes the community; and by eating and drinking the holy bread and wine, which also represent the sacrifice of Christ, believers share their faith, in an example of make-believe as a transitional phenomenon.

In theater or religion, children's play or storytelling, we assume a role different from what we are in our ordinary life. When we are playing or engaged in illusory worlds, we act as someone else. This personification releases some of our inner features, for a certain period of time and within a certain space, that we cannot, are not prepared to, or do not want to exercise in our daily life. Psychologically, Singer and Singer (2005) point out that make-believe helps us model our self, negotiating our early temperamental characteristics with those of people whom we admire.

Make-believe worlds are protected, but still porous, spatiotemporal spheres. We absorb and release information through personal and social filters. Each actor who impersonates Hamlet brings to the character layers of the actor's personal intentions, and when the play is over the actor returns to being an ordinary person but brings back within her or him the deepest contradictions and the dramatic flaws and strengths of Hamlet.

But it is not only by impersonation that one absorbs the qualities of illusory worlds. Myths tell universal stories that carry social and moral values. By telling, listening to, and being immersed in these stories and their imaginary worlds, we impart these values, we engage with the story and put ourselves in this mythical universe of morals, interpersonal bonds and disputes, the deeds of individuals and groups.

In all these cases, make-believe seeks to create some sort of empathy with the characters. Empathy creates the possibility of enhancing interpersonal understanding by seeing the world and others through somebody else's eyes. Make-believe allows us to impersonate somebody else, to live in somebody else's world, and shape our understanding of the world through somebody else's journeys; in essence make-believe is an exercise in empathy.

Fernando Pessoa (1931/2006), in the poem "Autopsicografia," writes:

The poet is a feigner
Who so completely feigns
That feigns to feel the pain
The pain that he truly feels[1]

The poem goes on to describe the reader not feeling the poet's pains but feeling the pain the reader does not have. Empathy does not seek a universal feeling, but rather to get us closer to the individual feelings and deeds of others, and by doing this, it reframes our own understanding of the world and of ourselves.

Make-believe thus creates the possibility of a deep engagement with the world. Role-playing games (commonly referred to as RPGs) are a fascinating example of this. RPGs are highly structured forms of mimicry. We all turn to worlds of our imagination in our childhood years. RPGs simply take the concept a little further. The most famous manifestation of this genre of games is of course Dungeons & Dragons, known to fans as D&D. It was created by Gary Gygax and Dave Arneson in 1974 and then enlarged in 1977 and 1979 to Advanced Dungeons & Dragons—or AD&D for short, as published by TSR Inc. Equally revered and vilified over the decades, it has been iconized by images of teenagers playing with multisided dice sets in their parents' basements. AD&D is essentially a series of booklets or modules that establish a shared rule set and basic lore needed to ground a social play session in a fantasy world. One person, known as the "Dungeon Master," uses the rule set and lore to devise and coordinate a play session shared among multiple players. Each player gets to define their game avatar and role. As the game progresses, the Dungeon Master vocally weaves a story of adventure and places the players' characters in it. The dice inject a layer of excitement by adding an element of randomness and chance to the choices made by the players. Little by little, a shared narrative unravels as both Dungeon Master and players cocreate their unique world of adventure.

While the genre was popularized in book form and was originally meant to be played in real-life sessions, the genre has also made its way into the digital realm as part of the video game revolution, with the computer performing the role of the Dungeon Master. Earliest examples were known as multiuser dungeons, or MUDs. They were developed at universities such as MIT and the University of Illinois, using basic programs originally developed for educational purposes. These RPGs had limited interactivity and used a text format since computers in the 1970s and early 1980s simply lacked the computational power to deliver richer experiences. By the mid-1990s, however, RPGs had become an established video game genre with a large variety of experiences developed mainly on both sides of the Pacific Ocean. Cultural differences leveraged endogenous cultural motifs and created fundamental philosophical divergences of game design, centered on the actual definition and representation of the player's avatar and its relation to the surrounding world. There is no better example of these differences than the role-playing video games created in Japan versus those created in the West between the 1980s and early 2000s.

In the Japanese RPG (JRPG) tradition, exemplified by established series such as *Final Fantasy* (1987–2019), *Dragon Quest* (1986–2018), and *The Legend of Zelda* (1986–2018), among others, the player doesn't really experience their own story, but rather one of a predefined character. If a person plays Hironobu Sakaguchi's *Final Fantasy VII* (1997), their character will always be Cloud Strife, the lead protagonist of Sakaguchi's vision; and no matter the in-game choices made by the player, the narration and perspective of the game will not deviate from Cloud's point of view. The same thing happens with any game in the Legend of Zelda series: it doesn't matter if it is the original *The Legend of Zelda* (1986), *The Legend of Zelda: Ocarina of Time* (1998), or *The Legend of Zelda: Breath of the Wild* (2017), the player will invariably take the role of Link, rather than a self-defined character or even the titular character. While decisions and interactions do affect how the character evolves, there is a lesser degree of overall freedom and greater linearity in the way that the character's story evolves over time, as everything follows a preexisting narrative. The JRPGs in question are indeed vehicles for their own encased stories, and progression is greatly defined by how much of them the player has experienced.

The Western RPG tradition, on the other hand, is contextually driven. Western RPGs such as *Baldur's Gate* (BioWare, 1998), *Morrowind* (Bethesda, 1999), *Fallout* (Bethesda, 1997), *Deus Ex* (Eidos, 2000), *Knights of the Old Republic* (BioWare, 2002), *Fable* (Lionhead Studios, 2003), *Mass Effect* (BioWare, 2007), or *Dragon Age* (BioWare, 2009) all work by establishing a place and lore where the player can project their own actions and decisions. It doesn't matter if the setting is fantasy, science fiction, cyberpunk, or postapocalyptic; all of these games follow the same structure of letting the player's choices aggregate to create an individual story. Sure, there are many in-game adventures, each with some particular story, and even a larger main quest line that the player may choose to follow, but that is usually beside the point, since their design philosophy is situational and often what truly matters is the creation of emergent narratives based on players' moment-to-moment choices, a form of narrative in action.

The player begins as a tabula rasa, given the choice to define who their avatar is. Characteristics such as gender, race, specialization, sexual preferences, enhancements, profession, looks, and many others are available to the player, a well-established mechanic that has now been exported to games from different genres. The ethos is that actions define who you are. Freedom of choice and exploration of consequences become their key characteristics. This embedded flexibility allows for a richer expression in the actual mechanical act of playing the game and in the available options for character leveling and progression. Perhaps more important is the way the character's avatar relates socially to other characters in the game, enriching his or her own in-game narratives in the process. Mechanics such as morality of choice or even explorations of unforeseen consequences that do not materialize until much further along in the game are not presented as black-or-white scenarios but rather as possibilities for dynamically weaving a story by adding tension, humor, romance, sadness, despair, and even a sense of wonder. RPGs are thus games formed by interlocking subsystems geared toward creating performant spaces that foster an expression of the self.

The performant spaces become catalysts for social interaction, where the goals and purpose of each player coincide or collide in a fluid coexistence that gives social meaning to shared moments. A good example of this is *Sea of Thieves* (Rare, 2018), a whimsical massive-online pirate simulator. The player begins by picking a pirate avatar of his or her choosing. The stylistic choices are all procedurally generated, so no two are alike. After the player is dropped in a random spot in the world, the goal of the game is never clearly defined, but the player has a few clues and items at his or her disposal: everything needed for seafaring and pirating (shovel, cutlass, musket, spyglass, and compass), along with a drum and a mandolin, in case the player wants to sing shanties while at sea. The genius of the game is that the world is as much a character as the player's avatar. Deserted islands, hidden caves, roaring seas, red sunsets, starry skies, dinghy boats, and the occasional sea monster are all that's needed to set off on an adventure.

The game aggressively sticks with the philosophy of always keeping its world "on-character." It actively removes most traces of an onscreen interface; in fact, by most modern game standards *Sea of Thieves* is stubbornly filled with nuisances from a predigital era. There are no maps on demand for the player, who must lay a map on a table and mark any desired destination. Afterwards, compass and even stars become crucial elements for proper navigation. Even getting a boat to move requires a chain of actions involving manually raising the anchor, raising and positioning the sails and mast, and finally directing the rudder wheel. Each one is a step of complexity initially unfathomable but open to experimentation. The world itself is the interface. The legibility of the place is key, and as a consequence the game slows down but simultaneously becomes more intense.

Groups of players can man larger boats and go together in search of adventures. The system is profoundly democratic, as each player can communicate by voice and by vote. Smaller teams can become impromptu fleets. Positions are filled, roles are taken, and loot is divided. Little details such as a bottle in the sand can become a long adventure for loot and treasure, gaudy clothes on a pirate indicate an experienced player, any mast on the horizon can become either friend or foe, any cloud is a potential thunderstorm. As pirate mythology requires, one can sail in search of treasure, but finding it is only the first step, since treasure doesn't hold value on a deserted island but rather in civilization; therefore, it must be carried back to be deposited in a bank if one wishes to buy fancier boats or clothes. Every ship is therefore a target, since it can be easier to simply attack one and steal its loot. Captains are always on edge; after all, this is a pirate simulator, so potential treason and mutiny is always at hand. Parlay, alliances, and social skills are therefore as important as being good with a sword or a musket. Additional skills such as cooking and singing are highly appreciated, since the special moment of a good meal with grog and music under the stars is universally appreciated. Slowly the world unfurls to reveal a cohesive and complex stage for self and social expression. The shared world invites exploration, imagination and experimentation.

This process of self-expression by way of exploration through scenarios and self-created roles can go beyond mere communication and enjoyment. Because RPGs are in essence a mirror upon which we observe ourselves and develop variations of empathy and action, they are useful beyond worlds of fantasy. Saleem Alhabash and Kevin Wise (2014) use a role-playing video game to discuss biases and attitude changing in the Israeli-Palestinian conflict. *PeaceMaker* is a 2D persuasive game, in which game designers employ strategies to convey a particular message, with players needing to fill gaps to change level; by doing this players are directed toward a particular worldview. Based on their observation of 172 American college students playing the game, Alhabash and Wise showed that through changes in the game, players engaged in self-induced changes of opinion, switching empathy with both sides.

Make-believe creates empathy, and empathy can inform design. This goes beyond the standard and programmatic relationship that is commonly established between designers and clients. Make-believe and storytelling create a world of possibilities in which we can engage without social restrictions. All parties engaged in make-believe put their guard down to fully enjoy the play, and when they do so, creative possibilities may arise. In role-playing, being an assassin, a monster, a hero, or a prince is a temporary agreement between the players; without players assuming these roles, the play does not exist, so the vanities of royalty or the malignancy of bandits are accepted by all players as part of their characters. And by temporarily accepting that such shadowy characteristics of humans come to light, all parties involved can relate to their own portions of vanity and greed, passion and joy. Make-believe opens up the possibility of otherness, and by engaging with what is foreign to us, with the out of the ordinary, we become open to being surprised and to trying new possibilities.

Playing with and within the Rules

Down the rabbit hole, in Wonderland, Alice meets the Queen of Hearts, who invites her to play croquet. In Wonderland croquet, playing cards become soldiers, who double as arches; flamingos serve as mallets; and hedgehogs are used as balls. During the game, hedgehogs move nonstop to avoid being hit and constantly fight with each other; all the players play at the same time without waiting for their turns, and the Queen keeps yelling, "Off with his head!" or "Off with her head!" There are no clear rules, or at least nobody seems to respect them, and by the end of the game only the Queen and King of Hearts and Alice remain.

Games have clear rules that bind together all participants. As Sicart (2014) argues, there is a profound tension between the playfulness and the structures of games, and professional sports and serious games are often the opposite of playful. "Play welcomes opposites," ranging in a spectrum from ungoverned and improvised behaviors, to behaviors following strict and codified rules (Zosh et al., 2018, p. 1). And yet, even within highly codified games some players stand out: even within the rules' restrictions there is still room for freedom. For a play to be playful, it must be "accompanied by a particular positive mood state in which the individual is more inclined to behave (and, in the case of humans, think) in a spontaneous and flexible way" (Bateson, 2014, p. 100). For Sicart (2014), playfulness is marked by the elements of surprise introduced by excellent players, who, without breaking the rules, excel in achieving the goals of the game in unpredictable ways. During three consecutive Summer Olympic Games, from 2008 to 2016, Usain Bolt, a sprinter from Jamaica, won the gold medal in the 100-meter dash and repeatedly broke the world record, often his own. What enchanted everyone was not only his superiority as a sprinter but also how Bolt seemed to be enjoying the run, introducing playfulness in such a competitive environment while all other contenders seemed to be exhausted and even stressed. Likewise, the Brazilian soccer team has for years been considered one of the best in the world, even when it loses matches and championships. In spite of the negative results, the players seem to be having fun and frequently try unnecessary but beautiful and surprising movements in the game. In sports, playfulness is matched with talent.

Spotting and cultivating talent and playfulness is tricky—all the more so because playfulness and talent often seem to be based on subjective criteria. For a long time, baseball teams used to exclusively count on a group of scouts to form their teams. Baseball has long been arguably one of the sports that generates the most data, from more traditional metrics such as RBIs, innings, intentional base on balls, and assists, to other metrics provided by high-technology devices recently installed in the balls to measure the speed of the ball and spin of the bat, among other apparently nonconsequential metrics. Managers and coaches use these metrics to make informed decisions and enhance the performance of their teams. Still, most baseball players used to be hired by this small group of scouts who, by drawing from their personal experiences as former baseballers and closely following teams and players of different divisions, had a tacit knowledge of which players their team should draft and invest in. Underneath such playfulness, however, sit hidden structures. In *Moneyball: The Art of Winning an Unfair Game*, Michael Lewis (2003) showed that a winning team should not rely solely on the tacit knowledge of scouts, managers, and coaches, but rather on quantitative evidence and objective analytical tools, something proposed in the sabermetric approach (from the acronym SABR, for Society for American Baseball Research). In the early 2000s, the Oakland Athletics (or Oakland A's) were a team with a small budget that could not afford the players whom scouts suggested and therefore could not compete with teams whose larger payroll budgets allowed them to attract high-performance baseball stars. Amassing and analyzing a huge amount of data, such as on-base and slugging percentages and several other metrics disregarded by scouts, the Oakland A's put together a team of effective players, not stars. Better results came almost immediately, and the team ultimately made the 2002 and 2003 playoffs. Soon other baseball teams adopted the same quantitative strategy to form their teams and assess their performance. At face value, it seems that playfulness has been put aside for a cold and quantitative approach. Although the ultimate goal of the team and its supporters has always been to win, the moneyball approach effectively broke all the rules in regard to how the sport was traditionally managed and played.

Baseball's data has also led to the development of a parallel game: baseball betting. One example is fantasy baseball. Completely based on actual data generated during baseball matches, fantasy baseball has barely anything to do with the sport itself. Although there are different forms of fantasy baseball, in its most basic version betters create their team out of players from different teams that will be playing on a particular day. The number of teams can be virtually as large as the number of betters, who put together their fantasy teams' players from, say, the Oakland A's, the Yankees, and the Red Sox. After the evening, betters compare the statistics on how these players performed in actual matches, including eight basic parameters, such as home runs, batting averages (hits divided by at-bats), and saves. The winners are those whose fantasy team players accumulated the best results on these metrics. Regardless of the results of fantasy baseball, its outcomes do not influence or reflect the results of the actual matches. This is a situation in which mathematical analysis and calculations supersede the actual games. This a case in which we could apply to fantasy baseball Caillois's argument that the mathematical analysis becomes a game in itself, and "would exist even if there were no games to analyze" (1961, p. 174). We could argue that fantasy baseball has created for itself a set of rules detached from the rules of the game it is based on. Furthermore, fantasy baseball seems to be an attempt to reintroduce playfulness to a sport that risked being dominated by an overabundance of metrics. It is also a beautiful example of how play evolves naturally, shifting and swaying over and over in a constant dance of exploration and balance.

In a game, rules are necessarily established to constrain the infinite possibilities of action and play; but rules might also be arranged in such a way that playing with the rules creates novel possibilities. In a diagram or algorithm in which the rules establish the relations between its parameters, variations in these parameters generate multiple and unexpected results, to the point that they might change the structure of the initial diagram or algorithm. Félix Guattari (1995) proposes to use the concept of the "autopoietic machine," which has the power to free the diagram "from an identity locked into simple structural relations" (p. 44).

Guattari's autopoietic machine stems from Humberto Maturana and Francisco Varela's work in biology and cognition. The authors define a living organism as an autopoietic system that is a unity in space as long as "any structural transformation that a living system may undergo maintaining its identity must take place in a manner determined by and subordinated to its defining autopoiesis" (Maturana and Varela, 1980, p. 135). The loss of autopoiesis causes loss of identity and death—or the system becoming a stranger to itself, in which case it changes so much that it turns into an entirely new system.

Guattari expands the notion of autopoiesis to language. He proposes that the diagrammatic aspect of language opens up the possibility of having "ontologically heterogeneous modes of subjectivity" (Guattari, 1995, p. 45), unlocking language and its rules from a permanent link between signifiers and a unique form of subjectivity that would be "lodged" in such a permanent chain. Guattari gives jazz as an example: formed by a combination of African and Western musical traditions, it has been constantly changing within some basic rules. By often playing with these rules, stretching and folding and mixing them with other music, jazz musicians and composers keep jazz alive. Purisms tend to die or stay frozen in time, becoming a mere reenactment of the memory of a living music; others break the rules to create other living systems, other styles of music; but as long as the structural transformations do not disrupt completely the nuclear identity of jazz, we still have it as a living music.

Play always has a degree of uncertainty. If the results are known, the enjoyment ends, and to continue to play loses its purpose. In chess, checkmate indicates that one player is absolutely certain to capture the opponent's king and thereby end the game. Although the players can still move pieces around, with a checkmate the game loses its purpose, so the player with the threatened king declares defeat. So what happens when, by playing within the rules, one player achieves such supremacy that beating such a player is an almost impossible mission? This is what has been happening with board games such as chess and Go, in which computer algorithms have beaten the world champions. In 1997 the chess grandmaster Gary Kasparov lost to IBM's Deep Blue, and in 2016 DeepMind's AlphaGo defeated Lee Sedol, considered the greatest Go player in decades.

Go is a board game in which two players alternatively place white and black stones with equivalent values at the crossings of a 19-by-19 grid. The goal is to surround areas—pieces within surrounded areas are removed by the opponent. It is a highly complex game. In order to solve board games algorithms need to recursively compute the optimal value function in a search tree formed by the possible sequences of moves, which amount to b^d, or the number of legal moves per position (b) elevated by the game length (d). In chess, b is ~35, and d is ~80. In Go, b is ~250, and d is ~150. The possible number of configurations is greater than the number of atoms in the universe (Gibney, 2016).

Thus, while Deep Blue was trained within the rules of chess to perfect its game, AlphaGo used what is called deep convolutional neural networks and general-purpose algorithms, interpreting the patterns of 30 million positions from expert games, figuring out what victory means, learning from mistakes, and developing strategies to win the game (Hassabis, 2017). Before playing with Lee, AlphaGo won 99.8 percent of the matches against other Go programs—even when some opponents had four handicap stones. One of the features that made AlphaGo remarkable was the strategy developed to design the algorithm: rather than feeding the model complete games, the 30 million distinct positions were sampled from different games. The strategy was used to avoid overfitting, in which successive positions are strongly correlated (Silver et al., 2016). AlphaGo learned by playing.

AlphaGo became a landmark in research in artificial intelligence. Its final version ran 40 asynchronous multithread searches using 48 CPUs and 8 GPUs. When AlphaGo beat Lee, a question hovered over Go and AI communities: Would AlphaGo eliminate the enjoyment of playing Go? Some imagined that, as Caillois (1961) had proposed, "Whenever calculation arrives at a scientific theory of the game, the interest of the player disappears together with the uncertainty of the outcome" (p. 173). We could expect that the mathematics behind AlphaGo would become "a game in itself," with an incidental relationship with the game of Go.

However, in the case of chess, more people have been playing the game after Deep Blue defeated Kasparov (Hassabis, 2017); and the reactions of both Fan Hui, the European champion first beat by AlphaGo, and Lee, after losing to AlphaGo, also seem to tell a different story. After some moments of distress and lack of purpose, the players seemed to enjoy playing against the program and learning from it (Kohs, 2017). David Silver, the lead researcher behind AlphaGo, said that Move 37, the incomprehensible move AlphaGo undertook that eventually determined its victory, "was outside of the expected way of playing Go that humans had figured out over thousands of years. To me this is an example of something being creative" (Knight,

2019, p. 66). On the other hand, in the fourth game of the five-game challenge he had already lost, Lee produced what became known as Move 78, whose probability AlphaGo had estimated at 1 in 10,000, at which point the program immediately calculated it had a 70 percent chance of defeating Lee again—until Move 87, when AlphaGo accepted defeat (Chouard, 2016).

AlphaGo shows the limits of playing within and with the rules, when they are reduced to the minimum amount of information and play becomes a set of strategies to recognize patterns in space and time. Moreover, the popularity of AlphaGo brought to public attention the role artificial intelligence will increasingly have in our lives. In what Kai-Fu Lee (2018) sees as the third wave of artificial intelligence, the ubiquity of sensors and smart devices deployed in cities, homes, and carried by people are turning the physical world and the relations among people and between people and the world into digital data, data that can then be analyzed and optimized through deep-learning algorithms.

In fact, the recent incorporation into our daily routines of devices embedded with artificial intelligence—from autonomous cars to dating apps, from credit-score algorithms to voice-activated personal management gadgets such as Alexa or Siri—has given rise to "thinking machines," or machines that learn by themselves. They do that by incorporating new pieces of information in any interaction they have with people who activate them, with each online search they do to perform a task, and through the communication they establish with other AI devices that participate in the chain of machines necessary to fulfill their goal. In the beginning, the tasks are simple and the responses given by the devices are predictable, often a faster version of what humans would do. However, after a certain point not even the engineers and computer scientists who designed the initial algorithms for each of these devices would know their decision-making processes, because AI agents acquire new knowledge and behavior every time they interact with the world. They calibrate their internal parameters, consider new data, and change their internal workflow, often becoming black boxes even to those who initially conceived them. Rahwan et al. (2019) comment that understanding what they call machine behavior is especially difficult in an environment that is changing in part due to the results of the same algorithms one wants to decipher.

AI machines are based on a set of rules, or algorithms. While fantasy baseball separates the game from its rules to fix its attention only on particular and disconnected metrics, AlphaGo keeps a minimum understanding of the rules and turns its focus to the best performance to achieve the goal of the game. Fantasy baseball represents the disembodiment of the game, whereas AlphaGo seeks its full embodiment. However, by doing this, AlphaGo does not take into account that a body is porous; and it is its porosity to the external world that improves it. Obviously, this was not DeepMind's intention; but returning to the work of Maturana and Varela, autopoiesis also happens when one system exchanges information with other systems, contaminating each other. This is what happens with AI devices that communicate with each other and react to and learn from the environment, to the point of changing their algorithms.

We could argue that with "thinking machines" we are entering a world in which machines and humans play with each other. By taking something out of its state of equilibrium, making it react to other elements and its surroundings, play can produce unexpected results. This is the moment when play becomes a transformative act.

Playing with Space

Although the importance of play and of play space is frequently acknowledged as fundamental in children's development, including improving learning and social skills, outdoor play has been severely curtailed due to increased urbanization and motorization. Cities have higher densities and lack open areas; and street grids, building codes, and even parks are highly codified, constraining the possibilities of free play. Additionally, increasing motorization makes streets more dangerous, with parents preferring to keep children safe indoors. The dichotomy between the widely accepted understanding among specialists that play is vital to a child's neurological and social development, and the restricted possibilities of spaces in which children can play freely, might be boosting a resurgence in play studies (Whitebread, 2018).

Huizinga, along with several other scholars and practitioners after him, stressed that play happens within a singularity in space and time, or a spatiotemporal unit. The act of play defines a portion of space and a duration that creates a safe area. Play admits behaviors, personifications, and fantasies that do not make sense or are not admitted outside the play space or when the play is over.

The notion of spatiotemporal unit is easily understood with highly codified games. Think of a soccer match. It requires a defined space, in which
marks on the field correspond to a set of regulations embedded in space,
and a defined duration of two halves of 45 minutes each. In the case of professional leagues, space, time, and the roles of each player are highly codified. However, among amateurs, the constitution of such spatiotemporal
units is part of the play. When playing soccer on the streets, we define the
sideline by curbs and use chalk to draw the goal line. Two pieces of brick
demarcate the goal, and rather than two half-times defined by minutes,
we use the number of goals, usually changing sides after a team has scored
its fifth goal. During the match, we fiercely dispute each ball and cheer for
each goal, stopping only momentarily when a car crosses the field. As soon
as a team scores the tenth goal and the match is over, each player becomes
a regular kid and the field disappears, giving way to an ordinary street.

Game is a form of play, generally with well-defined spatial inscription.
It is as if the rules of the game had been crystallized in space, and play
happens within this game space. But before discussing game spaces, in this
chapter we want to discuss how play creates new spatialities—spatialities
understood as unique appropriations of a certain space that are strong
enough to resignify our understanding of such space, but without interfer-
ing in its physical constitution. It is important to note that new spatialities
are more than the evanescent spatiotemporal unit that children and adults
alike form while playing. Such spatiotemporal units are the safe space for
those playing but do not change the perception or understanding of space
for those outside the play. New spatialities emerge when the play changes
how space is perceived and spatial possibilities emerge.

Sports are particularly keen in creating new spatialities. Oftentimes,
sports are performed in spaces dedicated to this particular activity. In these
cases, play creates discrete spaces when it becomes a game—a particular type
of play with defined rules agreed upon by the players. In games, the play
revolves around attaining specific goals within a set of allowed behaviors
and a discrete space and time. Huizinga (1938/1950) uses the term "playground" (p. 10) for this sort of "temporary sphere of activity" (p. 9), in
which an absolute order reigns for a discrete period of time. However, it is
helpful to denominate such play spaces as game spaces, in which the rules
of the game are reflected in space, combining form and function. This is
the case with board games, such as chess or Go, in which the placement

and movement of the pieces are restricted to certain positions, and also in more complex and bigger spaces, such as soccer or cricket, in which functions and particular actions are linked to the configuration of the field. For example, in soccer the goalkeeper can only use the hands inside the penalty box—outside it the goalkeeper is only allowed to use the feet, basically becoming a regular player. The infringement upon this rule brings a penalty against the goalkeeper's team, and the goalkeeper might be put out of the game if he or she breaks this spatial rule twice during the same match.

However, sports that are not tied to structured game spaces have the potential to create spatialities for their own sake, and also (and more importantly to our discussion) to demonstrate how play can open up unexpected spatial possibilities within existing spaces. Diane Ackerman (2000) argues that activities such as mounting climbing, scuba diving, and parachuting (all of which produce a certain degree of vertigo) are close to religious and artistic experiences in providing ecstatic and transcendent sensations—qualities that characterize what she calls "deep play." Surfing and mountain climbing are two forms of "deep play" that create spatialities while they are performed, and part of the players' deftness is linked to how they find spatialities where others don't.

In the second half of the twentieth century, surfing became a global phenomenon, somehow combining its countercultural aspects with a stronger presence in mainstream media, from movies to TV shows to magazines. Still, as part of the thrill is the unpredictability of the play space, in the global era of surfing it became "about the search, the journey, the discovery" (Laderman, 2014, p. 44) of the perfect wave—one that would never be found because it's ephemeral.

Surfers cannot control waves, nor even completely predict their formation. Surfing requires steep unbroken waves, and the best surf occurs at the breaking crest of the wave. A good wave involves swell directions, wind conditions, and the shape of the reef. On top of these natural conditions, the bodies and boards of the surfers in the sea interfere with the shape and form of the wave. Beyond dexterity, good surfing requires the surfer to select the right wave, which is indicated by subtle differences in the shape of its face and its vortex length. Although researchers have been studying how coastal geology, climatic cycles, and coastal interventions affect wave formation (Butt, 2014); and other researchers have been developing mathematical models to identify the intensity of surfing waves (Mead & Black,

2001), surfers need to select waves on the fly. Also, choosing a good wave does not mean much if the surfer doesn't ride it exploring its full potential, in a fleeting alignment of technology (surfboard), human (surfer), and nature (waves). Surfing happens in a play space where others might not see anything but beach and sea with breaking waves. In this play space, surfers create spatialities that depend on their own performance while shaping them, and as soon as these spatialities come to their full fruition, they disappear.

Mountain climbing became a sport in the nineteenth century. By 1865 all the highest peaks in Europe had been summited, and mountaineers started a race for mountains in exotic locales such as Africa, the Arctic, and the Himalayas. Mountaineers found some of these places impregnated with cultural aspects: for inhabitants living in these regions, especially in the Himalayas, the mountains are spiritual places that house their deities. Western mountaineers do not share the same cultural and religious background, and initially lamas advised against expeditions to the Himalayas, which would be a profanation of a sanctuary. Based on interviews with sherpas, the locals who guide mountaineers in their expeditions to the Himalayas, Maggie Miller (2017) sees high-altitude climbing as a combination of narratives of risk and strength, personal development and pride, power, freedom, and death.

Balancing risk, self-control, and freedom, mountain climbing is driven by a "wish for finding private and autonomous spaces" (Pereira, 2009, p. 166). Finding autonomous spaces in such inhospitable and ever-changing environments increases the appeal of mountain climbing. Mountain climbers, especially those dedicated to high-altitude climbing, also create spatialities to reach the summit. They use cords, pulleys, ice screws, spikes, and carabiners to chisel their way up the mountain, combining different climbing techniques. Falling rocks, strong winds, and snow avalanches often change the shape of the mountain ahead of them. It is a journey teeming with liminal moments. Again, there is a combination of human abilities, technological development, and nature often changing in unpredictable ways. Speaking about his mentor, Mugs Stump, Conrad Anker said that "he had taken what was unshapen and given shape to it" (Chin & Vasarhelyi, 2015). Like the ocean waves, mountains are an ever-changing environment, and each climb demands the creation of temporary spatialities, which will not be impregnated on the mountain.

While surfing and mountain climbing create their play space within environments prone to unpredictable changes, skateboarders create their play spaces within highly codified environments: streets and other urban areas.

Skateboarding boomed in Los Angeles and other Californian seaside cities in the 1950s and 1960s. Skateboarders used the wide and long streets in calm and boring (at least from the youth perspective) suburban developments to "re-enact the sense of being on the sea . . . down the tarmac drives and roads of its undulating residential sectors" (Borden, 2001, p. 29). In the 1970s skateboarders took the backyard pools of Los Angeles suburbia and concrete pipes used for drainage and water supply as their playground; and in the 1980s they turned their attention to the ordinary terrain of public spaces, using stairs, ramps, benches, and handrails.

In all these cases, skateboarders create alternative spatialities within highly codified spaces. Streets, swimming pools, drainage pipes, and benches are designed and built to perform specific urban functions. There is a strong association between form and function, which gives these elements precise and stable social meaning, and these meanings impregnate space, determining the expected and socially accepted use. Skateboarding is a destabilizing factor. Skateboarders peel off these established meanings and approach space through a performative play centered on the amalgamation of the body of the skateboarder and the skateboard. This single entity composed of humans and technology explores urban furniture and architecture for their potential to stimulate new sensations, to provoke vertigo. Skateboarding does not physically change space, but it alters our perception of space.

Skateboarders are often viewed as illegitimate in certain urban contexts, and they have long been facing a mix of bans and defensive architecture, in which urban furniture is designed to prevent its appropriation by skateboarders. On the flip side, cities have tried to leverage the positive role skateboarding can play in education and community cohesion by creating skate parks, in which pools, pipes, ramps, and other elements are redesigned to become a playground for skateboarders. Although some of these parks are highly used, and skateboarding competitions have a global scale, they are frequently built far from city centers and have strict regulations, which represent the spatial codification of skateboarding practice. Not surprisingly, skateboarders still explore urban landscapes as a contesting spatial practice (Chiu, 2009) and for the thrill of creating novel ephemeral spatialities out of traditional spaces.

It is as if surfers, mountain climbers, and skateboarders were the builders of Tlön, a world imagined by Jorge Luis Borges (1962). In Tlön, the world is not a "concourse of objects in space; it is a heterogeneous series of independent acts. It is successive and temporal, not spatial" (p. 8). In the southern hemisphere of Tlön, there are no nouns: the word *moon* is not part of the residents' lexicon, but the verb *moonate* is, because for the residents of Tlön space does not persist in time. Surfers, mountaineers, and skateboarders do not play in space but rather create spatialities by playing.

In the case of skateboarders and other urban sports, such as BMX or parkour, the semantics of architecture are "always provisional, pregnant with the possibility that lies beyond their apparent closure" (Borden, 2001, p. 8). By challenging architecture and other physical elements of cities, urban sports are also challenging the moral fabric of society and some mindless habits that guide our behavior toward space. They are challenging approaches that create and recreate play spaces but are outlawed within game spaces, in which the rules of the game determine the spatial configuration.

The last decades have seen part of play activities that were usually done outdoors turning indoors, with children, adolescents, and adults spending more time playing with electronic media. Among the electronic media, video games have a prime space when discussing the importance of play. The ways in which video games inform spatial design will be discussed in the chapter "Learning from Video Games." Here we just want to point out how spatial features drive how players experience video games.

Video games are implicitly connected to the notion of game spaces, a well-defined realm with clear rules that guide the play, the expected outcomes, and the players' behavior. At first, space in video games must theoretically be conceived as game spaces, not because of the rules and goals of any particular game but because all of them are products of computational coding. Their constraints and freedoms are encoded. Their space, time, characters, and behaviors are encoded. In principle, video games could be seen as the utmost example of the spatial characteristics of play as proposed by Huizinga (1938/1950): its "secludedness," a "temporary sphere of activity" in which "absolute and peculiar order reigns" (pp. 9–10).

However, some video games transition from the secluded and overruled game space to the openness of play spaces. They range from games in which players can roam more or less freely, exploring spaces that are not related to the main goals or narratives of the game. This is the case of the Grand Theft

Auto series, frequently mentioned in game studies as an example of a game in which players create and recreate their narratives virtually endlessly. As Gordon Calleja (2011) describes it, it is "a virtual environment with a number of games embedded in it and a linear storyline that players can progress through by completing a sequence of gamelike activities" (p. 8). Other video games, such as *SimCity* and *Minecraft*, extend this openness by allowing players to create their own play spaces. The game design stops being a mastermind behind any possible action and instead becomes a "stage setter," stimulating designers and players to negotiate and cocreate the play (Sicart, 2014, p. 90). And here enters another aspect that challenges Huizinga's argument of play, and even games, being performed in spaces that are separated from real life. If play has the social importance of forming our interpersonal, intellectual, and social characteristics, play influences and is influenced by the external world constantly, even during the act of play. The crowd at the sports venue has no role within the rules of the game. Still, any soccer or basketball player knows that the crowd influences their performance and consequently the possible outcomes of the game.

The active interaction between what happens within games and external life has deeper consequences than the crowd influencing players' performance, and it also happens with video games. Going back to Winnicott, video games are transitional objects. Studying adolescents and video games, Marsha Levy-Warren (2008) argues that they use video games to escape but also to make sense of the world; transitioning between reality and imagination, "adolescents play at being who they are becoming" (p. 78).

Video games, especially those using immersive technologies, also influence our physical interaction with the external world. Playing video games requires the use of devices that range from simple keyboards and joysticks to more powerful VR headsets, and all of them create audiovisual-haptic feedback loops to different degrees. We always play video games through human-technology assemblages, in which the players are not apart from the intricacies of the game, but as "situated and embodied subjects" (Keogh, 2018, p. 40), whose subjective and objective experience of the game transcends and transform the game space.

In spite of the variation that exists among the unmarked and ephemeral spatialities created by surfers and mountain climbers, the challenging approach of skateboarders toward established uses and meanings of spaces, or the highly coded game spaces, from soccer to video games, we agree with Huizinga that play creates temporary space within a larger space. This temporary space is modeled by the play itself, porous but still somehow apart from ordinary spaces (even when it happens without physical demarcations). However, Huizinga (1938/1950) considers that play does not have an important role in plastic arts, in which he includes architecture. For him, plastic arts are characterized by the "absence of the play-quality" (p. 163) because the architect, painter, and ceramist all "fix a certain aesthetic impulse in matter" (p. 167), while with art forms such as music, the work of art comes to life every time it is performed by an artist.

At first glance, Huizinga's comment seems appropriate: the work of architecture has a sense of completion. Buildings are more or less open to different fruitions, but eventually the building is there, solidly reflecting the architect's design. However, designers have been proposing architecture that responds and changes to its surroundings and to the interaction with users. For the 2016 Olympic Games in Rio de Janeiro, Estudio Guto Requena created an interactive skin made of 500 metal spinning discs, with different colors outside and mirrors inside. The discs move responding to stimuli collected by sensors, such as the beat of the music or the excitement of people inside the pavilion. For the Zaragoza World Expo, in 2008, Carlo Ratti proposed the Digital Water Pavilion, in which the façades were curtains of falling water that could be programmed and would create different patterns by controlling the opening and closing of 3,000 digitally controlled solenoid valves. Both projects will be discussed in chapter 3, "Tinkering with Spatialities."

Play has an intimate relationship with the idea of freedom. In learning environments this freedom has been explored in four typologies: freedom to explore and test ideas, freedom to fail and learn from failures, freedom to be someone else and by doing that experiment with one's own identity, and freedom of effort (Klopfer et al., 2018). Play can activate spaces and generate new spatialities, and the combination of human and technology can trigger novel experiences. But before discussing how media and other technologies can stimulate the creation of dynamic and responsive architectures, it is important to stress the conceptual point that, as proposed by Winnicott (1971/2005), it is "in playing, and perhaps only in playing, [that] the child or adult is free to be creative" (p. 71).

2　Embodying Fantasies

"Don't forget," he said to me, "the biggest attraction isn't here yet."
"What's that?"
"People. You fill this place with people, and you'll really have a show."
—Walt Disney to reporter Bob Thomas, as they looked over an unfinished
Disneyland in 1955

Harnessing Symbolic Meaning in Spaces

In the early nineteenth century, the German philosopher Georg Wilhelm
Friedrich Hegel gave a series of lectures in Berlin and Heidelberg that revo-
lutionized the way we understand beauty. Heinrich Gustav Hotho compiled
his notes on these lectures in a volume titled *Hegel's Lectures on Aesthetics*
(*Vorlesungen über die Ästhetik*). Hegel defined beauty as a direct sensuous
manifestation of freedom, postulating that different forms of beauty give
form to distinct forms of art (*Kunstformen*). Hegel underscored that while
art is capable of performing different functions, it still needs to maintain its
central role of providing an "intuitive, sensuous expression to the freedom
of spirit" (Houlgate, 2016).

Hegel believed that art should do more than just imitate reality and
nature; it can extend beyond the actual and instead show the possible. In
this sense, there is great power in the symbolic as an art form that eschews
the ideal and sensuous forms of beauty to instead focus on the abstract
world of ideas. In Hegel's terms, architecture as an art form can never aspire
to true beauty, since it must attend both form and function, which naturally constrains its potential aesthetic manifestation. Yet architecture is
a vessel of symbolic meaning, with each architectural object embodying

symbols that resonate with us, giving designers the power to encode meaning into the places we design.

As ideas and concepts become architecturally embodied, and when different architectural objects are spatially joined together (either by urban planners and designers or by chance over time), a gradual process of amalgamating buildings and symbols takes place at the urban scale. The planning process can weave a metanarrative that binds multiple architectural objects and therefore multiple symbolic narratives in place. In classical Athens, the Cecropia (now referred to as the Acropolis) was the focal point of religious life, the Agora served as the social and commercial nexus, and the Pnyx was where the ecclesia met to discuss, deliberate, and vote as they exercised their form of open democracy. These architectural elements embody the central principles of Athenian society and are examples of a particular set of values encoded in urban form.

Architecture and planning become a symbolic representation in which the designer can manifest agency. But unlike many other art forms, spaces are experienced socially and transformed beyond the designer's wishes and control. As a result, spaces continuously evolve through the events they host, with each one adding cultural, aesthetic, and social meanings to the story. The architectural elements become anchor points for what is ultimately a socially constructed narrative of place. Designers encode motifs for space in the present without really controlling what these motifs will be in the future, but they understand that these symbols can induce actions, behaviors, and stories that could influence future events and, in turn, the continuous transformation of the physical and symbolic aspects of spaces. In this sense, symbolic manifestation in the constructed form is akin to setting the stage for stories to unfold in space.

Powerful symbolic logic lies behind the designs of many capital cities. Pierre Charles L'Enfant's plan for Washington, DC, Oscar Niemeyer's Brasília, and Le Corbusier's designs for Chandigarh, India, all share a design coda that emphasizes monumentality, iconic architecture, and an aggrandized scale as a symbolic embodiment of the power residing in the state (Vale, 2014). All these cities and their symbols are designed around notions of power, and stories of power ultimately take place there; laws are discussed, decisions pertaining to the lives of millions are made, and thousands of people participate in marches and rallies. Even so, places are not permanent but rather in a constant state of flux, and over time their socially pre-encoded uses change, superseding the original intentions of the designer.

The main takeaway is that for the designer, there is power in symbols—not just in what they represent, but in what they can incite. What weaves them together is a narrative cohesive enough to resonate with individuals but flexible enough to include other narratives that can occur in these spaces. Along these lines, spatial design becomes an exercise in structured storytelling. The Disney theme parks and the cities of Las Vegas and Dubai are examples of how harnessing the forces of design as an exercise in storytelling can be an incredibly powerful tool for placemaking.

Fantasies, Storytelling, and Place

Imagination, storytelling, and placemaking often go hand in hand. In Italo Calvino's novel *Invisible Cities* (1978), Marco Polo describes to Kublai Khan all the cities in the Mongol ruler's empire he has visited, each with its own magic, mysteries, and uniqueness. But despite their particular wonders, each and every one of these cities have their origins in Venice, the real subject of Polo's fantasies. Polo is a great storyteller, capable of expanding the minutiae of his observations into fantastical tales of cities; in detail after detail, each place comes to life. Both men are complicit in creating these imaginary cities. Polo's storytelling is a design process in which reality follows fantasy and storytelling weaves them together.

Design is, therefore, a hopeful activity. We dream of fantastic places, then shape our values and desires into plans, and weave in narratives and stories to create the social, cognitive, and emotional glue needed to turn ideas into reality. It is not uncommon in spatial design to find a core value that anchors the rest, according to which every other element of design must be interpreted. In the case of the capital cities mentioned earlier, the core idea was power, but it could also be wealth or normative visions of the future. In this chapter we argue that fantasies, particularly those linked to leisure and play, can be liberating as well as attractive and powerful for the design and creation of spaces.

A fundamental process in placemaking is projecting aspirations and value systems onto plans. In Frank Lloyd Wright's Broadacre City plan (Wright, 1935), his vision encompassed an ultra-low-density continuum of built structures interconnected by the marvels of modern transportation across the plains of America. For Le Corbusier and his modernist peers in the 1933 International Congress of Modern Architecture, the vision of an urban future followed values of order: nature was messy, so modern man should not be (Le Corbusier, 1987). Le Corbusier's plan for Paris imagined structures that far surpassed nature in both scale and monumentality, where functions could be separated by technology and transportation networks centered on the automobile, the perennial symbol of twentieth-century modernity. The godlike power of the architect, who is capable of creating (imposing, one could say) a way of life for the future, is a seductive one, although of course it is an illusion. Unfortunately, it took us a while to understand this, and urbanism during this period was defined in no small part by variations on the fantasies and visions of men like Wright and Le Corbusier (Fishman, 1982). These fantasies were partially constructed in places as dissimilar as New Jersey and Chandigarh, often with dire consequences.

Although most visions and plans for new cities are not built, the media created for them survive across time. The images and ideas they contain are built around strong, clear, and appealing storytelling and visualization that spark social imagination over generations (Gell, 1998). Most renowned designers and architects know this, and many are natural storytellers able to weave desirable narratives, developing a "creative and symbolic dimension of the social world" (Thompson, 1984, p. 6).

Story development encompasses a "what," a "way," and a plot. The "what" is the content of the story and includes the events, actors, time, and location. The "way" is how the events are narrated, and the "emplotment" (White, 2009) is how the elements of the narrative are organized. Content and form go hand in hand, but the form is also linked to audiences and how they are expected to experience the content. Architecture itself is a story in constructed form, and the stories it stimulates are codeveloped with its users. There are no monologues from designers but rather continuous conversations between people and the space. Rich spatial design makes spaces evolve into places that can be relatable at a personal level while still maintaining their capacity to be socialized. So two questions to ponder are "What stories should we tell about our spaces?" and "What stories are spaces telling about society?" The response to these questions has important design and political dimensions, and successful designers enable both.

For example, the illustrations of daily life designed by Herbert Ryman for Walt Disney or those by Syd Mead commissioned by US Steel (both heavily inspired by the NASA style manual) went far in shaping the social discussion of what the future was going to be like for postwar America in the 1960s and 1970s. This was the apex of the space race, when America was expanding its global reach through the powers of individual freedom, democracy, and capitalism, manifested as a desirable "modern" way of life, which was provided by American corporations already harnessing that future.

Although flying cars have not yet become a pervasive mode of transportation, and some of these designs seem anachronistic today, twenty-first-century society still yearns for many of the ideas and notions illustrated in these visions. Again, framing the narrative and choosing the right values and elements becomes a crucial exercise when designing spaces. We often design our spaces with a focus on functional practicality, but it is emotions that speak to us, and play is a powerful force in eliciting emotional responses.

Emotions and Play as Spatial Narratives

Situationists in postwar Europe explored how our environments affect our emotions and behaviors. Guy Debord's "Guide Psychogéographique de Paris" (1955) described the city not just in abstract representations of space but rather through the emotions generated by different areas of the city. Debord's guide shows a subdivision of Paris based not on the traditional spatial representation, but rather on mood units (*unités d'ambiance*). Only *dérive*, individual drifting and wandering, effectively getting lost, can provide a truly intimate, emotional experience in the city.

As in the case of play in Huizinga's 1938 book *Homo Ludens*, the true goal of wandering is freedom: breaking the monotony of daily life, roaming the streets without destination or purpose. For Debord, this is defiance of the spatial monotony in the capitalist industrial city. Shifting the focus from the abstract component of symbolic representation to the sensuous aspects of the city, the situationists did not ask what the visitor or viewer thought but rather how they felt in the space. The idea was to understand the "choreography" of spatialized emotions.

In planning and architecture, the "work-live-play" triad of human activities needed for good placemaking is often referenced. But "play" is seldom truly acknowledged in urban development theory as being on the same level as the other two components. The constant propensity of designers and planners to focus on the "live-work" dyad inhibits our ability to fully reckon with leisure as a critical design dimension useful for fostering positive personal and social growth. In fact, "play" elements, such as amenities and culture, are often treated as afterthoughts, simply a consequence of the natural flow of cities. Ironically, much of the collective identity of a place resides in leisure and social spaces such as parks, libraries, and museums. Leisure spaces consider the complexity of the human psyche and social interactions, rather than only seeing people and society through the myopic lens of *Homo economicus* with his utilitarian rationale.

Acknowledging the relevance of play opens other perspectives for spatial designers, who understand that amenities add context and anchor experiences to particular places (Nichols, 2011). In fact, we have been intensifying places through amenities for ages. Carnivals and festivals have played central roles in amalgamating religious and cultural values. Entertainment facilities have been a permanent fixture of urban landscapes, from the Circus Maximus in Rome to the music halls on Times Square in New York. Humans like to be entertained, because entertainment takes us to a fantasy world where we can play with values and identities, and in doing so, reinforce or reform our presence in the world. Unfortunately, leisure activities are often disdained. Various religious and political groups have historically condemned entertainment as sinful, harmful, or wasteful (Nichols, 2011) and consequently unfit to be on the same moral and social level as capital or labor. Entertainment has also been overlooked because it has been difficult to quantify; for example, how can the effect of a park on a city's economic development be quantified? Until recently such questions have been almost impossible to answer and even silly to ask.

Still, amenities are important determinants of economic activity. The presence of a mixed offering of amenities in a region may make it desirable to a certain type of population, particularly the one Richard Florida (2002) calls the creative class. In the traditional development model, productive factors such as capital and other resources generate more jobs, which in turn attract more people and drive population and urban growth. In the creative economy, amenities flip this relationship by creating a desirable environment where a unique blend of spatialized pleasures is capable of driving consumption and attracting people, fostering economic and urban growth. This broadens strategic options for policymakers and gives designers the freedom to envision new spaces. By intensifying a place through events and leisure facilities such as museums, restaurants, parks, and shopping areas, cities can market themselves for their experiences and quality of life (Anholt, 2006). The creation of symbols and identity anchors become critical components in urban development as they make audiences identify with a given place and make them more receptive to its message (Rapaille, 2007).

For some, making pleasure and play the focal point of the design and development narrative is akin to fantasy, but intensifying these symbolic elements of pleasure and play reinforces the perception of spatial exceptionalism, making them unique. The following cases demonstrate how embodying fantasies using architectural symbolism is a viable strategy for urban design and development in harsh environments: the swamp and the desert. First, we explore the Disney theme parks as examples of a thriving culture-based development model that combines storytelling and fantasy to create a global destination in what was formerly a swamp. We continue with two desert cities: Las Vegas as a hedonic fantasy of unique architectural expressions and Dubai as a modern pop-up city of iconic excess. These examples provide a better understanding of the role of cultural anchors and symbols as primary catalysts for place-based experiences, which focus on leisure and can have major consequences in social, economic, and spatial terms.

The Swamp: Walt Disney and the Strategy of Symbolic Development

Walter Elias Disney was one of the most iconic business and media figures of the twentieth century. The Disney Brothers Cartoon Studio, later renamed the Walt Disney Company, began with commissioned animations, but it really took off on its own in 1928, after Disney drew (with the help of Ub Iwerks) a simple mouse named Mickey and animated it in *Steamboat Willie*, the world's first cartoon postproduced with synchronized sound. It was a smash hit, providing Disney with copyrights that gave his company financial freedom. Following the success of Mickey Mouse and friends (Minnie Mouse, Donald Duck, Goofy, and Pluto), Walt Disney had an even bigger breakthrough in 1937 with *Snow White*, the first animated feature film. In the following decade his company brought the likes of *Dumbo*, *Pinocchio*, *Fantasia*, *Bambi*, and *Cinderella* to cinemas, often appropriating stories in the public domain, sanitizing them for a more conservative palate, and linking them to the Disney brand.

By the end of the 1940s, Disney had turned himself into one of the most recognized public figures in the United States. Always a consummate story-teller and technologist, he was constantly refining a carefully maintained image that projected endless imagination and affability into the public consciousness (Thomas, 1994). Over the span of a few years, his creations became a fixture of American culture, used in everything from military training and propaganda to merchandising and education.

Disney's ambitions and interests eventually outgrew film and anima-tion. He had been interested in placemaking for a long time, influenced by his father (who had worked at the Chicago Columbian Exposition) and his affection for Americana. Disney had an affinity for an American Dream embodied in a romantic notion of the past and a hopeful vision of the future—perspectives that were invariably at odds with the realities of daily life in the country at the time. This made him critical of public parks and carnivals; he echoed the conservative views of the time in deeming them unkempt and unwelcoming to families. Even so, he was already planning his own park. When his wife asked about the project, he replied that they (amusement parks) were "dirty, unsafe and the people who work there are nasty. My park won't be anything like those" (Imagineers, 1996, p. 10). What began as a desire to create a clean and fun place where he and his employees could take their families gradually grew into one of his defining works: Disneyland.

During the late 1940s Disney and his team of designers began dream-ing up a park that borrowed heavily from nostalgia and iconography from popular media such as film and literature, mixed with his studio's creations. Walt Disney understood that creating another amusement park like Coney Island in New York City or Tivoli Gardens in Copenhagen would not be enough to carry his vision. He consequently decided to build not an amuse-ment park but a theme park, a place where each element would help tell a story; it would provide a "theatrical experience" (Hench, 2009, p. 2), a permanent show in which visitors would not be spectators but rather join in the play.

Disney purchased 160 acres of land in California, next to the new inter-state highway that was still being built. Many close to him thought it folly: "I could never convince the financiers that Disneyland was feasible because dreams offer too little collateral," Walt Disney said (Imagineers Group, 1996). He borrowed money against his own life insurance but eventually found creative ways to finance his venture: he produced a television show for the ABC network called *Disneyland TV* that helped him secure the needed capital while at the same time advertising the project to households across the country years before it opened. The recipe for Disneyland was a pervasive leitmotif of magic, adventure, and family fun translated into a space. As a storyteller, Walt Disney understood that the fantasy was far more attractive than reality and that being part of the fantasy would resonate deeply with the public. Merging storytelling in cinema with place-making effectively made Disneyland an exercise in transmedia, a place purposely designed to tug at people's emotional strings.

The park's designers envisioned multiple thematic areas, borrowing and combining popular references: Main Street USA with its nostalgic storefronts, awnings, and horse-drawn carriages; Adventureland, a window to the faraway exotic lands of novelists Rudyard Kipling, Edgar Rice Burroughs, and Rider Haggard; Frontierland, a piece of the Wild West (which itself was a very popular film and TV theme during the 1950s); Fantasyland, with its fairytale castle and rides inspired by Disney's animated stories of European folklore; Tomorrowland, a modernist vision of the near future that America was racing toward, foreshadowing the country's growing fascination with the space age; and Holidayland, a short-lived area that was the closest representation of an actual public park, with a playground, picnic areas, and a baseball field. Ironically, the area closest to daily reality was the one that did not survive the passage of time.

Disneyland was fundamentally a place that aimed to emulate stories. As with narratives, pace and tone are as important as specific words (or in this case, each constructed element). Disney created a choreography of activities spread across its entire area (Imagineers Group, 1996), making Disneyland a heterotopic place that juxtaposes different spaces, times, and styles and has a deeper, layered meaning (Foucault, 2004). The nexus of the park is located at the end of Main Street, where Sleeping Beauty's castle emerges as the heart and main landmark of the park—a reminder that the true locus of the place is situated in fantasy.

The task of designing the park fell to the recently created WED Enterprises, more commonly known as the Imagineers; over the years, they encoded the design principles and strategies that have shaped all the

Disney parks. What Imagineer Marty Sklar, who worked at Disney for 54 years, refers to as "Mickey's Ten Commandments" have effectively become the guide for theme park design (Imagineers Group, 1996, p. 11). These rules include core principles emphasizing empathy, namely "Know your audience" and "Wear your guest's shoes." The commandments also encompass rules for storytelling, such as "Tell one story at a time"; "Organize the flow of people and ideas," merging storytelling and experience; and "Avoid contradictions—maintain identity," in other words, don't mix contrasting content. They also discuss the use of icons in place design, requiring Imagineers to "Communicate with visual literacy" by using color, shape, forms, and textures; and in classic Disney parlance, "Create a weenie," an iconic visual magnet that serves as a guiding landmark. But it is the last two commandments that most clearly embody Disney's original drivers: "Keep it up" (everything must be clean and properly maintained), and above all, "For every ounce of treatment, provide a ton of treat," meaning that everything in the park should be about fun.

The Imagineers referred to themselves as 3D storytellers. A backstory was created in order to achieve consistency in design choices; as projects evolved during the development process, each attraction's backstory would serve as a focal point that permitted a grounded exploration of the design. Iterative design was the norm: just a hub-and-spoke layout required over a dozen design changes before Walt Disney approved it, according to Imagineer Lee Marvin (Malmberg, 2008, p. 66).

The design and development process borrowed many tools from traditional set design practices used in theater, film, and television. Each attraction and place was storyboarded, and every guest interaction and moment was illustrated step by step; unnecessary elements were removed. Everything that came into direct contact with the guests' senses was considered to be "on stage," from light fixtures to cobblestones to soundscapes. Imagineers used architectural tricks such as forced perspective, scale manipulation, gentle curving of paths to emphasize the skyline, and secondary and tertiary layers of visual elements that function as an unreachable background meant to increase the sense of scale and place.

While each attraction had a sequential storyline associated with it, the stories themselves were told in the details layered over the built environments. Even as guests stand in line, story sequences begin (the line space was often referred to as "Scene 1" by the Imagineers), preparing the guests for the ride experience by establishing story anchors through the scene-setting, props, and interactive features. Employees dressed in costumes parade around the park. Disney wanted the employees to be living in the story environment he had created, and they consequently had to be permanently in character: they were not employees but "cast members," making the fantasy come alive.

There were substantial differences between Disneyland and other parks around the world. Conceptually speaking, the former provided stories, while the rest simply provided amusement. After it opened in 1955, Disneyland became an instant phenomenon, a veritable pilgrimage site for the average American family. During its first year of operations, more than 1 million people visited the park; by 2018 it had more than 18.5 million annual visitors, making it the second most visited theme park in the world, after Disney World, which had almost 21 million visitors that year (Themed Entertainment Association and AECOM, 2019). Disneyland proved that people yearn to experience embodied fantasies, where the place cannot be dissociated from the stories. The theme parks became a core business enterprise for the Walt Disney Company and a key component in the company's strategic development (Zenger, 2013)—as illustrated by Walt Disney himself in his 1957 "Synergy Map," arguably one of the earliest known examples of synergistic corporate management theory.

The success of Disneyland allowed Walt Disney to set his sights on a much larger ambition: he wanted to create a city of his own. This was not the first time Disney had thought about future cities; he featured the American highway system on *Disneyland TV* in 1958, and years later his team helped design several pavilions for the New York World's Fair of 1964–1965 meant to showcase the bright future ahead. Disney had previously partnered with Monsanto to build the House of the Future in Disneyland's Tomorrowland, a collaboration that also included MIT and was meant to highlight the impact that futuristic inventions like microwave ovens and modern plastics would have on daily life. Disney was also instrumental in creating functional transportation prototypes that over time became attractions of their own, such as the park's futuristic monorail and a personal rapid transit system (PRT) known as the PeopleMover.

At the same time, Disney was secretly acquiring over 28,000 acres of land in Florida through various dummy corporations for his city of the future. In November 1965 Disney and Florida officials announced the creation of

Disney World. Part of the deal entailed political support from the governor and the Florida legislature to create a new ad hoc district where the new city would be built. In 1967 Florida established the Reedy Creek Improvement District (RCID), effectively a privately run district, which allowed Disney to issue tax-free bonds for public projects. These would include a "larger and better" Disneyland (later named the Magic Kingdom) and several theme hotels, but the centerpiece was a project the Environmental Prototype Community of Tomorrow, or EPCOT. This was Disney's vision for a city of the future, a home to 20,000 residents that would be a center of industrial creativity, showing off the fruits of American ingenuity. EPCOT would be a place where new technology was pervasive and continuously evolving, a space for ongoing urban experimentation, and an indefinite urban lab.

Walt Disney did not live to see any of this: he died of cancer in 1966, and Disney World opened its doors in 1971. Soon afterward the Walt Disney Company decided to fully redesign EPCOT as a theme park called EPCOT Center, a permanent exposition space meant to demonstrate the technological prowess and ingenuity of American companies and provide a stage for showcasing cultures from around the world in an easily digestible form (see figure 2.1).

Over the years, the Imagineers' design principles have guided the creation of the various parks and other facilities operated by the Walt Disney Company around the world. Disney parks are a showcase of how technology has been used for several decades to enhance storytelling and embody fantasies. From the 1950s to the 1970s, the rides used mostly electromechanical rail systems with pneumatically actuated audio-animatronic characters; in the 1980s and 1990s the parks introduced early motion simulators, such as Star Tours and Mission Space, which utilized digitally controlled hydraulic platforms and centrifuges borrowed from the aerospace industry and synchronized with audiovisual material to create a multisensory experience around stories. In the twenty-first century, attractions such as Sum of All Thrills at EPCOT Center use fully programmable KUKA robots to deliver an individually tailored simulated ride, which can be designed by each user, and virtual reality (VR) attractions allow guests to ride Aladdin's Magic Carpet at DisneyQuest, a park facility fully devoted to virtual experiences. The design evolution of Disney parks—from Disneyland and its later iterations in Orlando, Paris, and Tokyo, to EPCOT Center, to Tokyo's DisneySea and the latest parks opening in China—demonstrates how technology has

Figure 2.1
Walt Disney's EPCOT Center, a theme park with a mixed identity that ultimately
diverged from Walt Disney's original vision, keeping its modernist utopian spirit but
eschewing the central goal of developing a new kind of urban prototype.
Source: Brian McGowan, 2020.

broadened the design tapestry and enriched the language of the Imagineers,
primarily in three vectors: enhancing perceived realism, environmental
responsiveness, and user interactivity.

Na'vi River Journey is located in Disney's Animal Kingdom's recently
opened Pandora area, which is inspired by James Cameron's film *Avatar*.
The ride is to some extent an updated version of the classic Jungle Cruise
boat ride at Disneyland's Adventureland, which was filled with some of
the original pneumatic robots (also known as animatronics) performing as
wild and exotic beasts from the wild. For the Na'vi River Journey modern
technologies provide gains in perceived realism, responsiveness, and interactivity from the riders. Init multilayered digital projections bring three-
dimensional depth to hyperrealistic animated renderings of alien fauna that
interact with the gigantic bioluminescent flora of Pandora, fully surrounding the boat as the journey unfolds. The ride reaches its climax when the
Shaman of Songs, itself a state-of-the-art animatronic, comes alive in an
eerily realistic manner, singing and interacting with the riders; it is a far cry

from the limited movements of the early animatronic characters used in the classic rides, but it retains the basic idea of using technology to embody fantasy in space.

Nearby, Flight of Passage invites guests to step into the mind of a Na'vi avatar and ride a flying Banshee creature through the skies of Pandora. This attraction is the evolution of the Soarin' ride, which debuted at Disney California Adventure in 2001. Both use very large dome screen projections that envelop the riders and are synchronized with motion-controlled platforms and pneumatic actuators that inject gusts of air, water vapor, and scents. The goal of both attractions is to simulate the sensation of free flight. Riders are primed throughout the line area with scenarios and props meant to recreate a futuristic base. In Flight of Passage, the guests are digitally scanned and assigned their avatar, while a video explains their mission, making them active participants in the story and creating a sense of agency; all of this happens before the guests enjoy the ride itself. This attraction replaces the mechanical sitting hang gliders of Soarin' with autonomous robotic individual seats that move more freely and are more responsive to the audiovisual material, while mimicking the form factor and even the breathing of the Banshees via controlled lateral motion actuators and side air blowers. For a full five minutes guests fly across vast alien landscapes at full tilt in a ride so exhilarating that some guests are willing to wait in line for more than six hours.

Perhaps a more fitting comparison can be made between the two most iconic rides inspired by the Star Wars movies. Star Tours opened at Disneyland in 1987, while Star Wars: Millennium Falcon—Smuggler's Run debuted in 2019 as the main attraction of the newest Star Wars–themed area (at both Disneyland and Disney Hollywood Studios). The old and new rides are essentially the same, with one critical variation that is only possible through technological advances: real-time interactivity. Both attractions are electronically controlled motion simulators that use synchronized video to increase the sensation of presence. In both rides, guests sit in a spaceship cockpit environment and the audiovisual material is projected outside, creating an external immersive environment. The difference, however, lies in how the projected audiovisual is generated.

For the original attraction, Disney worked with Lucasfilm and Industrial Light & Magic to produce a short film showing space views, full planets, and space battles between the Rebel Alliance and the evil Galactic Empire, all with the cinematic quality of a Hollywood blockbuster. Smuggler's Run also projects audiovisual material outside the cockpit but uses dedicated servers with state-of-the-art graphics processing units to render the visuals (which are produced by a 3D graphics engine borrowed from the video game industry) alongside dynamic spatial audio technologies. These tools give designers the freedom to include real-time responses to the guests' in-experience behaviors, which means that Imagineers can enhance the power of storytelling by turning them into actual characters participating in the adventure. Where in the original Star Tours, guests were simply passive passengers with no input or control over their experience, in Smuggler's Run they are assigned roles as pilots, gunners, and engineers. Buttons and levers create responses that look and feel real: pilots can engage the ship's hyperdrive to surpass light speed, gunners can shoot lasers and missiles at the Empire's TIE Fighters, and engineers can harpoon cargo to smuggle across the galaxy. The adventure is responsive and consequently different every single time. For park designers who have attempted to make fantasies believable for decades, few things are as empowering as fully ceding the stage to the guests. For a place that relies so heavily on tight choreography, this is akin to improvisation.

These examples do not imply that only cutting-edge technologies should be applied when designing place-based fantasies. On the contrary, many of the best experiences have always relied on a combination of new and traditional technologies paired with good design principles that stand the test of time. There is a great deal of repurposing discarded technologies in the creation of new spaces, and over the years Disney's Imagineers have learned the hard lesson of coping with the fast pace of technological evolution. When technology becomes too complex to maintain (or worse, ceases to amaze or tell the story), it must be discarded. A good example is when available home technologies such as modern video game consoles and VR headsets became capable of rendering more detailed and richer experiences than many of those at DisneyQuest, which made the parks obsolete overnight and forced their closure (Williams & Mascioni, 2017).

Disney parks have very sophisticated tracking technologies embedded in their spatial fabric and worn by the visitors, which are fundamental for optimal operation of the parks as well as better guest service. For example, automated guest reservation systems (FastPass+) have been used for years to balance attraction loads. The company even developed its own proprietary Internet of things (IoT) and wearable technologies to provide a seamless vacation experience and to obtain data on guests' behavior. Visitors can purchase RFID/NFC-powered MagicBands as collectibles; these can be used for cashless payment in any store within the parks, to reserve a spot on a ride or in a restaurant, to purchase photos taken by the cadres of professional photographers in the park, or even to interact with park rides in unique ways that extend beyond the average park visitor experience. In a sense, Disney parks have integrated a series of spatialized technologies that create a digital layer of data to automate processes, optimize operations, and track visitors in real time to personalize services, so that the smart attractions respond differently to each guest.

Disney's experiments hold many lessons for spatial designers and urban planners. As Sharon Zukin (1995/2005) argues, they overturn the assumption that production is the sole driver of the economy and show the power of culture and entertainment.

Disney's success shows us a development model based on creating and exploiting cultural content as a primary value while creating a space for consumption (Zukin, 1990) that has proven to be quite resilient and expansive. Today, Disney World is the main economic driver of the city of Orlando and the surrounding counties. Over the span of fifty years Orlando has become one of the fastest-growing metropolitan areas in America, surging from 500,000 inhabitants in 1970 to over 2,500,000 today. It is also a global tourist destination that welcomes more than 75 million visitors per year[1] (expected to exceed 100 million per year within the next decade[2]), making it the country's most visited destination by far. And with each tourist spending close to $500 per visit, some $284 million in tourism development tax revenues are added to the Orlando coffers each year.[3] Not bad for a place that up until a few decades ago was mostly a vacant swamp.

Yet ultimately, the genius behind Disney's theme park design philosophy lies not in its pursuit of the authentic but rather in its careful representation of perceived fantasy. The fantasy clearly creates a place as we want it to be, not as it is. Criticisms often leveled at Disney parks describing them as artificially staged environments devoid of cultural significance often miss the point. The power of their design lies precisely in their obsessive pursuit of curated artificiality as a requirement to make the stories feel real. Such design power lies in embodying the fantasy: after all, people naturally gravitate toward the exceptional.

Deserts: Metanarratives of Pleasure and Opulence

It is ironic to think that deserts—natural habitats at the edge of human activity that are inhospitable due to scorching heat and lack of water but also have strikingly surreal vistas, with flora and fauna that are simultaneously beautiful and alien—are home to two of the most successful yet unlikely global destinations of the twentieth and twenty-first centuries. Las Vegas and Dubai are two cities designed around fantasies of glamour, wealth, and desire; both are surrounded by a natural environment of extreme beauty and harshness, in stark contrast to the man-made artificial pleasure and opulence on offer. Like the Disney parks, these cities are symbolically performative, with unique forms of storytelling and branding. If Disneyland is a theme park for families, Las Vegas is "the most aggressively branded and promoted concatenation of adult theme parks in the world" (Fox, 2007, p. 9). As places they both resonate deeply with different audiences.

Half a century ago, Robert Venturi and Denise Scott Brown conducted a studio class with a small group of students from the Yale School of Architecture to analyze and learn from the famous Strip in Las Vegas, Nevada. Their study centered on architectural form and meaning, and their observations of the commercial architecture on the Strip led them to distinguish different architectural archetypes there: the duck, where the shape of the building itself is designed as a symbol, and the decorated shed, a nondescript building with external symbols applied to it. Venturi and Scott Brown argued that ducks and decorated sheds were effective counterweights to the functional formalism of twentieth-century modern architecture, often devoid of any meaning.

Architecture in Las Vegas was a seemingly incoherent mish-mash, a juxtaposition of styles described amusingly as "Miami Moroccan, International Jet Set Style; Arte Moderne Hollywood Orgasmic, Organic Behind; Yamasaki Bernini cum Roman Orgiastic; Niemeyer Moorish; Moorish Tudor (Arabian Nights); Bauhaus Hawaiian" (Venturi et al., 1977, p. 80). The architecture's cultural pastiche, as bizarre as it seemed, had a lot to say against modernist architecture with its tendency to churn out massive quantities of homogenized, sterile, and anonymous non-places of circulation and consumption (Augé, 2008). For Venturi, Scott Brown, and their coauthor Steven Izenour, the key was to see Las Vegas without contamination by any previous judgments, eschewing the debates on high vs. low culture that are common in elitist architecture circles. Only in this way could the amount of architecture in the city with symbolic meaning be determined. The city seemed to hold clear lessons for designers in terms of how they could enrich the symbolic meaning of postmodern architecture. Unlike the Disney parks, with their carefully designed symbolic synchronicity and choreography, Las Vegas achieved a coherence of place by establishing a metanarrative that everybody could build upon, layered historically and told through cultural, legal, architectural, and programmatic means as the embodiment of opportunistic laissez-faire.

The spatial design of iconic Las Vegas cannot be dissociated from the culture and legal arrangements of the city. The anything-goes attitude that permeates Las Vegas architecture (which was already present in the 1960s and continues to this day) is the result of geographical and historical conditions. During the Great Depression, Las Vegas was a small town in the middle of the Mojave Desert, the driest place in North America with summer temperatures hovering around and even exceeding 120 degrees Fahrenheit. This harsh and inhospitable location stunted urban and economic growth in the region, leading local officials to encourage economic development by deregulating legal codes on social matters such as gambling and marriage as well as building codes and standards. Most notably, the current gambling regime was put into place in 1931, formally legalizing casinos and allowing them to evolve from the wide-open saloons and illegal urban gambling halls of the early twentieth century into the sun-drenched pleasure palaces that exist today (Schwartz, 2013).

The opportunistic nature of a laissez-faire spirit allowed the city to effectively capitalize on everything, from the key transportation infrastructure connecting it to the world to ill-reputed sources of capital needed for growth. When California authorities cracked down on illegal gambling in the state in 1938, many gambling tourists simply went to Las Vegas, which was ready to welcome them and was now easily accessible by the Union Pacific railroad line, the recently opened airport (McCarran), or Highway 91, which became the famous Strip and also connected California with the Canadian border across several states. Unlike the smaller casinos located around Fremont Street in downtown Las Vegas, the new casinos were larger, glitzier, neon-lit modernist monoliths. Opportunism even led Las Vegas officials and hotels to take advantage of the continuous atmospheric nuclear blasts at the nearby Nevada Test Site. These symbols of American modernity and might were visible from the Strip, which led Las Vegas to market itself as America's "Atomic City."

The coming decades brought an explosion in scale and themes. Investments from the likes of Howard Hughes and Kirk Kerkorian funded architectural design innovations. Unlike the smaller motels and casinos of yore, the new megaresorts had thousands of rooms apiece, casinos, and entertainment and shopping venues—as well as gardens, multiple pools, and grand, iconic, and glamorous lobbies. The city's gradual evolution from casinos to megaresorts turned it into a popular cultural icon (Jaschke & Ötsch, 2003). Elvis Presley filmed *Viva Las Vegas!* (1964) there, married his wife Priscilla in the Aladdin Hotel in 1967, and returned as a resident performer for the International Hotel a few years later. Other Hollywood stars also married in Vegas, lived in Vegas, and became performing residents. The Vegas residency has been a fixture of the city's entertainment scene for years, attracting many world-renowned performers, from Liberace, Frank Sinatra, and the Rat Pack to Rod Stewart, Elton John, Céline Dion, and Britney Spears. Utilizing internationally known figures from the film, music, and sports communities to obtain glamour and social respect through association has been a successful strategy in elevating the city's public identity beyond the seediness often linked to gambling and other leisure activities.

The same year the Nevada legislature legalized gambling, it also relaxed its marriage laws, making them the most lenient in the country. While most locations required blood tests and long waiting periods before granting a license, Las Vegas's Clark County allowed people to get married the same day they obtained the license. This new law followed divorce laws passed in 1911 that permitted a "quickie" divorce after just six weeks of residence. Together, these regulations established Nevada as a place for marital freedom in a historically repressed and culturally conservative nation. Pleasure as a design and development guideline leveraged laissez-faire attitudes with their clear connections to sex in order to create spaces that glamorized Las Vegas's image as a place for sexual freedom. It is no surprise that the city's attitudes toward prostitution mirrored the liberalization of social norms around gambling and marriage, particularly in the 1930s and 1940s, after Prohibition ended and alcohol was again permitted. Male workers rushing to complete key infrastructure projects like the Hoover Dam on the Colorado River, as well as servicemen stationed at the nearby US Army gunnery school (now Nellis Air Force Base) required such services; the legacy of open sexuality must not be overlooked, since is a critical aspect of the city's identity.

To this day, Nevada remains the only state in the union with legal brothels, and although it is formally forbidden in Clark County, prostitution is still classified as a misdemeanor (and not a felony) in the city. Unsurprisingly, this region still accounts for nine out of ten cases of prostitution in the state. The rise of the leisure economy has effectively propelled sexuality into the heart of the city as a tourist destination (Brents et al., 2009). As Linda Chase (2009) says in her take on the city, anybody looking for on-demand sex can easily find "more than 120 pages of listings and ads [in the yellow pages], a Freudian smorgasbord of sexual fantasies. Every ethnic and age group is represented: blondes, brunettes (including blacks), Asians, young and old. Clients can enjoy an evening with a French maid, a Catholic schoolgirl, a kitten with a whip—the choices are virtually limitless" (p. 98). Sex and hedonism became culturally reinforced motifs for "Sin City" in 1966 with the opening of Caesars Palace, inspired by Roman culture with its rows of nude statues, white marble columns, detailed mosaics, and bas-reliefs all welcoming the visitor into an exuberant palace of pleasure and excess. The hotel, which has continued to expand over the decades into a sprawling complex of almost 4,000 rooms across several towers, including a 4,000-seat colosseum theater (originally built to host a permanent nightly show by Céline Dion) and a large ultra-luxury shopping mall, truly spearheaded the combination of larger-than-life architectural structures that fully embodied the cultural appropriation of their sources while successfully legitimizing adult hedonic culture as a central value in the Vegas narrative.

The coming decades would bring a greater degree of publicly traded corporate control over the long-standing properties on the Strip. New owners sought to adapt to the changing demographics in the city (Rothman, 2015) and expand the types of experiences offered to tourists. They did it by intensifying the thematization of the hotels and more widely diversifying content through long-term exclusive partnerships with leading performing artists and groups as a strategy for growth. The aim was to transform Las Vegas into a more palatable destination for tourists across all age groups. Investments went to new properties that emphasized clear and distinguishable thematic characteristics. As a result, in the early 1990s there was an explosion of resorts such as the Luxor, inspired by ancient Egypt with its gigantic pyramid containing the world's brightest beam of light; the New York, a pastiche of motifs from the city that never sleeps; the Excalibur, a medieval fantasy castle; the Monte Carlo, based on the eponymous European casino; Treasure Island, inspired by Caribbean pirates; and the Mirage, a tropical paradise featuring a volcanic eruption every hour. The turn of the twenty-first century saw a new generation of theme properties with investments exceeding one billion dollars each, which increased the degree of design complexity and detail, luxury, and entertainment content offered to visitors. There was the Paris, evoking the fin de siècle City of Light with a half-sized replica of the Eiffel Tower; Mandalay Bay, another tropical paradise; the Bellagio, with fountains and architecture borrowed from villas surrounding Italy's Lake Como; and the Venetian, with its climate-controlled canals surrounded by stores, restaurants, and bars and replicas of the Palazzo Ducale, Piazza San Marco, and Rialto Bridge.

From a design perspective, the combination of functional elements in each megaresort is fundamentally the same. A massive piece of sculptural architecture establishes the theme and motif for the outside world. A grand foyer and lobby impose the message of luxury and pleasure on the incoming visitor according to the hotel's theme. A very large casino, usually filled with bustling movement, noise, and lights, provides the fantasy of effortless wealth through the probabilistic mirage of a game of chance, where even visitors walking past the high-roller tables can still partake in the excitement by playing a coin slot machine. The entrance to the hotel elevators is accessible yet subdued, meant only for the staying guests who have access and know the way. Retail space, bars, and restaurant facilities for all budgets are sprinkled throughout but concentrated nearest the casino area. And often some large-scale conference facilities and meeting rooms are tucked in the back, adjacent to the massive parking structure. The realization and distribution of these elements, however, follow the thematic guidelines as a way to maintain stylistic coherence.

Today Vegas is still pushing to become a high-end cultural and architectural destination, albeit with mixed results. The cultural performing arts content offered in the city has made it a global destination for theater and concert goers, following a long legacy of world-famous artists and large-scale spectacles from the likes of Cirque du Soleil. Meanwhile, the city has struggled to earn the same level of respect for its museums and art galleries, some of which hold highly esteemed collections; these include the Bellagio Gallery of Fine Art and the ill-fated Guggenheim Hermitage Museum designed by Rem Koolhaas for the Venetian (this featured a spacious 64,000-square-foot gallery, which closed after only a year of operation, and a smaller space destined for masterpieces, which only lasted a few more years). Fine dining is a big hit, and most top chefs have a restaurant in the city: Joel Robuchon, Charlie Palmer, Michael Mina, Nobu Matsuhisa, and other big names are treated like stars by hotel owners willing to invest millions to add these exclusive brands to their catalog of venues, turning the city into a multiple-Michelin-star paradise for foodies.

But amid the constant maelstrom of development in the city, "starchitects" have found it challenging to compete with the monolithic and thematized neon-lit towers of many hotels on the Strip. Rem Koolhaas, Frank Gehry, and Norman Foster have developed projects that either failed to materialize or (even worse) failed to capture the attention of a visiting public that is still more entranced with the volcano at the Mirage, the Eiffel Tower in the Paris Hotel and Casino, and the gigantic dancing fountains of the Bellagio. Even the $8.5 billion CityCenter, owned by MGM Resorts International and Dubai World, has struggled to find its footing among the more established resorts in the city, despite its 76 acres of mixed-use towers with designs by such stars as Ehrenkrantz Eckstut & Kuhn Architects, Foster+Partners, Gensler, and Helmut Jahn. This complex is capped by the Aria, a 61-story, 4,004-room pair of sensuous interconnected glass-and-steel towers designed by Cesar Pelli's architecture firm and containing one of the largest casinos on the Strip, connected to the city's most exclusive high-end mall. All of these projects failed to generate the excitement one would expect from their scale and design quality (see figure 2.2).

In other words, beyond the (perhaps clichéd) marketing motto "What happens in Vegas, stays in Vegas," what explains Las Vegas is a place-narrative with a historical origin compelling enough to attract billions of dollars of investments in real estate, infrastructure, and urban development to the unlikeliest of places. There is a degree of honesty to the statement, and the architecture reflects this coherently by delivering spectacle and pleasure. The constant thematic renovation of the city reflects the fluidity of reinterpretation and the Vegas tourism industry's capacity for reinvention. As architect and scholar Stefan Al (2017) relates, over the decades this stylistic evolution has emulated everything from the Wild West to modernism, corporate steel and glass, and even theme parks, eventually becoming a

Figure 2.2
The Lou Ruvo Center for Brain Health in Las Vegas, designed by Frank Gehry (*top*);
night scene of the Las Vegas Strip, showing the CityCenter complex and the Aria
Hotel designed by César Pelli (*bottom*). Both are examples of "starchitect" projects at
odds with the traditional theme architecture of the Strip.
Source: Nick Ferwings, 2018.

playground for contemporary starchitects: this can only be explained in a place where the central cultural and social narrative states that "in this place, anything can happen." The literal embodied fantasies of Disney parks targeting children and families are here replaced by metaphorical ones aimed at adults, delivered through a myriad of styles but all containing the same basic elements of adult fantasies: glamour, sex, desire, wealth, permissiveness, and freedom from social judgment.

As we have discussed in this chapter, dreams are potent when combined with vision, willpower, and a good story. Las Vegas is not the only city in the desert that changed its destiny by devising and following through with a localized narrative of opulence. Flying into the Dubai International Airport, the first thing visible from the airplane window is the city's imposing and ever-growing skyline of roughly two hundred skyscrapers (see figure 2.3), capped by the 829-meter Burj Khalifa, which is by far the tallest building in the world (at least until the 1-kilometer Jeddah Tower being built in Saudi Arabia claims the spot a few years from now). The skyline seems like a mirage stretching along the coastline as well as the desert. And a mirage it is, one designed and built as a fantastic hyperluxurious global techno-oasis in the Persian Gulf. But is Dubai's showcase of fantastic and even outlandish architectural designs and wealth narratives a manifestation of crass excess or a shrewd development strategy?

Figure 2.3
Dubai's impressive skyline, built mostly in the last two decades, capped by the Burj Khalifa, the world's tallest building and a statement of opulence and futurism.
Source: Jake De-bique, 2019.

In the 1970s the small port city of Dubai, capital of the Emirate of Dubai, faced a challenge: as in many places across the Arabian Peninsula, oil had recently been found in the emirate (in the Fateh Field in 1966). While this oil field was sizable, Fateh (meaning "Good Fortune") was a far cry from the great fields in neighboring Abu Dhabi or the massive ones discovered at the turn of the twentieth century in Saudi Arabia. Still, Dubai benefited as a result, with oil funding the emirate's development through the following decades. Oil revenue accelerated Sheik Rashid Bin Saeed Al-Maktoum's infrastructure plans for the city, which in turn boosted the population growth. But by the mid-1970s it was clear that Dubai would run out of oil much sooner than its neighbors, and this posed a problem. The city was enjoying its riches, but when the oil dried out it would go back to its original reality: a small fishing and pearling community, a regional port city stuck in a desert, surrounded by sand.

"My grandfather rode a camel, my father rode a camel, I drive a Mercedes, my son drives a Land Rover, his son will drive a Land Rover, but his son will ride a camel," Sheik Rashid Bin Saeed Al-Maktoum famously said again and again to illustrate the city's dilemma. How to keep driving Mercedes and Land Rovers, not in the global cities of London, New York, or Paris, but in Dubai? The response to this question required a shift away from understanding the emirate as a local/regional entity and toward viewing its potential transformative path through the lenses of globalization and neoliberalism. Even so, Dubai was not alone in its dilemma; other cities in the Gulf region, such as Doha and Abu Dhabi, had more natural resources and competing ambitions, so speed was of the essence. The answer was to transform Dubai into a global city overnight, as if it were bursting out of the desert sands.

The decision that would create a gradual transition of regional power was made in the mid-1970s and sent ripples far beyond the Persian Gulf, creating a socioeconomic project defined not only by the geographical boundaries of the emirate but also by a post-oil development strategy framed around the region's geopolitical complexities (Davidson, 2008). In a region famous for its riches as well as its notorious instability, an oasis of steadiness and calm is a prerequisite for any development narrative. The project, as Bromber et al. (2016) describe, created an altogether semantic construct that blended concepts of politics, programming, marketing, and utopianism.

The first step was clear: Dubai needed to be linked to the world. This required key investments in maritime ports, logistics, and airport facilities.

The development of the Jebel Ali Free Zone was important for landing for-eign investment by providing a tax-free area with a unique legal system that permitted a certain measure of legal rights for foreign capital invest-ments, a model akin to contemporary China's Special Economic Zones. Dubai's position near the tip of the Strait of Hormuz made it a strategic port as a gateway to the Persian Gulf and a key stop for ships navigating toward the Indian Ocean. Nonetheless, because the global world of the twentieth century was defined by its air connectivity, becoming an air power was also necessary (Brooks, 2013).

At the time, however, it was difficult for countries in a region encum-bered by constant warfare and conflict to land important foreign invest-ments beyond those involved in extracting strategic natural resources such as oil and gas. It was even harder to recruit the foreign talent needed to be competitive in the global economy. In order to place Dubai on the map as a destination for talented immigrants, the city invariably needed to move toward a multicultural cosmopolitanism capable of providing space for personal growth and development. This was a challenge for Dubai's con-servative Muslim society; but thanks to the city's historical role as a port with a certain degree of familiarity with foreigners, the emirate was better prepared for this than its neighbors. In order to meet its goals, the emirate framed a strategic narrative in which the city of Dubai was marketed to global companies as an oasis of legal and economic stability in the region, while simultaneously reinforcing a narrative that created a perception of wealth, opulence, and cultural accessibility designed to boost the desirabil-ity of the place at an individual level. Here, the power of symbolic archi-tecture alongside a few creative legal and institutional arrangements have been fundamental in achieving Dubai's position in the global competitive arena. Developing tourism, logistics, and finance as key industrial sectors proved critical to branding Dubai as a destination for success (Hafeez et al., 2016), as did a savvy international mass-marketing strategy emphasizing positive messages as part of a soft diplomatic approach that separated the city from conditions in the region (Govers, 2012) and even some global cities (Coombe & Melki, 2012). The city is run as a corporation (Kanna, 2011), while its marketing still projects a certain traditionalist and even orientalist vision to the West, as a holdout where Europeans are still served by Asians—even when this runs counter to the official public rhetoric of anticolonialism and the historic narrative of nationalism as a force to counteract British containment (Davidson, 2008).

At first glance, discussing many of the architecture and urban development projects launched by Dubai's authorities and investment arm over the past thirty years would seem to describe the epitome of Persian Gulf excess over and over again. At face value, projects like the Burj Al Arab hotel (considered one of the most luxurious in the world, with ten exclusive restaurants and a private fleet of Rolls-Royces and helicopters available to its guests) seem to be just the conspicuous expression of a nouveau riche operating with resources available only to Arab oil barons. The same logic would seem to follow many of the now famous development projects that the emirate has built over the years. The palm tree–shaped Palm Jumeirah and the Juzur al-Ālam ("World Islands"), with its hundreds of islands representing the world, are massive artificial archipelagos of dredged sand located a few miles off the coast of Dubai and seem to defy common sense; considering that the city had plenty of land available when they were planned, why create monumental artificial islands? In fact, one could ask the same question with regard to the Burj Khalifa. Yet it is precisely the superlative aspects of these projects that underscore what represents a shift from the old centers of the Arab and Middle Eastern world, such as Cairo, Amman, and Lebanon, toward the new cities in the Gulf (Elsheshtawy, 2009).

Lack of subtlety is precisely the symbolic objective of Dubai's architecture. Similar to baroque and churrigueresque architecture, the point is to display excess wealth and generate a human emotional response centered on desire. It is the audacity of the projects that makes them compelling. Such audacity only reinforces a narrative relating an environment of excess, not of scarcity, and a maximization of symbolic anchors is fostered to reinforce the central storyline. This is the underlying logical justification for ATM machines that dispense solid gold bars on the observation deck of the Burj Khalifa,[4] or a police force famous for its fleet of exotic cars, including a Lykan Hypersport, a Ferrari LaFerrari, a Pagani Huayra, an Aston Martin One-77, a Rolls-Royce Wraith, and dozens of other luxury vehicles used as patrol cars to police tourist areas.[5]

Alongside these seemingly outlandish projects and displays of opulence, a series of commercial destinations flourished and converted Dubai into a shopper's paradise. Large malls were often designed with theme park principles in mind; examples include the Souk Al Bahar, Ibn Battuta Mall, and Dragon Mart, a popular destination catering specifically to Chinese and East Asians. The culture of constant consumption fits in perfectly with the narrative of wealth and leisure. The story has clearly resonated: in just a few decades Dubai's population expanded 300 percent, from 900,000 in the year 2000 to a little under 3 million today.[6] At the same time it has become one of the most cosmopolitan cities in the world, with an expat population of Iranians, Russians, South Asians, Filipinos, Indians, more recently Chinese, and some Westerners making up between 83 percent to 95 percent of its population (Davidson, 2008), making native Emiratis a tiny de facto minority living in their own land.

This is not to say that mirages and visions of wealth are the only cause of growth; an empty narrative without substance will not be sustained over time. The scale and complexity of Dubai's infrastructure projects have fueled a job bonanza across the spectrum of skills and professions, from highly technical and managerial roles (usually filled by European or North American–educated professionals) to lower-skilled construction, domestic, and service jobs that are frequently filled by seasonal immigrants from East Asia and lower-income countries on the Indian subcontinent (Schindhelm, 2017).

Parallel in importance to the construction boom was the creation of legal and financial systems designed to attract and retain flows of foreign capital. These include the Dubai International Finance Center, a special economic zone created in 2004 that strengthened Dubai's role as a financial connection between the Middle East and Central Asia and the world beyond, assuring a relatively stable flow of capital into the city. They also include a 2002 land reform permitting foreigners to own land in the emirate. It is important to note that this reform came immediately after the September 11 terrorist attacks in the United States, which prompted a series of mandated regulatory control systems for foreign capital and the financial services industry in the United States. For many wealthy foreign individuals, especially those from places now perceived to be antagonistic to the West, the United States' new regulatory framework created risk by making their assets vulnerable to seizures and restrictions. The natural response among many wealthy Arab, Russian, Iranian, and Indian individuals (among others) was to move their assets out of the reach of US authorities, with Dubai becoming a preferred destination for parking capital assets. In a way, much of the real estate boom of the recent decades was not financed with oil money, but rather through the flows of foreign capital in a post-9/11 environment.

The influx of money created a booming real estate market that nearly quadrupled Dubai's urban footprint in less than a decade, creating enough room for outsized development projects signed by famous architects. Computer-designed architectural fantasies, showcasing the trend of leveraging 3D computer-aided design (CAD) and visual manipulation, were an attempt to influence economic interests (Sommerlad, 2016). The artificiality of Dubai's design, which is sometimes criticized, echoes symbols of aspirational globalism as it makes the place real based on the story created around it, and has become an important urban reference, a philosophy iconized in the Dubai Frame (see figure 2.4), an enormous building that is simultaneously the world's largest picture frame, ideal for taking selfie photographs with the rest of the city properly "framed" in the background, a clear architectural reference to the way stories are made in the age of social media.

Figure 2.4
The Dubai Frame, located in Zabeel Park, Dubai. The largest frame in the world, at over 150 meters tall, it stands as a physical manifestation of urban glamour for the Instagram generation.
Source: Mukund Nair, 2018.

To a certain extent, other cities, such as Singapore, have followed similar strategies of development and growth: connect the city to the world, drive a narrative of wealth and progress, manifest these values architecturally, increase global cultural standing via association with established players, focus on pleasure and conspicuous consumption, and reframe your legal and institutional arrangements accordingly. Perhaps the last element in the Dubai metanarrative has been what Brooks (2013, p. 367) describes as a "come-as-you-are ethos." In other words, the Dubai story line is not just one of wealth and luxury but also one of relative freedom. The multiculturalism manifest in the city's architectural and urban form belies how spatial design and development are followed by institutional forces. In Dubai different legal systems apply according to place; so depending on where in the city a person is at any moment, he or she may be governed under different systems and norms. Dubai's taxation and visa system has created a gilded cage of conflicting values (Ali, 2010), with a population of "flexible citizens" (Kanna, 2010).

In Dubai, adapting and changing one's own cultural norms is not required. In a city where no culture is effectively mainstream, the ability to establish a shared value system of ethical norms is greatly diminished, and as a result the social and legal coda is rooted within each unique place on a practical level, effectively making Dubai a place of places. Each is uniquely different, and there is sufficient diversity to provide residents with enough behavioral options to fit their lifestyles—forming a complex tapestry of stories in the process.

3 Tinkering with Spatialities

Playing and Tinkering

The act of play carves and multiplies spatialities within ordinary spaces. Play spaces are sometimes built with the explicit purpose of embodying fantasies—theme parks are an example of such play spaces—but they also emerge from spontaneous acts, such as when children imagine a cardboard box is a spaceship, or when skateboarders use handrails as slides. In these spontaneous situations, players define spatialities in which play occurs. Play creates a zone that is simultaneously safe and experimental; the rules that organize ordinary spaces do not apply to play spaces (the cardboard box is a spaceship during play). But play spaces are porous and can be used to experiment when alternative users interact with spatial elements (for example, we look at handrails differently after seeing skateboarders use them). This is because play permits behaviors, personifications, and fantasies that do not make sense or are not allowed outside the play space, or when play is over. However, by fostering explorations that go beyond functionalism, play can be so powerful that it triggers changes in the way we use and design spaces, opening up possibilities to create spaces that emotionally resonate with people.

This is particularly important in cities, which are composed of multiple intertwined spaces and are used by people with diverse interests, habits, physical abilities, and cultural backgrounds. In this sense, play spaces challenge Huizinga's (1950, p. 10) notion of the "magic circle," a spatially and temporally protected area in which the act of play is somehow isolated and protected from its surroundings. In writing about pervasive games that explore urban elements through technologies, Eddie Duggan (2017) argues that they "blur the boundaries between ordinary life and the ritualistic game space inside the magic circle" (p. 112). Huizinga's magic circle is not just a spatiotemporal container but also a mental state in which players experiment with values by willingly joining in play (either as participants or as spectators). This confirms the above argument that play spaces are always porous to the external world, and that exploring the porosity of play spaces can reveal aspects of the city that are often buried under established functions, habits, and meanings.

Playful attitudes can subvert the strict meanings of spaces. Skateboarders and parkour practitioners (called traceurs, the French word for "tracers"), for example, engage with the physical properties of space, putting aside the functional or symbolic meanings that are usually attached to it. Staircases, walls, handrails, bollards, and curbs are urban elements often ignored by the general public (and not the top priority of most designers) but become focal points for skateboarders and traceurs. They use urban spaces playfully and in doing so demonstrate other possibilities for these usually ordinary urban elements and spaces. Some urban games based on locative media (also known as pervasive games) also incorporate common urban features into their activities—urban features that are fundamental for playing the game but that are seldom noticed outside of play. Pervasive games are often triggered by GPS coordinates or other machine-read codes like barcodes or QR codes, which are embedded in the city and read with mobile devices. In all these cases, playfulness is seen as a strategy to appropriate spaces in unexpected ways, revealing perceptual and affective qualities that are usually subdued by established functions and uses.

Yet regardless of how radical these activities are in resignifying urban spaces by emphasizing aspects that we take for granted and don't bother to pay close attention to, the materiality of spaces appropriated during urban sports or pervasive games remains the same before, during, and after these activities.

What if spaces could dynamically respond to how people appropriate them, and playfulness transform and even generate spaces purposely designed to foster emotions, not efficiency?

A board used for chess or checkers has a very simple spatial structure: an eight-by-eight grid with alternating black and white squares. The differences between these two games depend on the role assigned to each piece, its position on the board, and the rules of the game. Most buildings have the same rigid organization and only come to life and reveal their potential for creating spatialities when people use them. Even when two people use the same building for the same purpose, they perceive the space differently depending on their behavior and individual physical and social characteristics (for example, children and adults can have very different perceptions of the same place). Although some spaces are adapted to different users, space does not usually react to these different users or their behavior. The spatial adaptations are preestablished and permanently encoded in space.

Now imagine a chessboard that could respond to the presence of each piece on it, to the movements of these pieces, and to the relations established between them. Black and white squares multiplying themselves, expanding or contracting in size, gaining verticality, merging with each other. This is a responsive space, one that reacts to users and to different behaviors.

The term "responsive architecture" comes from the work of Nicholas Negroponte; in his seminal 1969 paper outlining a theory of architecture machines, Negroponte discussed a future in which machines would learn from past architectural data as well as from data generated by users and their surroundings and respond to them, generating spatialities without the intermediation of a designer. In his view, responsive architecture would rely on "machines that someday will wander about the city" (Negroponte, 1969, p. 12), acquiring information autonomously and responding accordingly. Responsive spaces require technological devices that mediate the relationship between users and the surrounding environment through a combination of sensors and actuators, which Negroponte predicted would slowly take over buildings and urban spaces.

Thirty years later, in his book *E-topia*, William Mitchell (1999) noted that things would not "just sit there," but rather be aware of their surroundings and react to these multiple stimuli. Mitchell is another important scholar of the role played by information and communication technologies in transforming architecture, from singular buildings to cities. The Internet was still a novelty to the general public when Mitchell (1996) proposed, in *City of Bits*, that digitalization of services and information would decouple the close relationship between form, function, and symbolism that has characterized architecture. Mitchell observed that the value of literature, films, and music lies in the information they carry, not in the medium they use to carry this information. He added that architecture designed to host literature, films, or music was adapted to accommodate the medium, not the information: schoolhouses would become virtual campuses and bookstores would become bitstores. Mitchell's (1996) description of a possible near future is now a daily experience for many of us: when you arrive home, "One window on your screen connects you to a database on which you are paid to work, another shows the news from CNN, and another puts you in a digital chat room" (p. 101).

But part of Mitchell's forecast is still in its early stages: "distributed computational devices will disappear into the woodwork. . . . buildings will become computer interfaces and computer interfaces will become buildings" (Mitchell, 1996, p. 105). Another prediction that is still forthcoming in daily design activities is Negroponte's (1969) idea that "whenever a mechanism is equipped with a processor capable of finding a method *of finding a method of solution*" (p. 9; italics in original), even the authorship of the design would belong to the machine itself. However, both ideas are currently being explored by designers and researchers. When AlphaGo beat world Go champion Lee Sedol, Move 37 was a critical moment in the debate over whether machines can be creative; nobody (not even AlphaGo's creators) could understand what the computer was doing. What looked like a mistake proved to be the most important move in winning the match. It looked like AlphaGo was taking risks—like it was actually playing the game, not merely churning out probabilistic calculations.

Artificial intelligence (AI) is transforming architectural design. Machine-learning algorithms trained on large image databases can recognize objects and often label images more accurately than humans. In the other direction, instead of labeling images, algorithms called generative adversarial networks can create them, based on descriptions or labels that are fed into the system, by combining features from a plethora of images. This process generates photorealistic portraits that are consistently difficult for humans to classify as real people or not, even when the mechanism is known. A similar process is underway in architectural design: using large databases containing images of existing buildings, architectural plans, and characteristics of materials (ranging from color to textures to thermal performance), and fed with plot dimensions and client preferences, AI software can generate many options for floor plans, 3D models, and renderings.[1] These groundbreaking technologies in using AI to generate architectural design still yield highly biased results since they are driven by whatever information is present in the database (Leach, 2019).

However, the underlying question still remains: do these AI-based architectural design techniques propose new spatialities or mainly automate the design process? They seem like an AI version of Italo Calvino's Kublai Khan, who described possible cities to Marco Polo based on descriptions of many other existing cities without actually coming up with different urban experiences. Generating architecture plans and renderings is different from generating novel spatialities. In this chapter we are concerned with designers who are tinkering with technologies to create new possible spatialities at different scales.

All the projects discussed in this chapter are characterized by a playful approach: designers and users together explore a variety of technologies while not fully aware of the resulting spatialities. This is a serendipitous approach to architecture, in which the results are only known when the built spaces, surrounding environment, and users interact with each other, mediated by technology.

The role of technology in defining spatialities was a cornerstone in modern architecture, which was marked by the architect as a Promethean figure (Ratti and Claudel, 2015). Prometheus, the titan of Greek mythology who stole fire from the gods, gave it to humans, and taught them to work metal, is the metaphor for the architect who provides top-down, comprehensive, and authoritative design marked by pure rationality. True, Prometheus was punished by the gods, chained to a rock as an eagle ate his liver every day, over and over again. Today, with technologies infiltrated into our cities, the advantageous standpoint of a godlike architect is being put aside and replaced with collaborative urban experiences in the production of space. We could say we live in the era of Protean spaces. Proteus was a shepherd of sea creatures; he could foresee the future but would only divulge it if captured, and he would escape all attempts at capture by metamorphosing—changing shapes and assuming different characters. Play space is a Protean space, one that can constantly metamorphosize.

For years now, sensors and actuators that respond to environmental conditions and to human presence have become as routine as automatic doors, heaters that adjust ambient temperature according to thermostats, or lights that change brightness depending on the number of occupants in a room. More recently, the market for home devices has been inundated with another range of AI-embedded home-assistant technologies that respond to user behavior and commands, such as Google Home and Amazon Alexa.

These devices are connected to the Internet; when someone approaches or arrives at home and their smartphone automatically connects to the network, the home assistant turns on the music and dials up the heater. Similarly, a combination of internal light sensors, personal preferences, specific uses, and actuators on windows and lighting systems can adjust brightness for family movie time by closing the blinds and dimming the lights.

However useful, so-called smart-home technologies are mainly gadgetry. They are devices added to space in a purely functional way. And sometimes such responses mediated by the human-machine interaction can go off the rails. Jacques Tati expressed a humorous criticism of modern life and particularly of modern spaces in many of his movies, through his character Monsieur Hulot. He made a mockery of automated home spaces in *Mon Oncle* (1958), of office buildings in *Playtime* (1967), and of highways and car-centered society in *Traffic* (1971). In *Mon Oncle*, M. Hulot wanders through his relatives' modern villa, which is full of automatic gadgets. Hulot's exploration is motivated by genuine interest in these modern machines, but he is also amazed by their apparently unpredictable behaviors and the outcome when he does not follow the script in the operating manuals. In Tati's movies, humans need to adapt their behavior to machines in order to enjoy the modernity these new technologies provide, which eliminates any spontaneity or unpredictability. By playing with modern houses (in the case of M. Hulot) or the current smart-home solutions, we bring back moments of serendipity in our relationship with space, discovering or rediscovering spatial qualities masked by efficient machines.

Ubiquitous computing has become part of our city services and spaces, and many aspects of our lives now rely on software and data processing. The TV program *Black Mirror* often explores the characteristics of these systems that are "inherently partial, provisional, porous and open to failure" (Kitchin & Dodge, 2011, p. 11), creating what we have called urban phantasmagorias (Duarte and Firmino, 2018). "Be Right Back" (season 2, episode 1, 2013) begins with Ash's death. Martha, his pregnant girlfriend, decides to keep communicating with him via an AI-powered service that uses his entire past social media history to reply to text messages and phone calls in Ash's style and using references they both shared. Eventually Martha adopts another service that uses all Ash's data, including images and voice and video recordings (some of which she feeds), to create an android that looks almost exactly like Ash. Martha even allows their child sporadic interaction with Ash's android. Another episode, "White Christmas" (season 3 special, 2014), combines AI, personal surveillance, and smart homes. One of the central technologies in the episode is an egg-shaped "cookie," which contains a chip with the client's entire consciousness. People voluntarily sign up for a service that implants the chip in their brain for a few days (enough time to collect the person's entire memory, habits, and tastes) and then creates the person's digital clone within the egg. The data-based conscience organizes and schedules their daily activities, controlling everything from room temperature to how the client likes their toast. The absurdity of the situation is that everything in the smart home that seems automated is actually controlled frantically by an embodied conscience, a miniature of the client within the egg.

In all these cases, from the trivial automatic doors to the paraphernalia that eventually took over our modern houses, the basic features of these spaces remain unchanged: we still lag behind Mitchell's idea of buildings and computer interfaces. But what if the chessboard could change according to the movement of each piece? What if buildings could change, or only come into existence, according to the presence and behavior of people, and in relation to the surroundings? Or only materialize via biomaterials encoded to come into existence when certain environmental conditions are present? Architects have explored some of these possibilities before. The problem is that technologies and buildings mature at different paces; in fact, "new" technologies become old pretty fast, and what first made a building look innovative can make it seem obsolete relatively soon. By tinkering with new technologies, designers are using elements of play to test their ideas and engage users. By exploring interactions between people and space through technology, they often provoke or foresee radical transformations in how we engage with space. Some designers go even deeper to change the very materiality of space, creating building materials that react to the environment and to users, or that self-assemble, creating spatialities according to specific codes when triggered by external stimuli.

Similar to transitional phenomena and objects used by psychologists to study the importance of play in the formation of a person's character or social group behaviors, transitional spaces are safe (albeit porous) zones within ordinary spaces; they become catalyzers for social interaction that gives social meaning to shared moments. Designers of transitional spaces sometimes imbue them with artifacts that trigger the imagination, disconnecting from established meanings and functions for urban and architectural spaces. Elements of make-believe permeate play spaces, and when players are engaged with these transitional play spaces they enjoy a shared complicity. Play spaces create empathy, and empathy can inform design.

In this chapter we discuss four approaches that are converging to make spaces responsive to the presence and behavior of humans. First, we present projects that use technologies as tools to explore aspects of the city that frequently underlie daily habits. In the tradition of the situationists, artists and technologists use locative media, digital codes embedded in cities, and communication devices to provoke new ways to navigate and explore the city and to engage citizens in critical thinking about urban issues. Second, we focus on the critical and yet playful approach in using the same artifacts deployed in smart-city projects, such as control systems and urban infrastructures embedded with sensors, and provide examples of two initiatives: the hackable city and the playable city. Third, we discuss examples in which the human–machine interaction creates architecture. Here, designers use technology to enhance people's experience of these spaces, to the point that the space would not exist without human experimentations through technologies, or the architecture would be an empty box. Finally, we explore the creation of building materials that self-assemble and alter their behavior according to the surrounding environment and predefined instructions encoded in their materiality. In all these cases, spatialities are created by experimentation with new technologies in playful ways, and we argue that playfulness is used as a way of engaging people to experiment with these technologies and to awe people with unexpected spatialities that are created by the relationship between people and technology.

The City as a Playground

Amid the rise of the automobile and the full-fledged modernist cities and districts that marked the mid-twentieth century, a group of European intellectuals and artists launched a movement known as situationism. Guy Debord (1955/2007a), one of the main figures among the situationists, wrote about the quest for "observation of certain processes of chance and predictability in the streets" (p. 8) and the idea of random but attentive wandering through the city as "total insubordination to habitual influences" (p. 11). The situationist proposal included the *dérive*, defined by Debord (1958/2007b) as a "playful constructive behavior" in which one or more people abandon their regular activities to let themselves discover the city, "drawn by the attractions of the terrain and the encounters they find there" (p. 62).

Drifting through the city far from the well-worn paths was seen as a political act, questioning the principles of efficiency attached to the modernist city and modern life. Some critics point out that the situationists failed to recognize that only some privileged individuals who enjoyed such unrestricted movement could engage in the act of dérive, while walking ever-longer distances to find work was a necessity for the majority of the population (Flanagan, 2009). Even so, the situationists criticized precisely the functionalist aspect of the modern city, arguing that a collective of individual resisters engaged in exploring nonquantifiable and nonfunctional aspects of the city could become a broader social movement (Schrijver, 2011). In fact, some of the situationists became key figures in the social and cultural movements that erupted in France in 1968 and influenced the political landscape.

The situationists are frequently mentioned as the predecessors of a contemporary form of structured urban exploration: urban games.[2] Both dérives and urban games explore, question, and subvert the superstructures of urban life. The dérives explored the modernist city, which was organized around temporal and spatial functionalities and consisted of urban highways, skyscrapers, monofunctional zoning, and industries that dictated the rhythms of daily life. Urban games work around GPS and mapping technologies, communication networks, and pervasive computing, which increasingly organize the social and economic aspects of cities. These technologies are not simply another layer of cities, but rather are infiltrated into the urban fabric to such a degree that we cannot simply detach ourselves. Contemporary cities are a combination of intertwined physical and digital elements.

Urban games based on locative media have two characteristics: they are imminent and pervasive. They utilize everyday devices like cellphones, so people can start playing anywhere at any time, because the "chessboard" of urban games is always there—it is the very informational infrastructure of digital technologies. For instance, activities are triggered by specific latitudes and longitudes: when a certain location registers on the GPS of a personal mobile device, new potential activities emerge and users can start playing. Since this informational infrastructure exists to allow a flow of data, the same activities can appear at different geolocations or can migrate between locations, and new activities can be generated indefinitely. As a result, because the underlying structure of urban games can pervade any space, and anyone with a smartphone can engage in the game anytime and virtually anywhere, these games are imminent: any situation can be turned into a play space.

Although the image of people staring at their handheld digital devices has come to define a generation disconnected from the world around them, with locative media our location determines the information we retrieve online. Eric Gordon and Adriana de Souza e Silva (2011) argue that locative media actually makes us more aware of people, things, and events happening around us. We consume this information through a digital medium as if we were partially in a virtual environment, but the information itself is not necessarily dissociated from space and human meaning.

In 2002, back when Starbucks providing Wi-Fi access in its stores still made the news, teams playing *Node Runner* raced one other to reach as many Wi-Fi hotspots as possible in cities like New York, Paris, and Seattle, pinpointing their locations on online maps and posting photos of their achievements online.[3] Just over a decade later, Wi-Fi and the Long-Term Evolution (LTE) standard provided high-speed wireless connections for mobile devices in various cities. A powerful industry centered on pervasive communication and geolocation emerged (from ride-hailing to self-tracking apps). In 2014 Pan Studio introduced a game app titled *Run an Empire*,[4] which used tracking to gamify running; after players finish a run, the area within the perimeter of the run becomes a territory. The same run can be repeated to reinforce the player's ownership of the territory, and other runs expand their territory—but other players are simultaneously trying to do the same thing. In teams, players can establish banners or build castles that are displayed to all runners, and they can increase their own area or wrest control of territory from competitors by running between borders.

In *A Machine to See With* (2010), Blast Theory introduced what they call locative cinema.[5] A player signs up online and goes to a point in the city on a specific day, at a specific time. From this point, since Blast Theory knows the player's position in real time, instructions are sent: the goal is to rob a bank. The player is instructed to obtain tools, meet an unknown partner in another location, go to the bank, and act out a narrative composed of thrilling activities and ethical decision making, with the real city as a background. The game takes place in different cities but is adapted to the fabric of each one, and people begin their journey at various locations to converge at several points while unaware of the participation of other players. In some cities, cultural adaptations have a deeper influence on the design and goals of the game; for example, the version for Taipei (where heist narratives and their corresponding clichés are not part of the culture) required ten days of preparation and a major rewrite of the entire experience.

In 2016 Blast Theory and the theater company Hydrocracker ran another urban game that combined role-playing and communication technologies. In *Operation Black Antler*, players engage in an undercover operation that involves building bonds with another player with opposite political and moral views. They impersonate police officers who infiltrate protest groups and question this activity from the inside. This sort of locative game combines the physicality of the city with the immateriality and flexibility of digital communications; some actors play undercover officers who eventually meet participants in real bars. The blurred reality triggers meta-moments when real life spills into the fictionalized version of the game, creating permeable membranes between the player and her fictionalized persona—a characteristic that is common in play.

Pokémon GO (2016), created by Niantic Labs, was the first popular urban game to combine locative media and augmented reality (AR). *Pokémon GO* leverages digital maps of hundreds of cities on a single platform to embed Pokémons and PokéStops into thousands of geographic coordinates. Pokémons can be found inside schools, parks, or even one's own home. The AR interface is triggered by geolocation and includes Pokémons within real ordinary spaces, stimulating players to chase them in areas of the city they don't usually pay attention to, building on what Anthony Townsend (2006) calls context-aware computing.

Critics argue that most of these urban games have a loose relationship with the space they use as a playground, relying on an abstracted version of it and treating urban landscapes as commodities (Flanagan, 2009). Another long-standing criticism is that locative media artists tend to take a commercial approach to their art, employing technologies of surveillance and control uncritically (Tuters and Varnelis, 2006). As Mary Flanagan (2009) acknowledges, the challenge is to create compelling play environments that can simultaneously engage players in critical thinking about human life and urban spaces. Despite such shortcomings, Marc Tuters (2012, p. 271) suggests that urban games should be seen through a "locative epistemology," one that does not address space as a container for social relations and proximity only in terms of physical distances, but instead as an epistemology that views objects as well as the constitution of places as composed of networks of associations that are malleable and metamorphic in time or space.

Urban games question Huizinga's idea of the magic circle—a protected area within space where the rules of the game prevail and only specific actions are accepted. Anton Nijholt (2017) points out that when players are engaged in urban games, bystanders not participating in the game may be uncomfortable or see the event as suspicious rather than play, which has been observed with nondigital pervasive urban play such as parkour. When traceurs spontaneously begin to play using ordinary physical urban elements—climbing vertical walls barehanded and jumping from one roof to another—they could be mistaken for burglars in the act. Digitally based urban games are triggered by digital information, which also constitutes contemporary cities. Some pervasive games are introduced to engage residents and visitors with the city. But on the whole, even for those who do not play, urban games present some disturbance to the ordinary ways we use urban spaces, showing possibilities we might ignore when immersed in deeply rooted habits and making us all conscious of the multiple digital datasets that permeate cities as well as social relations.

Playing with the City

Smart cities have an unquenchable thirst for data. Rob Kitchin and Martin Dodge (2011) argue that codes and software are increasingly becoming the cornerstones of city management and driving decision-making processes. But since not everything that happens in cities can be translated into data, smart cities inevitably narrow urban experiences and civic participation down to a limited number of proposals that can stem from the combination of data, code, and software. This inevitably lets an enormous number of human experiences at the individual and social levels that cannot be captured or easily translated into data fall by the wayside.

Some other initiatives proposed by designers, technologists, and artists incorporate the same technologies deployed in smart cities but carry with them strong critical and political standpoints; some are meant to increase civic participation, while others engage people with these technologies in playful ways.[6]

The Hackable City initiative has a clear political purpose: use digital platforms common to smart cities to open up the city-making process to as many citizens as possible.[7] The program was begun in the Netherlands by Martijn de Waal, Michiel de Lange, and Matthijs Bouw, who built the conceptual framework of hackable cities on the idea that what they call platform society (digital mapping, social media, pervasive computing) is not a neutral connector and consequently requires a critical approach. This argument resonates with a broader notion of media activism, which ranges from movies and performances to video games that try to address the inherent imbalances of media (Flanagan, 2009): who has access to which media as both producers and consumers, who controls their content, and who monitors their use.

The Hackable City aims to build bottom-up participatory processes in city-making by playfully reappropriating these technologies beyond their original purposes (de Waal & de Lange, 2019). Ongoing questions in this field include the following: How are the data that constitute these platforms generated? Who has access to the data and to information technologies deployed in public areas? How do governments and private companies use this data?

Projects within the Hackable City include plug-in interfaces and portable interactive technologies temporarily deployed in urban spaces, or the use of street games for prototyping urban design proposals (de Waal & de Lange, 2019). Even though it was meant to include different levels of playfulness to engage citizens and featured iterative design and beta testing, one strand of the Hackable City project has been to develop methods, tools, and strategies ranging from dynamics to build trust among stakeholders to toolkits for organizing community meetings that sometimes seem overly structured for the freedom and spontaneity that characterize the playfulness they advocate as part of public engagement.

Since smart cities need data to operate, there have been massive efforts by companies and governments to generate data. One way to do this is to deploy sensors in urban infrastructures; these range from microphones that detect apparent gunshots and automatically call the police to surveillance cameras that monitor on-street parking and charge in a more accurate and dynamic manner or detect violations (like double parking).

In 2012 Playable City was introduced in Bristol, England.[8] The idea is that sensors deployed in cities and the data they collect can trigger responses other than those intended to improve the efficiency of urban systems. Instead, these same technologies can be used to stimulate serendipity and unexpected ways of seeing and interacting with the city.

Watershed Studio invited designers to propose novel ways to use the sensors deployed in urban infrastructures; in 2013 Pan Studio was selected for its project Hello Lamp Post. Urban furniture, from lamp posts to parking meters to trash bins, is at the same time omnipresent and invisible. These objects are everywhere, to the point that they blend with the background and nobody notices them. Moreover, they are ordinary; one traffic light is indistinguishable from any other. But the urban furniture in Bristol (lamp posts, bus shelters, and mailboxes) is tagged with unique identification numbers, creating a comprehensive inventory of urban artifacts that facilitates management, defining which lamp post needs a new light bulb or when the next bus will arrive at a specific bus shelter. At the same time, this provides individuality for each of these elements.

Pan Studio used these unique IDs to assign some sort of persona to each piece of furniture. People could send SMS messages with the object ID to a specific phone number, which would "wake up" the object and start a text conversation with the person. Sometimes the object would reply with simple niceties, and other times it would use previous comments to trigger a dialog. For example, a lamp post replied that someone had described it as a "badly drawn stick man," asking the current user what she thinks it looks like. These unstructured interactions disarm users and make them play with the system. Hello Lamp Post features a component of make-believe ("Is this trash can actually talking to me?") that engages each individual to exchange messages with objects and adds to the memory of these objects, to be used in subsequent conversations with other users. It also has an element of empathy: objects frequently mention what other participants said in a similar situation, creating anonymous networks of conversations between people through ordinary urban artifacts. Furthermore, since the system inevitably records the messenger's phone number, creating a unique ID, a network of dialogs mediated by urban artifacts emerges from the playful appropriation of the city. Since its first deployment in Bristol, Hello Lamp Post has been staged in a number of cities, including Astana, Kazakhstan; Bordeaux, France; and Singapore.

In 2014 Shadowing, by Jonathan Chomko and Matthew Rosier, received the Playable City Award. In this project, Chomko and Rosier animated streetlights. These omnipresent components of urban infrastructure were equipped with infrared sensors and cameras to detect the heat as people or other heat-emitters passed underneath, creating images of just their shadows, without the influence of surrounding light. These images were recorded and projected onto the pavement when other people crossed the same light cone, creating an unexpected encounter of shadows between those sharing the same space during the past and the present.

Memory is a form of temporal connection with events, people, and feelings—in short, experiences in our past that we can bring back and therefore assign to our present. By recording the shadows of another person's activities under a streetlight and projecting them back onto the same sidewalk later when another person passes by, Shadowing gives memory to places, connecting individuals across different times and creating shared memories. The project revives individual memories, introducing them into another person's experience of the city and thus constructing collective memories through different temporalities.

While interacting with Hello Lamp Post, participants actively engage with the urban furniture; in contrast, Shadowing frequently takes people by surprise. They might be just strolling at night when other shadows appear alongside their own under the streetlight. People soon realized what was going on and began to play with the shadows, creating a cross-temporal and playful interaction between citizens. Shadowing has appeared in many cities, including Austin, London, and Tel Aviv, and cultural differences enhanced the experience even further. In some cities it can take time to engage locals in the experience. For example, interpersonal relations between strangers are rare in Tokyo despite the newest technological devices in the market, whereas in Lagos people are more eager to explore technologies that foster interpersonal relations. In both cases, playfulness ultimately overcomes any barriers to create shared spatialities within the otherwise ordinary city.

The idea of a playful city was proved successful and followed by initiatives in Melbourne, Tokyo, London, São Paulo, and Seoul. Nijholt (2017) argues that the original idea, which took a critical view of urban technologies, became a marketing tool, a purely artistic initiative to attract visitors. In fact, when one of the designers, Jonathan Chomko (2014), was asked whether the playable city idea didn't risk over-organizing fun (which in principle should be free), he replied that he saw the project more as a "chalkboard than a game." Playfulness nevertheless has an inherently critical aspect of pushing the rules of the game to their limit and questioning monolithic views about habits, functionalities, and the meanings tied to spaces. In both examples, we can ask whether a lamp post is an object or a toy, a monofunctional artifact or a communication device. Ambiguity is simultaneously fun and critical, a central characteristic of play, and it can engage designers and users in freely creating and experiencing new spatialities.

Building Play Spaces

The main theme of the 2008 Expo in Zaragoza, Spain, was water and sustainability. One of the main attractions was the Digital Water Pavilion (figure 3.1), designed by Carlo Ratti Associati. Ratti had created the Senseable City Lab at MIT only a few years earlier;[9] since its inception, the Senseable City Lab has worked on how the increasingly pervasive sensors carried by people and embedded in the built environment can affect the way we understand, interact with, and design cities. The underlying idea is that the ubiquitous computers integrated into the urban fabric could sense and respond to events and environmental conditions. By learning from previous experiences and extending this knowledge to similar situations, they could also anticipate actions to enhance people's experience of space, in what has been called the sentient city (Shepard, 2011).

These principles found a playful expression in the Digital Water Pavilion.[10] From a purely material viewpoint, the building is a flat surface 40 centimeters thick covered with still water that looks like a mirror. The surface rests on 12 hydraulic moveable pistons that move the entire roof up to 4 meters high or down to the ground, depending on the prevailing winds and activities taking place in the pavilion. The pavilion has 3,000 closely spaced solenoid valves along the perimeter of the building, and dozens of pumps that open and close according to a digitally controlled system based on open-source software, creating the "water walls" that surround the pavilion. The patterns of these walls are generated by the public via the software, drawing shapes, writing words, and playing games. Embedded sensors detect people approaching the water curtains and close the pumps in these areas to create instantaneous passageways, allowing people to go in and out of the pavilion.

Figure 3.1
The Digital Water Pavilion, a fully responsive building powered by digitally controlled sensors and water actuators.
Source: Carlo Ratti Associati, 2009.

Digital water curtains have since been installed in airports, museums, theme parks, and hotels for uses ranging from illustrating logos and product outlines to art projects. This is the case of the 3D Water Matrix,[11] a computer-controlled installation featuring a grid of 30-by-30 electrovalves (or pixels/drops) that uses the multiple layers of parallel droplets to create shapes and water dances enhanced by lighting. Conceived by Shiro Takatani and Christian Partos, it was first exhibited at the Cité des Sciences et de l'Industrie in Paris as part of the *Robotic Art* exhibition.

Although interesting, most of these uses lack the playfulness of the Digital Water Pavilion, treating people as either consumers or spectators of what this interactive technology can do. As Ratti frequently acknowledges in interviews and presentations, children playing games or trying to outsmart the technology seem to have actually understood the powerful and playful relation between sensing and actuating technologies. The pavilion created an architecture that only existed through interaction between a sensing system, computer algorithms that interpret and actuators that respond to the user's behavior, and the materiality of the building (in this case, water) to create virtually endless potential spatialities.

In 2016 Guto Requena designed the Dancing Pavilion (figure 3.2) for the Olympic Games in Rio de Janeiro; this 300-square-meter building was a parallelogram with four faces supported by pillars. The ground floor was completely open, while the façades contained 345 round mirrors that formed a matrix, each capable of rotating 360 degrees in two seconds. This configuration allowed the pavilion to form graphic patterns and words, but it could also dance, as the name implies. Lidar sensors, which emit laser beams and detect people's movements, were located on the dance floor to measure movement and trigger the rotation of the mirrors. Dancing caused the mirrored panels to move, which in turn influenced the lighting by controlling the amount of sunlight that entered the pavilion, or by changing the intensity and color of the artificial light within. This feedback loop encouraged people to move, and the building not only looked like it was dancing but actually moved and danced itself, responding to how visitors playfully interacted with these changes in the architecture. In the Dancing Pavilion, the building did not simply contain the events within but was an active element in creating spatial experiences for the thousands of people who visited it during sporting events.

Figure 3.2
The Dancing Pavilion, created in 2016 by Estudio Guto Requena for the Olympic Games in Rio de Janeiro.
Source: Estudio Requena, 2016.

A year earlier, the Dancing Pavilion was preceded by Light Creature. In this project, Requena transformed the renovated thirty-story WZ Hotel in São Paulo with an interactive façade composed of moveable panels that display information and graphic patterns. Sensors on the roof of the building collect data about air quality (NO_2, CO, and CO_2), humidity, and temperature and translate this information into a range of data, from lower to higher values, which is then expressed by the building as the panels change color accordingly; microphones installed around the building measure noise level, which also is conveyed by the panels. Additionally, an app lets people interact with the façade. By displaying air quality and noise level on this large building, the goal is to create a collective environmental consciousness in São Paulo, one of Latin America's most populated, industrialized, and highly motorized cities.

As in Requena's other projects, the underlying idea is that digital technologies can allow people to connect and resume control of public spaces. He tries to do this by stimulating empathy (feeling someone else's emotions)—or, as he often says, through love. In other interventions, he had strangers sit side by side and played their heartbeats to each other through the installation. Listening to these heartbeats encouraged strangers to talk to each other, and Requena also generated live music based on this collective heartbeat. He has also 3D-printed objects, from pendants to sculptures, in real time based on people's love stories. Visitors were invited into closed chambers to tell their love stories; these chambers did not have microphones or cameras but instead featured sensors such as electroencephalography devices and galvanic skin conductors. Visitors expressed their love for parents, partners, children, and pets—although we cannot be sure, since none of their stories were recorded in images or words. But the electroencephalograms generated during these sessions, representing the raw emotions of love stories, were transmitted to a 3D printer, and visitors left the installation with material evidence of their emotions translated into objects.

Playfulness permeates Requena's work. One of the key evolutionary functions of play is the act of bonding and belonging, which occurs through ambiguity, a central characteristic of play (Sutton-Smith, 1997). A tool can be a toy or a weapon, and the act of impersonating somebody else can be a sign of craziness and ridicule or engagement with a shared fantasy. Playfulness works around "frolicsomeness, lightheartedness, and wit" (Sutton-Smith, 1997, p. 147). These characteristics disrupt established expectations while at the same time creating tense moments of uncertainty and stimulating mutual trust, with people relying on one another and their collective imagination to establish common ground. In these architectural experiments, when people open their emotions to others they create novel spatialities.

Constructing Building Blocks

The very nature of building materials can be transformative to architecture. The imagery of twentieth-century modernist buildings and cities is populated with skyscrapers competing to be the tallest in the world, long free spans that defy common structural calculations, fully transparent buildings, and curvilinear constructions that look like habitable sculptures. Behind the great works by Mies van der Rohe, Le Corbusier, Kenzo Tange, and Oscar Niemeyer are technological breakthroughs in material sciences and construction methods, which include large glass panels, steel and reinforced concrete, aluminum, and electricity. Controversial as it might be,

Niemeyer's gestural architecture features his aesthetic vision as well as the technological achievements of steel and reinforced concrete. Industrializing the production of aluminum and its alloys opened up the possibility of high-speed travel, transatlantic flights, and towering slim buildings, creating a "material culture based on aeriality, speed, and lightness" (Sheller, 2014, p. 85). Electricity (when used in elevators or artificial lighting) created contemporary metropolises as we know them.

Ratti's Digital Water Pavilion and Requena's Dancing Pavilion are exciting and provocative, and they point toward possible directions for an architecture that can reshape itself in relation to how people engage with space. But they still rely on the juxtaposition of sensors and actuators onto the sheer materiality of the buildings. What if building materials could self-assemble? And what if buildings could reshape themselves in relation to users and the surrounding environment, without the need for external sensors and actuators? Or what if the materialization of buildings could be directly encoded in the material components?

The digital technologies that make interactive architecture possible, and the computational power required to enmesh virtual figures into the physical world in urban games, actually rely on very tangible components that utilize gold, silicon, tungsten, and many other elements. Researchers and designers have been working in the opposite direction: rather than exploring the use of digital technologies to transform buildings, they have been using the computing logic of digital technologies to rethink and redesign what these materials are and how they can perform, sometimes synthesizing brand-new substances. Rachel Armstrong (2020, p. 40) calls these "wicked" experiments, because they trigger relationships between objects, bodies, and systems that exceed our capacity to fully observe or experience them outside their own realm.

These active new materials do not have microcomputers embedded in them but instead combine synthetic biology and material sciences that allow the materials to self-assemble, shift shapes, and change their physical properties in response to environmental conditions, user characteristics, or preprogrammed instructions without the intermediation of sensors, batteries, computers, or actuators. These new materials are responsive, in what has been called active matter. Skylar Tibbits (2017a) argues that active matter does not simply follow predetermined commands (like shape-memory materials or smart materials) but rather is guided by the properties of the digital world (like reconfiguration and error correction) and natural world (like growth and repair). In what he sees as the "renaissance moment of programmability" (Tibbits, 2017c, p. 339), natural materials can be fabricated digitally, synthesized, and grown, leading to new properties, while synthetic materials can incorporate characteristics and processes of the natural world, such as adaptation and reconfiguration.

Designers looking to complex natural processes for inspiration is nothing new; the novelty here is that computers now allow designers to encode the power of agency that nonhuman agents have in the biological realm during both the ideation and fabrication phases of their work. Alisa Andrasek (2016) has developed algorithms that simulate biological processes, incorporating agents alien to design (like cell division and morphogenesis at the cellular scale) in furniture design. For the 2012 Olympic Games in London she designed "urban toys" which have since been deployed in many cities (Andrasek, 2015). These toys, part of a project titled Bloom (figure 3.3), allow users to experience the complex forms derived from algorithms inspired by natural processes, changing the user's perspective of what urban furniture can look like. The awesomeness commonly described by users derives from the translation of everyday biological processes at the cellular scale up to the scale of urban furniture. Andrasek (2019) argues that the initial surprise,

Figure 3.3
Bloom, designed by Alisa Andrasek as a piece of collectively assembled, playful, and dynamic architecture for public spaces celebrating the 2012 Olympic and Paralympic games in London.
Source: Alisa Andrasek, 2012.

followed by excitement about experimenting with the objects, occurs because this approach exceeds the human capacity to recognize patterns in complex natural phenomena—what she calls superhuman intuition. Rather than mimicking biological processes, Andrasek uses them to incorporate complexity in design, proposing a counterintuitive aesthetic.

While Andrasek's early design is inspired by biological phenomena and continues with physical phenomena to introduce complexity as a generative design tool, other researchers and designers are creating building materials not simply as the physical output of design, but instead considering the creation and self-assembling characteristics of these materials as agents of design, or "generative collaborators" (Tibbits, 2017b, p. 12).

Neri Oxman, director of the Mediated Matter group at MIT,[12] encodes biological processes found in nature to induce the design and the material qualities of her work. Typical digital design protocols separate ideation and construction into two consecutive phases: generation of form, followed by optimization of construction performance. Even if iterative systems use performance optimization as a feedback to inform design, they are commonly seen as two processes. In nature, design and construction take place simultaneously through the interaction between the innate properties of the materials used, the external environment, and performance criteria (Oxman et al., 2013). Mediated Matter's Silk Pavilion (see figure 3.4), built in 2013, combines digital fabrication technologies with the work of 6,500 living silkworms (Bombyx mori).[13] Inspired by the fact that silkworms can generate three-dimensional cocoons with a single linear thread, the generative algorithm of the pavilion defined its overall geometry along one continuous thread with different densities, which was used to guide the work of the silkworms. Besides the different densities of this single continuous thread, Mediated Matter also altered ambient illumination and temperature, inducing the silkworms to move across the basic geometry of the pavilion and simultaneously guiding the design and construction processes.

Wearables have become a fertile area for the exploration of biomaterials; their smaller scale (in comparison to buildings) seems favorable for experimentation and user-experience assessment. Living Mushtari,[14] another project developed by the Mediated Matter group, is a 3D-printed skirt-like wearable filled with synthetic microorganisms (see figure 3.5). It comprises 58 meters of fluid channels filled with autotrophic and heterotrophic microorganisms in a "microbial factory" (Bader et al., 2016). Autotrophs

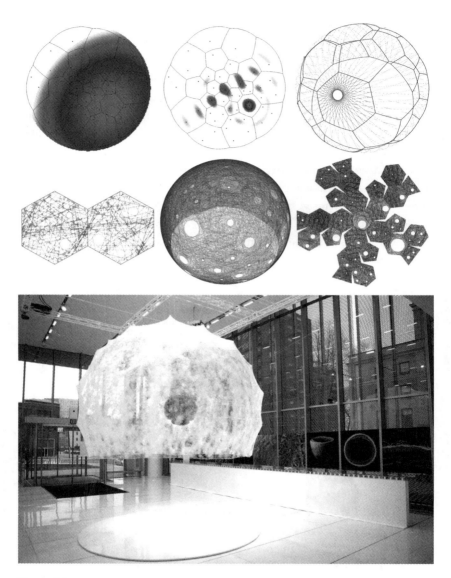

Figure 3.4
Top: Digital form-finding process and computational tools used for the Silk Pavilion: solar mapping, aperture distribution mapping, aperture generation logic, spinning range calculation, overall distribution, and unfolded panels for fabrication.
Bottom: A perspective view of the completed Silk Pavilion and the basic research exhibit focusing on fiber-density-distribution studies.
Source: Mediated Matter group, MIT Media Lab, 2013.

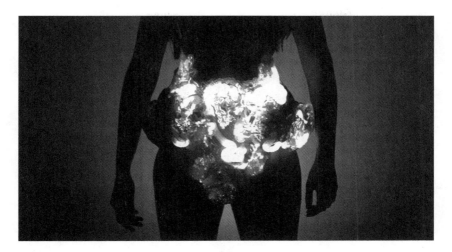

Figure 3.5
Mushtari filled with chemiluminescent fluid.
Source: Paula Aguilera and Jonathan Williams, 2014.

such as cyanobacteria convert sunlight into the nutrients consumed by the heterotrophs, which then produce compounds used as building material. Mushtari's channels are molded around the human body. The geometry of its 3D-printed fluid channels is generated by algorithms that emulate biological growth, encompassing the overall shape of the wearable as well as the local meshes, which have different densities in different regions. The channel diameter varies between 1 and 25 millimeters, and transparency also varies to control which areas receive light and consequently trigger photosynthesis among the autotrophs inside the channels, which will eventually nourish the heterotrophic microorganisms that literally grow this wearable.

The Self-Assembly Lab,[15] also at MIT, works with the idea that structures could build themselves with active matter and could adapt to ever-changing environmental conditions following three principles: geometry, energy, and the way elements connect with each other. The pneumatic objects developed by the Self-Assembly Lab are sculpted with a liquid material inside a tank of gel suspension. When ready, they are inflated to assume their intended shape, whether a vase or a sofa. In Liquid Printed Pneumatics (see figure 3.6), the Self-Assembly Lab collaborated with BMW to develop inflatables that can expand and morph into multiple shapes, creating linear actuators, changing from cubes to spheres, and expanding

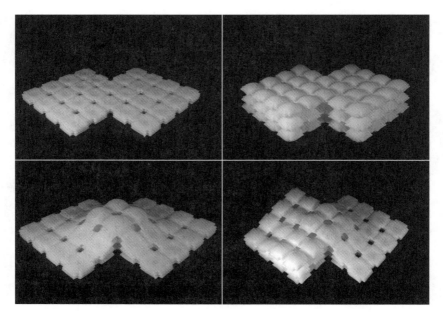

Figure 3.6
The Self-Assembly Lab's Liquid Printed Pneumatics project, which explores the use of flexible materials and air for multiple form configurations.
Source: Self-Assembly Lab, 2018.

800 percent in size. First displayed at London's Victoria and Albert Museum in 2018, the piece displayed as part of "The future starts here" exhibition is a three-layered, of two partially overlapping four-by-four grid of inflatable cells. The general structure can be elongated, and each individual cell can rise independently to create many different shapes (for example, in a house this structure could reshape itself as a bed, a couch, or a sofa), and each cell and the overall structure are always able to return to its original state. For the Cooper Hewitt, Smithsonian Design Museum in New York, the Self-Assembly Lab created a responsive environment with active textiles. Here, small perforations laser-cut in a composite textile open and close in response to a light source, without the need for external sensors or actuators to control their movements. The composite textile creates active mosaics of shadow and light inside the space, either maintaining the desired luminosity or playing with it to actively change the qualities of the space.

If curtains can respond to sunlight to control luminosity, change façades, and adjust light in interior spaces, high-technology glass panels can increase their opacity to reduce the amount of light that enters a room, or they can become almost fully transparent. Initial commercial deployments have been made in some airplanes; current laboratory versions can become fully opaque or reach 82 percent transparency in the visible spectrum, while also constantly harvesting solar energy (Goldschmidt, 2018). Turning transparent surfaces in our cities into active architectural elements by simply changing their opacity could minimize energy use at the building level. By also harvesting solar energy, glass façades could generate electricity and reduce the incident heat load. This technology could also be applied to personal electronic devices (for example, smartphone screens could generate power when exposed to light).[16] Combining all these applications could "substantially offset fossil-fuel consumption worldwide" (Traverse et al., 2017, p. 849).

Here as in many other fields, nanotechnology has led to new frontiers in building materials. One group of researchers has poured a mixture of quantum dot semiconductors that filter different light wavelengths into thin sheets of glass (Meinardi et al., 2015). This solution reaches optical energy conversion efficiency of 3.2 percent, still far from the 6 percent that would make this material commercially viable, but results are promising: if 12,000 windows in New York's One World Trade Center were coated with the quantum dot photoluminescence glass, they could power more than 350 apartments (Vilvestre, 2016). Other research suggests applying a one-atom-thick layer of graphene onto glass panels to harvest solar energy (Song et al., 2016). Graphene is highly conductive, flexible, transparent, and made from carbon, which is abundant and inexpensive. Moreover, these graphene-based organic solar cells can be applied to any surface, generating abundant energy as a byproduct.

Building surfaces could also harvest water from dew, fog, and moist air, which is easily done in humid zones. In Warka Tower,[17] by Arturo Vittori and Andreas Vogler, a mesh net collects droplets of dew that form along its surface. Initially utilized in dry regions of Ethiopia with local materials and designed to be easily assembled with simple tools, the idea stems from the fact that temperature difference between nightfall and daybreak is the critical factor in collecting water from condensation. However, local conditions are still important. Recent research has shown that a porous metal-organic framework could harvest water in regions where relative humidity is below 20 percent—some of the driest conditions in the world. One kilogram of this metal-organic framework can harvest 2.8 liters of water each day, using only the ambient temperature (without any external source of energy) for condensation (Kim et al., 2017).

Building materials could also be made of thin air (or something close to it). Simon Park, a bacteriologist at the University of Surrey in the UK, has cultivated the largest collection of bacteria and fungi for use in the arts, called C-Mould, with thirty different microorganisms.[18] These microorganisms can produce electricity, pigments, biomaterials, and even elemental gold. *Gluconacetobacter xylinus* (commonly called GXCELL), a bacteria species common in rotten fruit, can produce cellulose. Park used it to produce a paper-like material, on which he printed, using pigmented bacteria as ink, Charles Darwin's *On the Origin of Species*. He also uses cyanophytes, a group of photosynthetic cyanobacteria that grow in air and water when exposed to sunlight. One specific species, *Oscillatoria animalis*, produces a biomaterial with microscopic filaments that feature a unique oscillatory motility that allows them to self-weave and self-repair. Park is working with artists and clothing designers to incorporate these biomaterials into textiles.

These scientists and designers are constructing the building blocks of architecture. Their work is marked by trial and error, by exploration of unknown areas of knowledge. Not surprisingly, the works discussed in this chapter are temporary, either because they were only mounted as installations in art galleries or published in scientific journals. Their beauty lies in the fact that they indicate new possibilities for spatial design and construction, as designers and scientists play with multiple possibilities for the future.

*   *   *

One risk in writing about new technologies is that examples quickly become outdated. The Institut du Monde Arabe in Paris (1988), a cutting-edge work of responsive architecture, is one such example (see figure 3.7). This building was designed by Jean Nouvel; its south façade recreates a mashrabiya (projecting oriel window with latticework) composed of mechanical diaphragms that could adjust their aperture individually in response to hundreds of light sensors; as Mark Meagher (2015) commented, the building

Figure 3.7
Close-up of the façade of the Institut du Monde Arabe in Paris.
Source: Sophie Vinetlouis, 2020.

seemed to have become "a sentient creature capable of movement and intelligent behavior" (p. 164). Soon after the museum opened, however, the diaphragms were already only controlled centrally (without relying on all the sensors), and the technology itself, containing hundreds of thousands of pieces moving mechanically to adjust the lighting conditions, became outdated.

Even so, the Institut du Monde Arabe highlights the poetics found within the relationship between building, users, and the surrounding environment. What remains is the possibility of play between these elements, the idea that architecture can be a living organism—whether via active textiles or a single-atom layer of graphene applied onto glass. In both cases, the response to light can be embedded in the very material used in façades.

The projects discussed in this chapter still may be subject to the conundrum of high-tech obsolescence; some outstanding technological marvels fade quickly, as soon as the next technological marvel shines. However, they also point to another aspect that can radically change architecture and create new spatialities: designers will not need to add sensors and actuators to buildings but instead will leverage the sensors and actuators embedded in our phones, clothes, bodies, and buildings, and the distributed intelligence that makes them sense, respond, and adapt to the users and the environment. This brings us to the idea of ubiquitous computing introduced by Mark Wieser (1991): technology is powerful when it disappears, seamlessly integrated into the world.

The symbiosis between the physical and digital elements of the city, between bricks and bits, triggers the augmentation of space, the creation of new spatialities that do not depend on specific and deliberate acts of individual or collective groups but constitute our daily experiences of space (Duarte and Firmino, 2009). Although blending with the context and becoming invisible seems the inevitable path of technology, we can become aware of these transformations when they reveal their presence and their effects on people's behavior. The technological developments discussed in this chapter feature a range of materials that not only actively respond to the environment but are also part of a broader ecosystem that nurtures spatial design— which for far too long has been mostly constituted of passive objects. In many similar works that explore biomaterials, a multidisciplinary team is involved in cocreating technologies, techniques, concepts, and design.

Another part of what Remko, Requena, Tibbits, and Oxman do is to engage users in discovering the immanent power of ubiquitous computing through playful activities. Any game is a social technology, usually composed of specific rules and artifacts: even a hopscotch grid drawn on the sidewalk is a social technology that contains rules and artifacts. But any game loses its allure without the element of play and its inherent possibilities of surprise. Engagement is triggered by what is out of the ordinary, even if this only happens for a short period in a specific space. Play combines the freedom to be amazed by walls made of water that appear and disappear, by buildings that seem to dance along with visitors, by wearables that grow around the body. Through awe, play gives us the freedom to understand the science and technology that are behind what seems magical: there is no right or wrong in play, only experimentation. Play allows us to explore novel spatialities that might only last for short periods of enjoyment, but these experiences also indicate one possible future for spatial design in which technology does not prescribe behaviors but rather provokes unexpected ways to engage with space.

4 Artifices of Self-Deception

Artifices of Self-Deception as Intellectual Tools

The Romance of the Three Kingdoms, written sometime in the thirteenth century, is considered one of the four great classic novels of Chinese literature. Set in the second and third centuries CE, it is a historical novel that tells a sweeping tale of an age when kingdoms, larger-than-life warlords, cunning strategists, and massive armies fought for supremacy at the end of the Han dynasty period. Grand strategies, politics, and perhaps more importantly, the art of deception are all used to gain a stronger position in a landscape of ever-changing alliances and perils. In one of the early chapters, the book describes the Battle of Red Cliffs, one of the largest naval battles in human history. The massive armies of the warlord Cao Cao, numbering more than 800,000 soldiers, threatened the existence of the states of Shu Han and Wu and forced them into an uneasy alliance.

In one key episode, the leader of the Wu forces, Zhao Yu, fears that the master strategist of the Shu Han forces, Zhuge Liang, will eventually become too dangerous for the future existence of the Wu state. He devises a strategy to have him killed without destroying the alliance. Faced with a shortage of arrows, he tasks Zhuge Liang with finding 100,000 arrows in ten days. When the strategist responds that he will do the task in three days, Zhao Yu asks him to pledge to this result (convinced that this impossible task will force Zhuge Liang to face execution). The strategist, however, has other plans. He devises a plan to load twenty boats with straw soldiers. On the third day, he sails the boats in the middle of a foggy night, moving them close to Cao Cao's forces, who are camped on the other bank of the Yangtze river. Once close to the bank he signals his sailors to beat the war

drums, sending the enemy forces into a frenzy. Since the enemy command-
ers are incapable of clearly seeing the attackers in the fog, they order their
archers to indiscriminately fire their arrows toward the sound of the drums.
Soon Zhuge Liang's boats are filled with thousands of arrows that get stuck
on the straw men, while he shares tea inside one of the boats with Zhao Yu's
advisor, Lu Su, who clearly realizes the strategic brilliance of his opponent.
In the end, Zhuge Liang returns to his camp with more than enough arrows
to fulfill his wager. His masterful deception is able to manipulate both Cao
Cao and Zhao Yu—the former into seeing a nonexistent danger and over-
reacting accordingly, the latter into showing his true intentions.

Religious texts, historical accounts, strategy treatises, and iconic pieces of
literature all warn us about the dangers of falling for the trickery of deception. It is not surprising to find that deception holds a bad reputation in
our collective consciousness, being often equated with cheating, lying, and
subterfuge. This view, however, is often a mistake.

Indeed, deception implies inducing someone to consider as true what the
deceiver knows to be untrue, often for the deceiver's own benefit. However, all
is not what it seems, since deception may be hardwired into our biology and
as such is part of our nature. In his provocative book on self-deception, Edu-
ardo Giannetti (2000) argues that deception is often observed as a survival
and reproduction strategy among microorganisms, plants, and animals.
Nature has by way of evolution created plants that produce pseudo-flowers
with the scents and colors of true flowers (but without reproductive functions) to attract and trap insects; at the bottom of the sea, octopuses will
sometimes flex their bodies and change both form and color to look like
rocks, part of the seabed, or even a larger predator; in rainforests, chame-
leons rapidly change their color by actively tuning special layers of skin cells
to blend in with the environment and avoid predators. Similar phenomena
also happen during reproductive cycles, with animals making themselves
more attractive during courtship. Nature, it seems, frequently uses deception
as part of its toolkit.

Our bodies are no different. Deception plays a key role in some of our
biological processes, which is why we sometimes use deception to our advantage. For example, we can trick our immune system to enhance our resistance to disease. That is how vaccines work: by injecting a small amount of
a nonlethal virus, we deceive the body into producing antibodies against a
possible harmful infection by that virus in the future. Meanwhile, modern

anesthesia is simply a deceptive strategy to convince the nervous system that we are not feeling pain. While it would be a mistake to view these natural processes as anthropomorphic and consciously devised by organisms, something that Giannetti cautions against, these examples demonstrate that inducing someone to act upon the premise that something is, when it is not, can be beneficial not only to the deceiver but also sometimes to the deceived. The logic of deception is based on the asymmetry of information between different parts; however, when properly encoded and designed, deception can have positive effects for all parts involved. Deception is a survival tool in many areas of life.

The asymmetry of information between different parts that characterizes deception essentially works by inducing someone to think something is true when the other person knows it to be untrue. Although it is obvious that this is a common dynamic between different entities, self-deception would seem to be an epistemological impossibility: I induce myself (the deceived) to believe something is true though I (the deceiver) know it is not. This makes no sense, and yet we do it all the time. Our minds are incredibly adept at tricking us into interpreting information in ways that make no sense and are decoupled from reality—but we constantly enter into self-deception for our benefit. In our modern, overstimulated environments, our cognitive processes frequently tap into our capacity for disbelief, our biases, and our deceptive internal logic to create mental shortcuts that allow us to navigate the world. We make sense of the world using pieces of information that make sense to us even if we are overwhelmed with information that we know is there but does not fit into our perceptual or intellectual frameworks. A common example is our understanding of the day cycle marked by sunrise and sunset. Although we know that it is Earth's rotation that marks the passage of days, we still use in our daily life the notion that the sun rises and sets on the horizon. To this extent, self-deception is not only a possibility but also a common feature of our daily lives. Moreover, it is essential for our inquisitive spirit and constant querying of the world.

In this chapter we argue that self-deception does not simply exist in nature or in our mundane habits, but that we actually purposefully create artifices of self-deception that eventually become powerful intellectual tools enabling us to broaden our understanding of the world—in the particular case we consider here, our understanding of space. More than simple illusionist stratagems, which can deceive our spatial perceptions, artifices of self-deception can profoundly alter how we perceive, understand, represent, and conceive space and how we can project possibilities of spaces over time. Moreover, we argue that, just as fifteenth-century linear perspective impacted our representation, understanding, and projection of space, technologies that engage in self-deception, such as virtual and synthetic realities (encapsulated in the notion of immersive realities), may become key landmarks in the quest to create artifices that mediate our critical approach to spatial design. Play and self-deception form the core conceptual argument of this book. In fact, playfulness is the attitude that helps us differentiate between ethical self-deception and sheer manipulation: the structure of the artifice of self-deception is open, and we still engage with it as a way of understanding a phenomenon.

The importance of self-deception as an intellectual tool, primarily for the investigation of the self, has been raised before, and scholars have argued that it should be viewed as more than an apparent pathological condition. As Alfred Mele (1997) explains, people enter self-deception when they believe that something, p, is true although it is false. Such a belief is grounded in the motivationally biased treatment of data and involves biases that might lead people to believe in an improbable p. It is relatively common to use self-deception as a strategy to cope with difficult personal or social situations; for example, to hide (or protect) oneself behind a more comfortable untruth in order to avoid reviving persisting traumas. According to a broader understanding of self-deception, the self is made equally of disclosures and disguises, and "deception and self-deception are part and parcel of our engagements in the world including, not least, in the development and maintenance of our image and sense of ourselves" (Solomon, 2009, p. 32). Thus, part of what constitutes our understanding of the world and our understanding of ourselves in relation to the world is built upon beneficial untruths we tell ourselves.

While we often discuss self-deception as an involuntary strategy, we can also benefit from other uses of self-deception, such as projection of the self in moments of emotional intensity. Our capacity to envisage ourselves and others in situations apart from our current reality is key to our survival since it is by doing so that we perceive danger outside of the immediacy of the now. This capacity goes beyond simple imagination because it is triggered and triggers instinctive responses to unexpected situations. It is in this context that particular methods and technologies of spatial representation that are artifices of self-deception interest us: artifices that induce us to think a certain space is, when we have evidence showing that it is not. Furthermore, we argue that rather than diverting our attention from a presumed reality to a deceptive representation, these artifices actually unveil important aspects of the represented space and help us understand how we perceive and conceive spaces we live in. Thus, our focus is not on people's deceptive behaviors toward one another or themselves but on the means we consciously use to represent the world around us in deceptive and nonharmful ways, ways that would not be possible without such artifices. The world reaches us, and makes sense to us, through such artifices of self-deception.

In fact, deception and self-deception are incredibly powerful artifices that humans have created to establish and maintain relations with each other, to understand the world, and to share this knowledge. Language, in general, relies on aspects of self-deception. It is almost never self-referent; on the contrary, the power of language lies in the fact that it signifies something external to itself, through its "ontological absence from itself" (Baudrillard, 2000, p. 71). Any scribble, any groan, any stroke is a form of expression but not a language, which requires some level of codification and agreement among those who share its codes. The signifier is not the phenomenon (a feeling, an object), and it is not the signified (the mental concept of a phenomenon) either; and the links between signifiers and the signified change in time and are informed by contextual elements not directly related to either of them. But, still, we understand and communicate phenomena through the employment of signs. Language is the common element a community shares to make sense of the world. Thus, language's worth resides in its being an element that connects different entities and phenomena. Language is a pass-through, a medium, an in-between tool, a connecting artifice that brings the world to us through deception: I accept that something is something else when I know that it is not. The artifices of self-deception that we discuss here also have this in-betweenness, a liminal characteristic connecting us to worlds both real and imagined in ways that would not be possible for our senses and minds if such artifices were not employed as intellectual tools.

To give an example of the common agreement necessary to use language as an intellectual tool in order to understand a phenomenon even though none of the signs of the language are actually part of the represented phenomenon, let us consider the language used in mathematics. A mathematical formulation does not have any value in itself, its power residing instead in the shared social codes used to express concepts and phenomena and the relations between the terms. In $E = m \cdot c^2$ the equals sign represents the concept of equivalence between different terms and a relation between them; E, m, and c are each a particular phenomenon (E represents energy, m mass, and c the speed of light in a vacuum). Energy is a conserved quantity that cannot be created or destroyed but only transformed from one form to another (for instance, heat can be transformed into movement). Mass[1] represents resistance to acceleration or the gravitational attraction of an object to all other bodies in a particular gravitational field, and c is a universal constant. Finally, the superscript 2 and the dot represent relations between terms: the 2 indicates that, in this formulation, the speed of light in a vacuum should be multiplied by itself, and the dot indicates that c^2 should be multiplied by the mass of an object. The relations between these terms are a quantifiable expression of equivalence between two phenomena: mass and energy. Thus, the value of the graphic/written expression $E = m \cdot c^2$ resides in its socially shared ability to encapsulate a common understanding of natural phenomena and the relations between them by the use of a previously agreed-upon set of symbols and associated syntax.

The same goes for more trivial uses of codified representations of the world, such as the use of the words *house*, *casa*, and *maison*, which, although graphically and acoustically distinct, represent the same general idea of a livable space shared by people with close, usually family, ties. These three examples use the same set of graphic signs: the Latin alphabet. However, it would not really make any difference if the word *house* were written in other languages that use different symbols or structures, such as Arabic, Hindi, or Chinese; the concept of "house" would still be there, even if the language or the physical form of the house were different. The idea of a livable shared space would remain.

Now, what does language have to do with spatial design and the artifices we use to mediate and investigate our perception of space? Just as mathematical formulations and written and oral languages are used to represent the world, so artifices are used by geographers or designers to perceive, understand, conceive, and communicate spatial experiences and proposals. Drawings, paintings, photographs, maps, videos, and virtual reality are all used to represent space, and each does so according to its intrinsic ability to engage our senses, influencing or even manipulating which spatial characteristics are captured, observed, and communicated to viewers.

Representations are thus artifices used to present an idea or experience conceived or lived by someone to someone else—often to someone who has not had the same experience. In this chapter we argue that some forms of representation not only represent space (making it comprehensible) but also have the power to change the way we perceive, understand, and conceive it. Moreover, we argue that radical forms of representation, such as immersive technologies, are simultaneously powerful artifices of self-deception and intellectual tools because of their capacity to engage our senses in a way that we are unable to control—although our mind knows we are not experiencing a situation, our brain and body feel it as real.

Deception as an artifice to induce someone to accept as true what is known not to be true becomes powerful make-believe when the deceiver masters the conventions of a specific language. In such cases, deception can position its product within a social context in which such make-believe affords advantages for the deceiver and the deceived. In the long history of art forgery, the most impressive cases are those in which the deceiver mastered the language of the copied artwork in a context in which the deceived saw benefits in accepting the produced work even when in hindsight all the elements consistently pointed to a forgery. This is the case of one of the best-known cases of art forgery: Han van Meegeren's fake Vermeers. In retrospect it is difficult to understand how some of van Meegeren's works were accepted as Vermeers by connoisseurs, given that he lacked the technical and artistic skills of master art forgers; still, those deceived by van Meegeren's forgery saw so much prestige and monetary gains in "discovering" a new Vermeer that they easily accepted being deceived.

Deception helps us make sense of the world. All languages, understood as any shared form of expression, rely on some degree of self-deception. We look at a painting and see a house that is not there (and might not even exist); what is there is paint and canvas. Language simply provides the informational structure by which we smear the paint in a specific order, such that our brain accepts it as a code for "house," and the neocortex—the part of the brain that processes visual data and mental abstractions—takes care of the rest.

In ordinary representational forms, however similar to the represented object or phenomenon, the medium, with its materiality and representational rules, is always present and evident; and we agree, consciously or not, to go beyond these so that we can decode, understand, and ultimately enjoy an experience that we might not have firsthand. Given that our bodies have evolved to understand space through all our senses, mastery of a medium—any medium, for that matter—can only be achieved if the designer or artist can creatively bypass the sensorial deficits imposed by the medium and human biology. A clear example of this is the frame. Physical realities envelop us, so in the case of spatial representation, a frame, be it in the form of a painting, a stage, or a screen, makes its rules, techniques, and materiality evident when conveying representations of space and time. We may go back and forth across the screen, swiping, dragging, zooming, and panning, but its limitations are always present, attesting that "this is not a person, but a representation of a person that can have a material existence or be an imaginary composite of what we understand as being a person."

Let us take three examples of representations of houses: a child's drawing, a medieval painting, and a photograph (see figure 4.1). In the case of the child's drawing and the medieval painting, we cannot be sure whether they are the result of transferring to the canvas what the child and artist were seeing when they depicted the buildings or a collage of their previous experiences of many houses embodied in a particular portrayal. In the case of the photograph, a photosensitive surface captures the chemical reaction caused by light reflected by an object that was actually present when the photograph was taken. What we see in this case is a unique spatiotemporal depiction of an object—a minute later, another image would depict a different, spatiotemporally unique house. Regardless of the techniques and skills used to produce each image, we see houses because we relate each representation to our cumulative experience of livable spaces shared by people with close ties, a well-accepted definition of a house in different cultures and times. The portrayals are representations, but not artifices of deception.

Deception plays with our physiological and mental perception of space. It is a visceral make-believe that extends beyond the conventions we accept and share with others. However, not all deceptions become intellectual tools in the sense we are exploring here. We argue here that an intellectual tool allows us to understand and conceive space in unprecedented ways but, no matter how powerful, never attracts or retains the viewer's attention. A representation becomes an artifice of self-deception when, even if the rules

Figure 4.1
Top: Houses represented in the Français 239, an illuminated copy (mid-fifteenth century) of Laurent de Premierfait's 1414 translation of Giovanni Boccaccio's *The Decameron*. *Source*: Bibliothèque Nationale de France.
Bottom left: Drawing of a house made by a child. *Source*: Volodymyr Hsyschenko.
Bottom right: A photograph of a house in Iceland. *Source*: Luke Stackpoole.

and materiality of the medium are present and we are aware of them, it still tricks our mental and physiological perception of space.

Without minimizing their importance, we could differentiate artifices of self-deception as being tricks or tools. Intellectual tricks also deceive our perception in visceral ways, but they seem to urge us to unveil their ingenuity, and they engage us because we take pleasure in being deceived. Intellectual tricks master cunning to the extent that even after we realize their workings, we actively engage in being fooled, enjoying not necessarily the results of the deception but the operation of the deception itself. The question "How does it work?" is always present, even after we realize the workings of the device.

The Ames room is a well-known example. It is a room that gives the viewer the illusion that two people of the same height in different parts of the room have dramatically different heights. First built in 1947 and frequently displayed in amusement parks and museums, an Ames room makes use of an optical illusion to trick our visual perception. Viewed through a peephole, all the angles in the room appear to be right angles, when in fact the walls are trapezoidal and the floor and ceiling sloped (see figure 4.2). Thus, we have the impression when viewing it through a peephole that the room is an ordinary cube, but when two people of the same height enter the room and occupy opposite sides at the back of the cuboid, one of

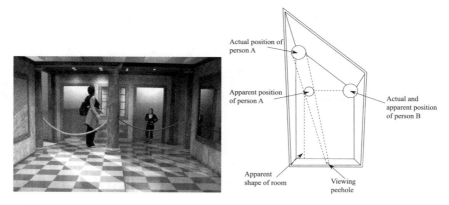

Figure 4.2
Left: A photograph showing the optical illusion of an Ames room located at the Cité des Sciences et de l'Industrie in Paris. *Source*: Mosso, 2015.
Right: Layout diagram of an Ames room. *Source*: Alex Valavanis, 2007.

them seems to be much taller than the other. Although we have seen the individuals before they entered the room, and although we know that the sides of the cuboid are not regular and that the angles are not right angles, our senses are still duped. Such self-deception happens even when an adult and a toddler enter the room and, when seen from the outside, the child seems to become taller than the adult—even though we are fully aware that this is impossible. The enjoyment here comes from being tricked by the artifice.

The fifty-second film *L'arrivée d'un train en gare de La Ciotat* is arguably the best-known and most powerful deception in cinema.[2] In the film, made by the Lumière brothers and first shown publicly in 1896, a train pulls into La Ciotat station and passengers alight from and board the train. The novelty of the moving images, however, took viewers by surprise, and some members of the audience are said to have fled the room in panic. Regardless of the veracity of such accounts, which are disputed by some film historians, this short movie has become part of the founding myth of cinema (Loiperdinger and Elzer, 2004). Even when it was clear that the train was not coming out of the screen, the effect still thrilled spectators, who rushed to experience it again and again. The Lumière brothers, aware of the dramatic effect achieved with the film, reshot the scene with a stereoscopic camera to obtain a three-dimensional effect; that film was first shown in 1935 but is now lost (Aumont, 1996).

M. C. Escher's depictions of spaces represent impossible architecture. His drawings, produced during the twentieth century, follow the rules of perspective with great accuracy. Escher (2007) said that mastering design so that he could depict what amazed him in his observations of the world around him led him to mathematics. Although precise, Escher's works instill a sense of wonder in the viewer because of their logical coherence. In one of his engravings, we see an interior space with a set of stairs looking out onto different views. Figurine-like people are climbing and going down the stairs effortlessly. However, some of the stairs are double-sided, and on one side a person is climbing the stairs while on the opposite side of the same stairs someone else is going down. In the top of the picture, there is a vaulted flight of stairs, where one person seems to be going up while another person appears to be going down the same flight of stairs. We are fully aware that these movements are impossible and even understand the tricks Escher plays with shadows and the positioning of objects to direct our perception. Our expectation is that some objects should follow gravity, as if gravity were synonymous with verticality in the picture, so that vases and people should fall if represented upside down. Although we know these are pictorial conventions, Escher's perspectives mesmerize us, enchanted as we are by the mastery with which he fools our perception even when we know the tricks.

Artifices of deception are more elaborate than mere illusionist stratagems. According to medieval Christian tradition, illusions were the art of the Devil: while God's miracles suspended the laws of physics, and nature astonished humans with its inexplicable wonders, the Devil could only create illusions (Warner, 2004). In the three examples above (the Ames room, the Lumière brothers' early films, and Escher's engravings), our spatial perception is deceived, as if we could not control our senses even though we are fully aware of the device's workings. The strength of these works lies in the use they make of artifices of deception as perceptual tricks.

There is another category of artifices of deception that serve as intellectual tools. The main differences between artifices of deception as perceptual tricks and intellectual tools are, firstly, that tricks draw attention to the trickery itself, making it part of the value of the deception and the means by which the viewer is engaged; and, secondly, that tools transform the way we understand, represent, and conceive space. However, this does not mean that when artifices of deception are intellectual tools their workings are hidden. We are in fact aware that such tools are artifices, and we even master and play with their rules, but we consciously use their self-deception properties for our own benefit. We accept self-deception as a way of acquiring knowledge about certain phenomena and, in turn, about the way we acquire such knowledge. Thus, self-deception becomes a tool for self-reflection.

Focusing specifically on the acquisition of knowledge about space—how we perceive, represent, and conceive space—here we discuss what we argue are two transformative artifices of self-deception: linear perspective and virtual reality (VR).

Space in Perspective

One example of an artifice of self-deception used as an intellectual tool is linear perspective, which became established in the fifteenth century. Artists had used perspective before with varying results, sometimes depicting what would today appear to us as obviously "erroneous" representations of space, sometimes showing space in visually impossible ways. In the fifteenth-century illustration shown in figure 4.1, all the doors and windows and the roofs of the two two-story buildings have nearly the same vanishing point, away from the viewer, while the larger room with the open entrance and the small room connecting the two two-story buildings seem to have a different vanishing point, toward the viewer. Although not architecturally impossible, this is an improbable arrangement. Furthermore, the heights of the ground and first floors and the sizes of the people inside the buildings, compared with the single individual outdoors, are also highly improbable. In spite of all these spatial improbabilities, which seem awkward to our contemporary visual sense of representation, this pictorial composition reinforces the story that the artist wanted to tell, with the focus on the person who seems to be hiding between the buildings and the difference in height between the floors of the two-story buildings indicating the relative distance from the viewer.

This form of spatial representation could vary from artist to artist and from scene to scene. Each artist would base their composition on their own perception of a particular scene. In contrast, linear perspective, the rules of which were first formulated between 1401 and 1425 by Filippo Brunelleschi (Kubovy, 1986), offered a standard procedure for representing any space. The main feature of linear perspective is the vanishing point toward which all lines in a given scene converge on the horizon. The mathematical principles were established by Leon Battista Alberti around 1435, and having been adopted rapidly in Italy and, later, Europe, the system was to lead to profound changes in modes of spatial representation.

A textbook case of linear perspective is Pietro Perugino's fresco *Christ Handing the Keys to Saint Peter* (see figure 4.3), painted in 1481–1482 and located in the Sistine Chapel in the Vatican. The horizon line divides the fresco in half, and the main theme (Christ handing the keys to the kingdom of heaven to Saint Peter) is centered in the foreground, while the doorway of the main building is centered in the background. The lines in the piazza perpendicular to the plane of the picture converge at an unseen point behind the main building (the vanishing point), while the lines parallel to the horizon guide the viewer and help the painter make all the objects and figures change size appropriately.

Figure 4.3
Christ Handing the Keys to Saint Peter, or Delivery of the Keys (1481–1482), a fresco by
Pietro Perugino located in the Sistine Chapel.
Source: Wikimedia Foundation.

The vanishing point, the quintessential element of linear perspective, is
an optical artifice used to organize everything in space and has illusionistic,
narrative, and structural functions (Kubovy, 1986). As Erwin Panofsky (1961)
put it, perspective structures space as infinite, constant, and homogeneous,
three characteristics that are "antinomic regarding the psychophysiological
space" (p. 38), characteristics that ignore the bodily perception of space.

Taking the fifteenth-century French illumination shown in figure 4.1 as
a reference again, the relative dimensions and spatial organization of the
figures and buildings in the scene, although improbable, still follow a symbolic organization: for instance, the figure between the two buildings is bigger than the other figures, which seems to induce the viewer to see him as
the main character of the scene. Obviously, painters who use linear perspective also organize elements in the pictorial space symbolically to emphasize
their intentions. However, regardless of the painter's intentions, all the elements in the scene are subjugated to the same internal spatial organization
governed by the vanishing points. In fact, centrality and infinity, two features of perspective, are essentially contradictory terms (Arnheim, 1974): if
a center exists, there is a start or end point, and if space is infinite, it has no

center. And yet, centrality and infinity become key procedural artifices to convey a realistic depiction of space based on linear perspective.

Imagine this scene: you are standing on a street corner, looking at a square lined with two- and three-story houses, trees, bushes, benches, and streetlights, with people walking around. Each of these elements apparently is an entity in its own right. Another person approaches the square. For you, standing at the corner, or for anybody present in the scene, this person seems to be another independent entity in the scene. But not when she is put into perspective, literally. In a sketch of the scene based on the rules of linear perspective, the person's position and dimensions would not be absolute values but would rather be relative to all the other elements in the scene and, moreover, would be defined according to the procedures of perspective. Perspective would determine her spatial relation with you, the observer, and with everybody and everything else present in the scene. Perspective creates an absolute space, an all-encompassing means of representation, in which nothing that enters the scene escapes from the vanishing points.

Because of its well-structured rules, perspective has been the subject of severe criticism. Some see it as a "monster unleashed on the art of the Renaissance," a "truculent . . . four-square grid," as explained by Kubovy (1986, p. 121), while Rudolf Arnheim (1974) considers perspective a "scientifically oriented" mechanical reproduction taking the place of creative imagery or "a violent imposition upon the world represented in the picture" (p. 294) because of the centrality it confers upon the viewer as a manifestation of the individualism of the Renaissance.

Linear perspective, grounded in mathematical expressions and empirical data, has become so prevalent as a tool for representation that we often take it as the only trustworthy depiction of a scene. In fact, perspective is an artifice of self-deception. However, unlike the tricks discussed before, perspective as an artifice of self-deception is so powerful that even when its workings are revealed, our perception of space does not change. We argue that this happens not because of the supposed truculence and violence imposed by perspective but rather, as posited by Hubert Damisch (2000), because perspective should not be understood as a code but as an epistemological model. Bringing the world into perspective means organizing all its elements in such a way that the relations between them make sense: this is the epistemological power of perspective. Facing myriad perceptual stimuli, we restrict ourselves to a set of rules that on the one hand might reduce our perception of space, but on the other hand allow us to understand and represent such space in a way that it can also make sense to other people.

Regardless of where the actual viewers are in the outside world when they contemplate a spatial depiction of it, perspectival representations create a virtual viewer that brings together all external viewpoints. All bodily eyes merge into a single mental, ideal eye. This privileged virtual viewpoint becomes the second center of the projection; it is the counterpart of the vanishing points that structure the depiction of the scene, and, together with these, it organizes the perception of space. Such an artifice hinders other physiological aspects of visual perception, as Panofsky (1961) explained: we do not see with a single fixed eye, but with two eyes constantly moving throughout the scene. Still, perspective as an artifice of self-deception is so powerful that we often take the spatial representations based on its rules as the "true" representation. Even Arnheim (1974), who criticized perspective for its violence and "deformation of the normal shapes of things," accepted that it is "by far the most realistic way of rendering optical space" (p. 283). Perspective is so powerful that, even though we understand that its rules might deform the shapes of the objects being represented in ways that sometimes contradict what our senses see, it is still the prevalent representational model.

Indeed, only a few decades after Brunelleschi's experiments and Alberti's formulation of the rules, perspectival representation became the standard way of depicting space throughout Europe, and training in linear perspective has long been mandatory in arts and architecture schools. Although modern art and architecture have repeatedly questioned the absoluteness of perspectival representations and have subverted and abandoned perspective at various times, architects have often deployed it to challenge the status quo of design. Some of the most radical designers who have questioned the aesthetics and ideologies of previous architectural designs have still employed perspective as an intellectual tool to think about space—even when their proposed designs would challenge the prevalent architectural norms of their times, including representational norms. Examples include Le Corbusier, Oscar Niemeyer, and Rem Koolhaas, each advancing design and critical thinking about architecture and cities but relying on fifteenth-century rules of perspective to convey their ideas. The rules of perspective and the artifices of self-deception associated with perspective are still powerful intellectual tools and epistemological models used to understand, represent, and conceive space even when the goals are to disrupt the prevalent aesthetics and functionalities of space.

The Virtual: A Conceptual Framework and Immersive Reality

A leap of more than five hundred years from the time of Brunelleschi and Perugino to the present day brings us to mixed reality (MR) technologies. Clearly, it would be absurd to suggest that in such a long period no other powerful media have been devised and used to understand how people perceive and make sense of space or how people represent or conceive space. Indeed, we have pointed out the effect the Lumière brothers' early films had on audiences as one of the artifices of self-deception created during this interregnum. However, in this case, the medium was part of the trick played on our visual perception of space, and the disruptive effect vanishes as soon as we understand the trick. Various other technologies—from photographs to computer tools—have been used to represent space, although Damisch (2000) observes that these modern technologies actually reinstated the power of perspective as a spatial representation; in fact, the massive use of these technologies has made perspective even more prevalent today than during the fifteenth century. MR technologies are different from what existed before simply because they shift our perception of space from representation to an experience that involves many of our senses. Presence is a key concept to understanding immersive reality (IR): we have a physiological perception of being somewhere we are not, either because the immersive space is alienated from the here and now in time and space, or because it is a space where it is impossible to actually be, such as an intracellular environment or an interstellar one.

The point we are making here is not simply about the media used to represent, analyze, or design space. Our interest lies in the artifices that lead us to accept as true what we know is not and the degree to which self-deception becomes an intellectual tool that informs the epistemological models with which we perceive, represent, and conceive space. Technology plays a definite role in this process, and in this sense MR can be considered a groundbreaking technology. The fact that other modern technologies did not become intellectual tools as powerful as linear perspective may perhaps be attributed to the fact that they were built upon the same or similar rules of perspective (photography and cinema, for instance) and therefore only achieved the same degree of similarity, or equivalence, with what is commonly perceived as the real world.

IR also achieves this degree of equivalence with the world, but in quite an interesting manner: it resumes a classic, pre-perspective form of spatial perception. In Panofsky's (1961) words, classic art was an "art of the body," concerned not only with what was visible but also with the tangible—the tectonics and plastics of the world. After five hundred years centered on the squeezing of space onto a plane mediated by the contradictory terms of centrality and infinity that characterize linear perspective, another artifice of self-deception has emerged that takes advantage of our fully bodily perception of space.

IR technologies make embodied simulations possible because they share basic perceptual mechanisms with the brain. The deception they practice happens at the stage of the senses, prior to mental abstractions. As Riva et al. (2019) explain, spatial perception is based on the brain creating a simulation of the body in the world and using this simulation to represent and predict actions, concepts, and emotions. MR works similarly, building multiple simulations of the body and the surrounding space with its many possibilities for interaction and working through our biology to have the body engage with the world. Thus, by altering experiences of the virtual embodiment of the self, regardless of the human scale, MR creates a "multisensory body matrix" (Moseley et. al, 2012) that serves to encode cognitive models of the world and, inversely, offers neurosciences embodied ways to understand how the brain functions (Parsons et al., 2017).

Immersive technologies are grounded in the concept of the virtual, which deserves to be discussed here, since it also grounds our argument that immersive technologies and perspective are equally powerful as artifices of self-deception conceived as intellectual tools. The use of the term *virtual* solely in relation to computer-mediated representations has been criticized because it limits the term as an operable philosophical concept (Friedberg, 2006). Building on Henri Bergson's theory of memory, Anne Friedberg explains that the virtual should be seen as an ontological distinction between, on the one hand, the possible and, on the other hand, the real and the actual—in her distinction, the real and actual are, and the virtual is the consciously perceived. Pierre Lévy, Gilles Deleuze, and Félix Guattari, among others, also make the distinction between the virtual, on the one hand, and the real and actual, on the other. Deleuze (1988) sees the possible as opposed and opposite to the real, and the virtual as opposite to the actual, for "realization involves a limitation by which some possibles" will be repulsed and others will be realized, whereas the virtual "does not have to be realized, but rather actualized," which happens by differentiation and creation (p. 97). In summary, while the real is "in the image and likeness of the possible that it realizes, the actual, on the other hand, does not resemble the virtuality that it embodies" (p. 97). The possible is derived from the real, "abstracted from the real once made" (p. 98); however, the virtual can take infinite forms, while the actual only exists in its single state. For Deleuze, new ideas—and the lines of differentiation—can arise from perceived experiences, and therefore the senses take precedence over objective reality.

Building on Deleuze, Lévy (1997, p. 3) posits that "the possible is a ghost of reality," for it is already defined, only lacking existence, whereas virtuality encompasses forces, trends, and constraints that may or may not be actualized. Guattari (1995) sees the virtual as "becomings . . . nuclei of differentiation" (p. 92) and says that it is not a matter of "representation and discursivity, but of existence. . . . carried beyond my familiar existential Territories" (p. 93). These nuclei of differentiation do not mimic or multiply a known reality, but open up other actualizations, other possible configurations. It would thus be wrong to liken the outcomes of virtuality to images without referents (these are simulacra). Underlying the philosophical approaches of the virtual is its purely etymological definition, derived from the Latin *virtus*, or strength, power, an act of becoming.

Friedberg (2006), advocating the philosophical use of the term *virtual* as a "marker of ontological property" (p. 11), argues against the enforced association between the virtual and the digital, as this approach makes the term a media-specific one. By rescuing the philosophical concept of the virtual, Friedberg develops arguments to illustrate the virtuality of other media, mostly moving-image media such as cinema and video. However, her arguments seem tailored to media that are specifically of interest to her because, although she gives examples of virtuality in other media, the absence of any discussion about what is commonly accepted as virtual reality (VR)—an immersive spatial experience built digitally in computers and mediated through optical, auditory, and haptic devices—is particularly striking.

We would argue that accepting a somewhat narrow definition of virtual reality as immersive representations of spaces built in computers and mediated by digital devices, in fact, strengthens the epistemological use of the term *virtual*. An all-encompassing concept seldom serves the purpose of guiding an intellectual endeavor. And going a step farther, we see digital technologies creating not only a parallel environment (which is currently the usual outcome of VR) but also an amalgamation of these technologies within our concrete space, as in the case of mixed realities. MR technologies act directly on many of our senses, affecting our perception of direction, balance, and scale in ways we respond to physiologically—in ways neither cinema, video, nor even holography are capable of. If the virtual is the "knot of tendencies or forces . . . that invokes a process of resolution" (Lévy, 1998, p. 24), it has the power to make myriad possibilities real and constantly produce variations and new dynamics of these possibilities, whereas the actual is one of the static outcomes of these virtualities. While the approach usually adopted when studying virtuality is to consider the transition from the possible to the real or from the virtual to the actual, Lévy (1998) proposes the reverse approach: movement toward the virtual. When this approach is adopted, the virtual reveals itself to be a playground of possibilities with sometimes unpredictable outcomes. Each actualization is followed by multiple virtualizations.

Contrary to Baudrillard's (2006) argument that intelligent machines are described as "virtual" because "they put thought on hold indefinitely" (p. 51), what Lévy shows is that the virtual is anything but on hold; on the contrary, it is a continuous actualization of myriad possibilities that stimulate our thoughts in novel ways. Baudrillard's generally Luddite approach to technology hinders his perception of technology as a tool to challenge and advance knowledge, whereas Lévy's argument has the philosophical strength to make the virtual an epistemological tool. Alas, only VR—understood as immersive representations of spaces built in computers and mediated by digital devices—can actualize the infinite possibilities that any space has when forces, trends, and constraints play against each other in ways that affect our bodily experience of space. Neither cinema nor video can do this.

This does not mean that when we are immersed in a VR environment we believe we are in a real space. Obviously we are aware that we are not—the clunky optical digital devices, up to now the most common VR interface, that make this spatial immersion possible don't let us forget. Still, when we are in a VR environment simulating the cabin of a jetliner flying over Manhattan or a free climb in the Grand Canyon, it is not only our rational mind but also our body and brain that respond to the spatial experience. VR affects our physiological responses to spatial experiences in such a way that our senses feel something as true when our rational mind knows it is not. In this sense VR is a radical artifice of self-deception.

And since VR affects our bodily perception of space, we also argue that as an artifice of self-deception VR opens up new possibilities as an intellectual tool that can transform how we perceive, understand, and design spaces. Consider, first, our perception of scale. As Nicholas Negroponte observes, although other media, such as photographs, films, or computer-generated images, can represent galaxies or microorganisms accurately, the intrinsic perceptual scale of the human body always mediates the enjoyment of such representations. In VR, everything is on a human scale or our bodily scale is also a virtuality, an actualization of multiple, dynamic possibilities. The limits of life-size or real places disappear, allowing VR to be used in different scientific fields to experience models of galaxies or the molecular structures of proteins. Negroponte (1995) argues that the compound term *VR* should be seen as two equal halves: "VR will allow you to put your arms around the Milky Way, swim in the human bloodstream, or visit Alice in Wonderland" (p. 199).

The speed with which VR went from being considered science fiction, high-tech gimmickry, or a device for teenage arcades to a serious technology that expanded the boundaries of research in molecular biology, medicine, and the cognitive sciences can be seen in scientific publications. In a mere twenty-five years, *Nature*, a major scientific journal, went from asking whether VR was not simply a verbal joke, arguing that VR was rooted in the "age-old craft of manufacturing illusion" and briefly conceding that it might have more serious uses in the future although these were still unclear ("Is Virtual Reality Real?," 1993), to describing many current applications of VR in the sciences and observing that the technology had come of age (Matthews, 2018; Skibba, 2018).

Even fierce critics of computer-based imagery, such as Jean Baudrillard, sometimes seem to build good arguments from the wrong perspective. Baudrillard argues that simulation has lost a referential being or substance because it is generated by "models of a real without an origin or reality"

(Baudrillard, 2006, p. 1) and that "the world and its double cannot occupy the same space, for the double is a perfect artificial and virtual substitute for the world" (Baudrillard, 2000, p. 70). So, what is the problem here? Nothing, if one thinks that artifices of self-deception are intellectual tools. Fifteenth-century perspective was essentially a model that worked without the reality: it is a set of rules and procedures that guide how one represents the world as seen, but also the world as it could be. Because its make-believe characteristics convey the message more strongly than previous representations, perspective gives the impression of reality even in an imaginary world. VR, as a computer-generated spatial representation, offers actualizations of multiple, dynamic possibilities—not a representation of reality as if there were any inherent truth, or goodness, in being real. Likewise, VR demonstrates that the world and its double can occupy the same space, as it can actually enhance our perception and understanding of space beyond what our direct sensorial experience would consider real. Go outdoors, look at an anthill: what you see is reality, a reality that can be easily crushed under your feet. Now become an ant, enter the anthill, march with your peers: it is the model, the VR model, that creates a sensorial experience of the anthill as if you were on the same scale as an ant, walking along with other ants. This sensorial experience changes your perception and, consequently, your understanding of the anthill. And by becoming an ant—or at least by perceiving the world from the ant's perspective, at their scale—you might grasp characteristics of this space you would not when viewing it from the human scale.

Virtual reality models are diagrams, in the semiotic sense proposed by Charles Peirce, who equates them with algorithms within the category of signs he named "icons." In this way, diagrams and algorithms are minimum arrangements of some essential characteristics and workings of a phenomenon that allow us to indirectly access this phenomenon and its multiple variations. Einstein's equation discussed earlier in this chapter ($E = m \cdot c^2$) is an icon: it encapsulates essential characteristics of each element in a particular organization that brings us the concept of energy without direct access to it. The equation does not intend to include all characteristics of a phenomenon (for one, the sensorial perception of the speed of light is absent), but placing these essential components in a particular arrangement makes energy virtual, and variations in the parameters result in multiple actualizations. A computer model that generates VR is a semiotic diagram, an algorithm with multiple parameters, that generates actualizations that affect our physiological responses to spaces. It is an artifice of self-deception that becomes an intellectual tool that helps us explore the world beyond our immediate mind and body capabilities.

The main argument of this chapter is that we voluntarily engage in different forms of self-deception as a way of making sense of the world—and making sense of ourselves in the world. Self-deception helps us cope with traumas, by creating the self-illusion that what we know happened, might not have happened; or to face dangerous, uncomfortable, and unknown situations. Self-deception also shapes many artifices we create to perceive the world, and some of them are so powerful that they deceive our senses even when we understand and master its workings. This is the case of linear perspective, which continues to be an artifice of self-deception even though we do not realize it, as it is so natural to our way of representing the world. But when we look at a drawing by M. C. Escher, we realize how powerful and deceptive perspective might be—and at the same time, how it is a unique tool to understand and represent the world around us. This is also the case of immersive reality technologies, such as virtual reality. When we are in virtual reality environments, our brain engages in accepting that something is, even though our mind knows that it is not—and we argue that this artifice of self-deception has the power to open up new possibilities of perceiving, understanding, and conceiving space. In fact, designers have been exploring the tool as deception of not only our bodily senses but also our social and cultural biases. Virtual reality allows us to feel the world as somebody else, either by adjusting how we perceive the world (by turning us into a toddler, for instance) or by adjusting how the world perceives us (if we become a homeless person, for instance). In both cases, this experience has the potential to change how we engage with and design spaces.

Virtual reality has the power to exponentiate Marshall McLuhan's (1962) argument that new media could expand the somewhat restrictive world of the written word toward what he called the acoustic space: his argument that the linear understanding of the world, characteristic of the written language, were being replaced by media such as radio, cinema, and television, which were bringing back our primal perception of the world through the use of many of our senses simultaneously. Virtual reality immerses our senses in this multisensorial apprehension of the world. And different from television or cinema, in which the medium was always there as a barrier between our senses and reality, virtual reality affects our brain directly. As we will discuss further, this is a groundbreaking technology, as linear perspective once was, in exploring novel ways to perceive, understand, and conceive space. Understood critically, artifices of self-deception can help us to open up new ways of making sense of the world.

5   Learning from Video Games

Playing Video Games

Games create self-contained spaces in which particular rules and behaviors are accepted and others are excluded, players assume specific roles while playing, and a common set of values is shared among all players during the game. This "manipulable and well bounded" environment enables us to explore how such behaviors and actions influence design (Habraken and Gross, 1988, p. 151). Although N. John Habraken's and Mark Gross's research concentrates on board games, some of the elements of board games are also present in video games, such as variable physical organization, control distribution, territorial organization, program, multiplayer action, and in-play development—in which it is not just the initial creator (or programmer) who determines the overall design outcome; the players themselves can, within the framework of shared values, establish new features, goals, and rules within the game. More recently, artificial intelligence has allowed video games to learn the behavior of multiple players and propose internal rearrangements that open up the possibility of ever-changing games (Togelius, 2018).

The playfulness aspect intrinsic to most games takes over the initial rules and opens up new possibilities within the game itself. The role of playfulness in changing the games from within has been incorporated by gamers and game designers, mainly due to a combination of technological improvements (computational power, parallel processing, cloud computing) and the social media culture of cocreation. All these possibilities have captured the attention of the design community (Koutsabasis, 2012), eager to explore qualities of the virtual worlds created by games, such as embodiment, copresence, and interaction.[1] Introducing a series of works that explore commercial computer games as tools for planning and design processes, Friedrich von Borries, Steffen P. Walz, and Matthias Böttger (2007) point to the potential of superimposing the social interactions of computer games over the physical spaces of cities.

The interest of the design community in video games can be seen in renowned museums' attention, such as the Smithsonian exhibition *The Art of Video Games*, which opened in Washington, DC, in 2012 and traveled across the country until 2016; or the acquisition of video games by the Museum of Modern Art (MoMA) in New York. Initially presented at the *Applied Design* exhibition (2013–2014), the fourteen video games on show at MoMA were part of a wish list of forty and included a range of games, from *Pac-Man* (1980) to *Canabalt* (2009). Interestingly, as John Sharp (2015) points out, the video games were acquired by the Architecture and Design department, not the Media and Performance department. In the press material MoMA acknowledges video games as "one of the most important and oft-discussed expressions of contemporary design creativity,"[2] and the curatorial selection included the elegance of the code and the player's experience.

Artists have explored video games as artistic media; examples include Cory Arcangel's *I Shot Andy Warhol* (2002), based on a *Hogan's Alley* mod, where the gangsters have been replaced by Warhol and the "innocents" by the Pope, Flavor Flav, and Colonel Sanders; and Mary Flanagan's *[giant-joystick]* (2006), a 10-foot-tall joystick, modeled after a classic Atari 2600 joystick, that requires collective work to move it, shifting the isolation that was often linked to video game players to a collaborative work, and the scale of the game experience to involve the whole body. From the computer science side, Julian Togelius (2018) has summarized the mutually beneficial relationship between video games and artificial intelligence. A developer himself, Togelius has developed an open-source AI benchmark tool called the *Infinite Mario Bros.* (see Karakobskiy & Togelius, 2012). This tool is used in AI competitions, in which participants need to beat the game (and each other) by developing increasingly sophisticated AI agents. The benchmark was created using a public domain clone of the original *Super Mario Bros.* game, and was created as a tool to help reinforcement learning and game AI development. Educators have also used games in learning practices, such as the Education Arcade at MIT. *The Radix Endeavor* (Klopfer et al., 2018) is a massively multiplayer online game that integrates STEM (science, technology, engineering, and mathematics) practices into the game environment. The game is built around five distinct biomes, where players engage by collecting data and performing experiments.

Another pool of video games that combine aesthetic, technological, and narrative experimentations are independent Games (also known as Indies). These games are usually developed with a limited budget and as such have a narrower scope than blockbuster games, however since they are usually developed and even self-published by independent ventures, they often have a more experimental approach in their narrative and gameplay, including features allowed by the freedom of development outside the traditional developer-publisher system. However, as Jesper Juul (2019) argues, in the history of independent games, they become a category in the period of maturation of the video game industry, at the turn of the twenty-first century, with the consolidation of venues, institutions, developers, and distribution channels, and offer now one of the largest blocks of intellectual properties in the video games marketplace

Although these initiatives are exciting, when using video games either to promote artistic engagement or to advance knowledge in computer science, their outreach is commonly restricted to small groups. Our goal in this chapter is to discuss video games that are commercially available, for if video games have the potential to change spatial design and placemaking concepts and methods, it is in great part because they leverage multiple technological, cultural, and social features of contemporary society. Video games are pervasive—after all, more than half of households in America have at least one dedicated video game system, and games are by far the most popular category of applications that we run on our smartphones—so there is no point in discussing their transformative potential as if they were a niche media.

The role that video games can have in spatial design and placemaking is not simply a matter of building and representing realistic environments. Space does not rely on just form but on how its qualities trigger people's responses to the elements that constitute space, responses that range from behaviors to affections—as Steven Poole (2000) puts it, "the inner life of video games—how they work—is bound up with the inner life of the player" (p. 11) Some video games are completely built around the responses that players have when interacting with different spaces. In these cases, video games "encode urban models that become understood through play" (Gil & Duarte, 2008, p. 262).

Three decades ago Will Wright made quite a splash with his game *SimCity* (Maxis, 1989), which became the seminal work for the "city simulation" genre. The game was very forward looking for its time, presenting urban scenarios for virtual mayors, such as a crime-ridden Detroit, an earthquake in San Francisco, a nuclear plant meltdown in Boston (see figure 5.1), or coastal flooding in Rio de Janeiro due to global warming. Its simulation software revealed an underlying logic of a machine city that emulated both urban planning and socioeconomic dynamics within its hypothetical scenarios using a multi-agent-based software (Weinstock & Stathopoulos, 2006). The game prompted discussions in both amateur and academic circles regarding the value of these simulators in city development and management processes. Likewise, the game, its future iterations, and similar games in the genre have been used to teach students to grapple with the complexities of urban planning, which involves several interrelated parts and interacting variables, and which have immediate formal and social reflections in the city (Gaber, 2007; Minnery & Searle, 2014). Luke Caspar Pearson (2019), cofounder of the Videogame Urbanism group at the Bartlett

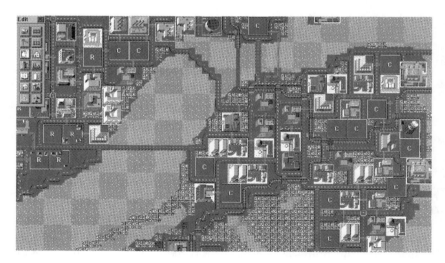

Figure 5.1
The Boston scenario in the video game *SimCity* (Maxis, 1989).
Source: Maxis, 1989.

School of Architecture in London, sees the isotropic three-dimensional space of video games as a possibility for reinvigorating architectural practices by creating quantitative utopias and atopias, in the vein of critical architectural proposals of the 1960s and 1970s, such as Archizoom, Archigram, and Superstudio.

At the time of *SimCity*'s commercial release, technology wasn't nearly powerful or mature enough to be used for serious work, an almost impossible task for a software package that came in a single floppy disk and ran using 512 KB of memory. The idea of it, however, remained intriguing; and though it was this piece of software that framed the initial interest from urbanists, the reality was that the video game industry had been experimenting with spatial design for quite a bit of time. Although more recent versions of *SimCity*, as well as other city-building games, such as *Cities: Skylines* (Colossal Order, 2005) and *Cities XXL* (Focus Home Interactive, 2015), allow multiplayer work and more complex spatial features, they still have two common characteristics. First, most of the cities designed within their environments tend to either replicate existing cities or mimic many aspects of existing cities and recombine them into new forms. Second, the most common interface for players is to engage from a third-person perspective, privileging a viewpoint from above. This perspective clearly emulates the bird's-eye point of view traditionally used by urban planners, who rely primarily on overhead maps and plans to perform their design functions. Daniel Golding (2013) comments that in these cases the player acts as a strategist and is somehow separated from the daily acts that create the life of a city; he instead advocates for a first-person perspective, in which the player becomes a tactician. Within this context, "individuals encounter the city not as a concept, but as an immediate experience" (Golding, 2013, p. 127).

This change in perspective would imply altering the game's narratives, giving room to multiple characters and unexpected events. Indeed, many contemporary games have been incorporating freedom of movement and multiple journeys within the game time-space. Taking a first-person approach to city building would also reflect a more critical and contemporary approach to planning and design. In multiplayer city-building games, the spatial characteristics, ludic aspects, and narrative functions of the game can all work in tandem to create a sense of place closer to the players' and designers' actions and intentions (see Picard, 2014).

Although city-building video games are relevant to our discussion, they represent a specific niche, and our argument is that general video games, not just ad hoc "city simulators," can inform spatial design. For this reason, we will discuss a wide range of video games, highlighting how their characteristics are relevant to design.

Early Experiments in Spatial Design and Representation

To say that the first video games were limited in their spatial design would be an understatement. Early games consisted mostly of some pixels crudely arrayed on a single screen. Computer hardware constraints and limited processing power forced their design approach to be contained within a minimalist territory (see figure 5.2), where only the essence of an object was used, and all nonessential forms and features were removed.

With simplified visuals came lean principles of interaction that aimed to maximize the choices the player could make in such primitive environments using basic input devices. Games such as *Pac-Man* (Namco, 1980) and *Q*bert* (Gottlieb, 1982) could create endless permutations of move sequences within their abstract worlds, with the player using just a joystick that could be pushed in only four directions. In both cases, the whole game space fit on a single screen, and while *Pac-Man*'s labyrinthic space was fully two-dimensional, *Q*bert* already presented a pseudo-3D effect by using isometric perspective. These games put forward the importance of the discipline of economy in screen "real estate" used for player movement, which would become one of the defining cornerstones of video game design. The

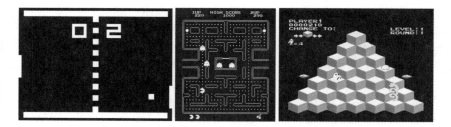

Figure 5.2
Three early video games: *Pong* (Atari, 1972), *Pac-Man* (Namco, 1980), and *Q*bert* (Gottlieb, 1982).
Source: Atari, 1972; Namco, 1980; Gottlieb, 1982.

success of both games, and many others of the late 1970s and early 1980s, also underline a common feature of video games: players are driven by the constant possibility of failure and surmounting obstacles, or phases, in which "frustration and anger binds us to the game" (Juul, 2013, p. 13).

Storytelling and Genius Loci: Early Efforts in Place-Based Narratives

In the early years of video games, the industry started to borrow archetypes from other media forms, particularly film. Storytellers have been using different channels to convey their stories, in what Jenkins (2001) calls transmedia storytelling. Michael Nitsche (2008) points out that the linearity that characterizes cinema has been described as incompatible with the nonlinear and interactive features of video games, but as he correctly concludes, storytelling in video games is not intended to tell a linear narrative but rather to use evocative means to engage the players.

Storytelling is also essential to one of the key characteristics of play: make-believe. Video games usually require that players assume the role of a specific character or have a set of characters that are part of the plot. Thus, the player is always moving between the immediate action, the short-term narrative of the part she or he is playing, and the overall plot of the game.

In some cases, the plot is based on existing stories popularized by other media, which serve as a hook to the game. This is done in order to bring some sense of identity to what could often be abstract images, or to lower the entry barrier to a new video game. Among the attempts to capitalize on the mental association with already established intellectual properties, some efforts are more successful than others. *Pitfall!* (Activision, 1982) was able to channel the iconic characteristics of the adventurer, inspired by the Indiana Jones movies, into a successful franchise; others, such as *E.T. the Extra-Terrestrial* (Atari, 1982), were abject failures that became an embarrassment for everyone involved, with millions of copies buried in the desert in New Mexico (Kent, 2001). Curiously, both were based on blockbuster movies directed by Steven Spielberg. These video games were created using sprite-based 2D graphics in which the whole game space is contained on a single screen. However, the difference in quality between them is at least in part on the storytelling: in *Pitfall!* it is possible to recognize cues that link it to the Indiana Jones movies, whereas in *E.T.* nothing links the game to the movie except the crude representation of the main character.

The visual limitations of early hardware created frustration in some game developers, who in the late 1970s and early 1980s kept trying to convey richer worlds that simply could not be displayed graphically at the time. Crucial among these efforts were the ones led by Infocom, a company founded at MIT, which sought to bring deeper storytelling techniques into video games (Briceno et al, 2000; Maher, 2013). Their first game, *Zork: The Great Underground Empire* (Infocom, 1980), narrated place details using only text. For example, the game begins with the following words: "West of House: You are standing in an open field west of a white house, with a boarded front door"; and if the player types "north," another text appears leading you to the "Forest Path," where there is a "particularly large tree"; and then the player might type "climb tree" and follow all the subsequent texts activated by the player's textual commands.

This level of detail in place description and gameplay choices, unheard of in the industry, showed players and developers the possibilities of imagining larger and richer worlds. Infocom's *Zork, Zork II* (1981), *Zork III* (1983), and *Planetfall* (1983) created the adventure and role-playing game (RPG) genres in the video game industry and demonstrated that a grounded sense of reality required both finer granularity and detail in spatial representation—even without images (one of *Planetfall*'s opening phrases, "This is a featureless corridor similar to every other corridor in the ship," disguises how rich and engaging narratives can convey the idea of complex spatialities). What is clear is that humans need variation of choice in order to buy into a parallel reality. In this regard, Malgorzata Hanzl (2007) argues that RPGs have been "a useful tool in consensus building programmes for decision making and planning professionals" (p. 297) and have been widely used in planning schools.

The Rise of the "Side-Scroller" Genre: Linear Systems and Design Tools

In 1983 Nintendo Co., Ltd., launched the Famicom System in Japan. The system arrived in North America in 1985, renamed as the Nintendo Entertainment System (NES). Bundled with the system came a little-known game called *Super Mario Bros.* (Nintendo, 1985), which became one of the top-selling games in history (Tassi, 2016). The game was a revolutionary piece of software that introduced a side-scrolling effect of lateral movement, which allowed game levels to grow dramatically in size and complexity. Although it wasn't the first game to feature levels that went beyond the confines of a single screen—others, such as *Defender* (Williams Electronics, 1981), *Moon Patrol* (Irem, 1982), and *Jungle Hunt* (Taito, 1982), preceded it—*Super Mario Bros.* effectively popularized the genre of "side-scrolling" games (also called "side-scrollers"), a name derived from *emakimono* (scroll) pictures in Japanese art, where the sequence of movement is often unveiled as the scroll unfolds (see figure 5.3).

The NES was well equipped for depicting these scrolling graphics. Video game spaces, once confined to a bounded area, acquired an infinite space with unknown possibilities. Overnight the system became flooded with side-scrolling games, which typically came in side and top-down perspectives, although isometric views were also used. Side-scrollers brought linear systems design skills to the industry. Games were usually divided into levels, where each level was generally a variation of a linear, often thematically inspired

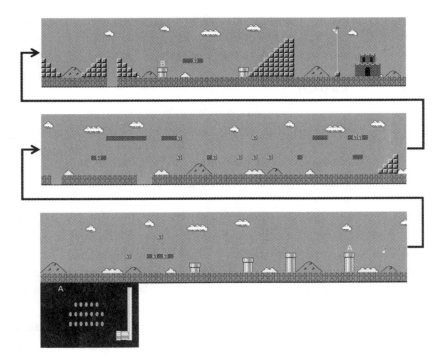

Figure 5.3
A section of Level 1–1 of the *Super Mario Bros.* (1985) video game for the Nintendo Entertainment System showing the linear scrolling layout.
Source: Image composition made by authors.

system with moving obstacles and enemies. Section drawings were used for creating these levels. Additional layers were added, which moved at different speeds in order to simulate parallax effect and add a sense of 3D depth to the levels. The added layers also gave the freedom to do linear design in different planes, where the foreground was used as the "play" level, and the background was used for design motifs that created visual variations on places related to the game's theme. Soon more intricate designs appeared. Games such as *Metroid* (Nintendo, 1985), *Castlevania* (Konami, 1985), and *Bionic Commando* (Capcom, 1988) diverged from the traditional linear form of the classic side-scroller and started to incorporate horizontal and vertical scrolling and multiple stacked levels, which would require maps for navigation due to the intricacies of their design. These games experimented with the notions of rhythm, spacing, and sequence, and their relationship with human interaction and navigation, while presenting the player a high density of activity and form. They would represent the apex of linear spaces in a 2D plane. Over the next decade, hundreds of side-scrollers would proliferate to become a dominant form of spatial design in video games.

Nonplayable Characters

As virtual worlds grew in size and complexity, they began incorporating nonsequential place-based activities where the depiction of monumental architecture was often used as identity drivers and storytelling devices. Many of the worlds depicted in these games also show actual division of activities in their spatial design. These strategies create a sense of place, in which players form subjective attachments to particular spatial features, helping them navigate game spaces of greater complexity. RPGs would integrate paths, courtyards, markets, upscale areas of town, shantytowns, temples, factories, and administrative and palatial environments. Architecture became another component of transmedia storytelling, in which stories flow across media and inform and enrich each other (Jenkins, 2003). The elements and principles used were not so dissimilar than the paths, edges, nodes, landmarks, and districts proposed as the core blocks for legibility of urban spaces described by Kevin Lynch (1960).

Gradually, maps and navigation principles, along with iconographic representations of places and streamlined interfaces, became fixtures of the video game landscape in order to help the player manage these worlds.

Overhead or isometric perspectives used to facilitate navigation became part of the visual language of the genre (see figure 5.4). With the spatial complexity and the use of placemaking as a strategy to engage the players, another aspect emerged: players became cocreators of spatial narratives. Although these features and functions are defined by the game designer, they are selected and arranged by each player while playing, transferring part of the control of the game space to the players (Nitsche, 2008).

Within this context of increasing the spatial complexity of games as part of the game plot, another important aspect was the introduction of nonplayable

Figure 5.4
An over-the-top world map of *The Legend of Zelda: A Link to the Past* (1991) showing Hyrule Castle as the center of the world.
Source: Nintendo, 1991.

characters (NPCs) as inhabitants of these virtual worlds. Since settlements are rarely vacant places, NPCs became crucial in driving the perceptive density of activity toward the game user, allowing places to become "alive." Populating towns and cities throughout games, NPCs would interact in very specific manners with players: some of them are key characters in the game narrative and plot; others are inconsequential, simply populating the space; and yet others might interact with the player outside the main plot of the game, creating parallel personal narratives that are experienced by each single player.

3D Worlds as Interactive Playgrounds

In the second half of the 1990s, economies of scale made possible the incorporation of low-cost 3D graphics processing to video games systems, which eventually displaced 2D sprite-based machines in the market. General consumer game consoles, such as the PlayStation by Sony and the Nintendo 64 by Nintendo Co., could render 150,000 or more texture-mapped, fully shaded polygons (a polygon is the basic geometric shape out of which 3D models are made in computer graphics). Overnight, gamers worldwide demanded new types of experiences from their virtual worlds. The video game industry had to respond by evolving some of the foundational disciplines on which it was based.

The late 1990s represented a period of experimentation regarding the development of a new vocabulary for the industry. Again, spatial complexity increased dramatically, since now developers had to think in terms of camera points of view and z-axis use while devising multiple levels of immersion. Simultaneous movement along the x-, y-, and z-axes effectively showed the limitations of traditional input devices available in commercial systems, which by then had been standardized as joypads that included just a cross-shaped digital input for movement across two axes. Gradually the adoption of multi-analog joysticks, capable of handling simultaneous movement of in-game characters and the virtual cameras and subtle feedback in the form of vibrations used to give haptic cues, allowed for precise traversal of 3D spaces represented using 2D screens.

Initially, many games simply recreated a 2D experience by replacing parallax layers for polygons to give a sense of depth using polygons. However, soon some games started exploring novel methods of interaction using 3D spaces. A YouTube compilation of the games in the Wolfenstein series from 1981 to 2019, put together by Andrew Louis,[3] provides a good overview of how the graphic capabilities of computers transformed the narrative of the game. Although the more recent versions have outstanding graphic resolution and camera movements, the most dramatic change happens between the 1984 (*Beyond Castle Wolfenstein*) and 1992 (*Wolfenstein 3D*) versions, when the game goes from a single-screen, maze-like 2D game, to a first-person 3D game. Other seminal 3D games include *Doom* (ID Software, 1993), *Mario 64* (Nintendo, 1996), *Tomb Raider* (Core Design, 1996), *Resident Evil* (Capcom, 1996), and *The Legend of Zelda: Ocarina of Time* (Nintendo, 1998); see figure 5.5.

The designers of these games understood the relevance of camera perspective to making the experience immediate and palpable. First-person-perspective games allowed the player to see the world through the eyes of a digital avatar, while a third-person perspective usually used an over-the-shoulder camera that allowed the gamer to see the game character in relation to the world; furthermore, fixed camera angles were also used in order to control the gamer's cinematic experience. Some of these games, such as *Resident Evil* and *Tomb Raider*, incorporated several moments in which the player was a spectator of actions and dialogues between different characters. These storytelling moments helped set up the plot, define the relationship between the characters, and engage the player in a plot in which he or she would also be a coauthor.

Game designers quickly understood that camera perspective deeply affects design and play decisions. First-person games, such as *Wolfenstein*, tended initially to be more claustrophobic experiences filled with corridor structures and frantic gameplay, whereas third-person-perspective games (such as *Tomb Raider*) were much more expansive, with larger levels overall and a slower pace. Soon, games started alternating camera perspectives according to different parts of the plot and giving options to the players.

Initial 3D spaces in game design, however, remained far from real in terms of both proportions and detail. Early 3D chipsets remained too weak to display high-quality, believable worlds. Most game worlds remained fairly linear in nature and had few emergent elements, giving them an artificial feel. *Tomb Raider*, which introduced Lara Croft, a now-legendary character in video games, would also pioneer the use of a grid design in which all surfaces would be identical squares of the same size, rendered individually,

Figure 5.5
Early examples of prerendered and real-time 3D spaces in console games. *Top to bottom: Tomb Raider* (1996), with real-time third-person camera; *Resident Evil* (1996), showing a fixed camera perspective over prerendered backgrounds; and *The Legend of Zelda: Ocarina of Time* (1998), a hybrid using both prerendered and real-time environments.
Source: Core Design, 1996; Capcom, 1996; and Nintendo, 1998.

Figure 5.6
First-person view in *Mirror's Edge* (*left*) vs. third-person view in *Sleeping Dogs* (*right*), showing different levels of immersion due to difference in camera perspectives.
Source: EA DICE, 2008; United Front Games, 2012.

several with the same patterns, allowing graphics processing of 3D spaces using the limited hardware and software of the time. Those few games that intended to simulate high-density, open-ended urban environments, such as *Grand Theft Auto* (DMA Design, 1997) and *SimCity 3000* (Maxis, 1999), still used 2D sprite-based graphics or top-down perspectives to hide the lack of graphical detail. Still, despite some technological restrictions, these games were exploring what Gordon Calleja (2011) calls processual games, in which variations of the story within the general plot of the game can happen in any enactment. These narrative enhancements embedded in new complex and 3D spaces make Calleja (2011) observe that to consider *Grand Theft Auto* and *Tetris* within the same general media category does not reflect the chasm that these new games were creating within the video game industry.

Creating Tangible and Hyperreal Spatial Interactive Simulacra

By the turn of the millennium several companies were trying to represent realistic-looking spaces in 3D form. A new generation of systems had the computational power to make it feasible. However, the leap from designing abstract 3D spaces, where the developers had a lot of creative liberty, to creating a believable virtual city in which players could assume different points of view and explore the space more freely, was still a daunting one.

There are three main aspects. First, from a design perspective, game developers had to learn to properly scale their designs to more human-related sizes. Particularly challenging were first-person games in which the character is not simply a hand holding a pistol but also carries a personal background—as Brendan Keogh (2018) writes, "the body incorporates the world into its habits" (p. 24). In *Tomb Raider*, for example, Lara Croft moves in space carrying her story: climbing rocky mountains, rappelling in waterfalls in the rainforest, killing enemies, or snowboarding through frozen landscapes are actions that reflect her personal saga.

The other two aspects are closely related to spatial design. Game designers had to learn to systematically capture the visual and spatial design elements of a place and combine them into coherent urban typologies. It was not enough to populate the games with generic buildings; since players would be strolling through a city, these urban environments needed to convey a sense of place, in which streets and buildings carry particular meanings. Finally, game designers had to figure out how to populate and recreate a sense of randomness in their worlds, while maintaining an optimal experience flow. In short, game designers were required to simulate staged chaos and serendipity. They had to learn how to manage the drab places that constitute a large part of cities and mingle them with points of high interest to the player. Players had become "situated and embodied subjects" (Keogh, 2018, p. 40), whose experience of the game required their immersion in a meaningful environment—not the abstract space of early games, but games built upon the creation of places.

This was crucial in order to ground believability in their environments while meeting their primary goal: to entertain. To do this they had to increase the density of activities and landmarks per area of coverage in the game space vis-à-vis the natural heterogeneity of activities and landmarks per a similar area in a real city. Game designers had to learn to distill the core identity pillars of a real place and amplify them, intensifying the player's experience by intensifying the essence of a place.

The first major breakthrough in the industry was a game called *Shenmue* (Sega, 1999), developed by Sega's legendary AM2 team. The game modeled an interactive and detailed 3D representation of mid-1980s Yokosuka, Japan. The game's director, the highly respected Yu Suzuki, named the design philosophy F.R.E.E. (Free Reactive Eyes Environment); it was centered on making every object, surface, and element in the simulation detailed and tactile. The player could not just look at buildings but also enter them, explore any room, open drawers to look inside, and make herself at home. The story of the place wasn't just told through dialogue but instead was embedded in thousands of microdetails (for the time) scattered throughout the synthetic environments. Equally important, the place was populated by NPCs, each of them with personal agendas and roles. The player-controlled avatar could walk through the market and hear NPCs gossip or argue over the price of fish. Although only small parts of the city were open to the player, *Shenmue* followed the RPG tradition of imbuing a diversity of activities into the game environment. The game infused NPCs' interaction with activities as a central play in the place dynamics. It allowed gamers to enter stores, pray at the local Shinto temple, play games in the neighborhood arcade, train at the dojo, go to work at the docks, and feed stray cats. Sega's team of developers understood that in order to ground a place it needed to look lived-in. The team at AM2 even simulated day and night cycles to alter the rhythm of the city, using old meteorological data from the 1980s to get the in-game weather "right." For the time being Shenmue became the gold standard of simulated and grounded place design.

Other games also tried to emulate city environments up close. *Metropolis Street Racer* (Bizarre Creations, 2000) allowed players to race supercars through highly detailed portions of London, Tokyo, and San Francisco; whereas *Jet Set Radio* (Sega, 2001) portrayed a stylized, cartoony version of Tokyo, where gangs of skaters would compete among themselves for the control of turf. Cities were rapidly becoming playing fields on screens around the world.

The second breakthrough was the highly controversial *Grand Theft Auto III* (DMA Design, 2001), launched only two years after *Shenmue*. The game creates a fictional city called Liberty City (modeled after New York). Unlike *Shenmue*, *Grand Theft Auto III* actually scaled back the detail shown on screen, but this loss of graphical flourishes allowed for a dramatic increase in size and activity density. The city was enormous; it had a game world that was designed to release players to do their will on it (hence its genre was labeled "sandbox games"). Few things were scripted; almost everything was procedurally generated in real-time. Virtual citizens would react in unpredictable manners, cars would roll through the streets while the weather randomly changed and affected everyone. Liberty City was divided into three major districts, which encompassed various typologies, such as industrial zones, high-rise office buildings, an airport, and residential zones, with corresponding linkages and landmarks as well as changes in social groups and ambiance. In a social and political analysis of the game, Stephen Duncombe (2007) explains the huge popularity of the Grand Theft Auto series, in which sex, violence, and cheating are part of the narrative, as being a "virtual arena in which to express eternal desires for sex and death we might otherwise play out dangerously on terra firma" (p. 54).

Temporal and Regional Aesthetics Integration

Throughout the history of video games, the industry has borrowed identity elements, as psychological and narrative anchoring devices, from different media, such as films, books, and photography (Lemke, 2009). Often, devices from other media would be incorporated into the game story, either directly—with characters taking some time to read a book, perhaps to find clues to the main mission of the game or perhaps simply for fun—or indirectly, making references to scenes and narratives evoking specific films or cinematographic genres to help create the proper setting of the game, or using sound effects and music to create an atmosphere that will trigger a sequence of actions.

With the advent of more intricate stories and worlds, designers understood the need to increase both the complexity of the inspired elements as well as their level of synthesis. They also understood that stylistic elements needed to give character to a place was needed to ground a narrative within a cultural and spatial context. The works of Fumito Ueda, such as *Ico* (SCE Japan Studio, 2001), *Shadow of the Colossus* (SCE Japan Studio, 2005), and *The Last Guardian* (SCE Japan Studio, 2016), are good examples; they borrow both stylistically and morphologically from the works of Giorgio de Chirico (1888–1978), whose metaphysical art was inspired by the unseen, "hidden" stories behind the arches and columns of Turin, and also from the drawings of Gérard Trignac (born 1955), an architecture-trained artist who illustrates the imaginative works of Italo Calvino and Jorge Luis Borges, among others. Another good example is *Grim Fandango* (LucasArts, 1998), whose story arc melded a noir comedy (clearly inspired by the 1942 film *Casablanca*) with the Mexican Day of the Dead festivities. Stylistically it required mixing inputs from both Art Deco and Art Nouveau with Mesoamerican iconography and Mexican folklore, incorporating cultural iconicity into the spatial-design process (see figure 5.7).

Other developers opted to follow a vein of realism. The second half of the first decade of the millennium saw an explosion of both closed- and open-world environments in the virtual space that would closely mimic real-world spaces as settings. Developers would apply many of the techniques used in games like *Shenmue* and *Grand Theft Auto III*, but with a higher level of detail. Gamers had the option to live in segments of cities such as Rio de Janeiro, Shanghai, or Tokyo. Actual art and topographic assets were often used in their development, but they were typically tweaked, and some spatial features were modified in order to enhance playability (see figure 5.8). Developers knew that borrowing from existing places—be they real or fictional—was an efficient way to help players insert themselves into the narrative, since most of them would have had some exposure to said places and their commonly associated narratives and cultural tropes through mass media such as film, TV, and books.

Figure 5.7
Top: Architectural, urban, and motif integration combining Art Deco and Mesoamerican aesthetics in *Grim Fandango Remaster*.
Bottom: A Favela Heights–inspired multiplayer level in *Max Payne 3*.
Source: Double Fine Studios, 2015.

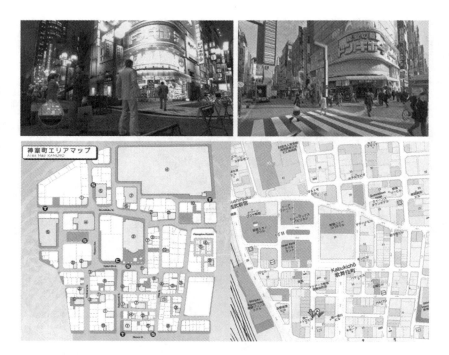

Figure 5.8
Top: Comparison between the fictional district of Kamuro-cho in the 2009 Sega game *Ryu Ga Gotoku 3* (*left*) and the actual Kabuki-cho district in modern Tokyo from Google Street View (*right*).
Bottom: The in-game map (*left*) vs. a map of the Kabuki-cho district in Tokyo as rendered by Google Maps (*right*).
Source: Composition made by authors.

Of particular interest was the effort of game developers to recreate diverse urban settings from different historical time periods, generating a set of activities that intensify their spaces and characterizations of virtual citizens based on historical figures to ground the proper representation of place. Games such as the Assassin's Creed franchise (Ubisoft, 2007–present) partake in what essentially is urban historic and archaeological research. Several cities, such as ancient Rome, Constantinople in the time of Suleiman the Magnificent, Boston during the Revolutionary War, and France during the French Revolution, have been carefully recreated using actual historical documentation such as maps, literature, and art. The architectural accuracy of these games received special attention in 2019, when the

Notre Dame cathedral, in Paris, was heavily destroyed by fire. In the effort to help reconstruct and repair the cathedral, Ubisoft made available the data used in their game to recreate such an iconic piece of architecture. It turns out that while not 100 percent accurate, it still is one of the most comprehensively researched and detailed 3D representations of the cathedral. What the synthetic borrowed from the real was now completing the circle and returning back to its origins.

In more recent years, the Assassin's Creed franchise has gone back further in time, to Ptolemaic Egypt (*Assassin's Creed Origins*, 2017) and ancient Greece at the time of the Peloponnesian War (*Assassin's Creed Odyssey*, 2018; see figure 5.9). In both games, the usual archaeological documentation was utilized for the research process, in order to recreate the iconicity of both places as they reside in our scholastic pursuits, while using the historical gaps created through the passage of time to explore a representation of Greece and Egypt in a coherent form derived from our cultural imaginations. The murky swamps of Crocodilopolis are only matched by the majesty of the Pharaohs in Alexandria, or the statue of Athena in the Acropolis. But more interesting places emerge in the design explorations of Hades, Elysium, and the visions of the Egyptian netherworlds, where

Figure 5.9
In-game representation of ancient Athens and the Acropolis during the Peloponnesian War in *Assassin's Creed Odyssey* (2018).
Source: Ubisoft Montreal, 2018.

the developers, released from their historical constraints, leveraged the lack of information from such ancient eras to fill in the gaps by blending history and myth, creating a modern rendition of each place's mythological richness. Ubisoft would ultimately release an educational version of both games' digital play spaces, littered with all the collected material used in their creation; curated by expert historians and archaeologists, these versions are now being used in schools and museums to augment their curricula with rich interactive media.

Beyond the stylistic and architectural, other aspects of a city continue to be explored by the video game industry. Games such as *L.A. Noire* (Rockstar Games, 2011) and the Mafia series (2K Games, 2002–present) recreate places such as Los Angeles in the early postwar period or New Orleans during the civil rights era to explore historical, social, and political dimensions through their narratives and interactivity. The games combine real-world cases, clue findings, interrogations, shoot-outs, fistfights, and all other elements of video games, with meticulous architectural recreations, sound effects, local accents, and soundtracks related to each city and period. Dialogue, mannerism, and performance are captured in a way not dissimilar from a modern motion picture. For example, *L.A. Noire* was the first game to employ a combination of motion scan and facial videogrammetry, which uses thirty-two cameras to capture both the motion and the performance of actors and enhance their dramatic performances as transposed to the digital in-game characters. Similar methods of motion and facial capture have now become the industry standard.

One of the most advanced "sandbox" urban simulations at the moment is *Grand Theft Auto V* (Rockstar Games, 2013). The game recreates a fictional city named Los Santos, which is based on modern Los Angeles and encompasses an area much larger than any other in the Grand Theft Auto series. It is so large that the in-game topography varies from desert to mountains, from suburbia to high-density urban landscapes and underwater environments. The game also recreates many of L.A.'s iconic destinations, such as the Hollywood sign, Venice Beach, and Mann's Chinese Theatre, in minute detail, not just architecturally but in terms of social activity, from both other players and nonplayable characters.

The urban design recreation of Los Santos utilizes many landmarks as well as ordinary spaces that are animated by NPCs, which gives a sense of place and drives players to explore different portions of the game space and the many possibilities of the plot. It seems that the main storyline missions are there mainly to provide an overall narrative for the game, while the real content of *Grand Theft Auto V* is provided through the wide variety of emergent real-life activities that have been "gamified" and that the player can do outside the mainstream game "missions" (see figure 5.10). A player's avatar can wake up in the morning, do a yoga session, or go to the gym in a fictionalized Venice Beach. The player can walk around the city, drive a car, or ride a bicycle while enjoying music broadcast from one of the nineteen in-game radio stations (each with their own unique DJs and fake advertisements). The player may spend the afternoon shopping or in a movie theater, walk their dog, watch multiple TV channels, get drunk, make money through stock trading in the in-game financial markets, or go scuba diving.

Figure 5.10
Examples of interactive urban activities possible in *Grand Theft Auto V* (2013) as a dynamic sandbox experience.
Source: Rockstar Games, 2013.

These activities can be coherently interlinked to form larger playing sessions where the players weave their own emergent narratives.

For example, a player may go shopping for a parachute, drive toward a helipad, pilot a helicopter, and perform a skydiving jump into downtown Los Santos, creating a particular story from their daily activities that they can share through social media channels such as YouTube, Twitch, and Instagram. Emergent narratives such as these can be created in both single and multiplayer sessions and are critical in providing a sense of "life" to the place—one that stems not only from the visual simulacra but also from the large amount of activity variations that the player can interact and experience. Emergent narratives can be seen as a sandbox, or an "authoring environment within which players can define their own goals and write their own story" (Jenkins, 2007, p. 59). Sometimes the player sees oversized street furniture, which is used to indicate places of action. As Pearson (2019) suggests, this symbolism is no different from the bollards-as-planters commonly displayed in front of embassies and government buildings.

Users also expand their emergent narratives by using modification tools (commonly referred to as "mods" in the PC gaming community) that give them full access to the game engine and assets in order to experiment with the play dynamics and level designs. This feature opens up the possibility of cocreation between the game design team and the players. As we discussed before, it transcends playing within the rules and instead becomes playing with the rules. In the case of video games, rules are encoded in the software, and any modification is either not allowed by the developers or might crash the system. In such multiplayer sandbox games, on the other hand, game designers foster the "coexistence of coded and socially negotiated rules" (Calleja, 2011, p. 13)—a characteristic that is (or should be) extremely relevant for urban design. In fact, many of these experimentations in sandbox games become so popular with users that developers opt to integrate them into the games via online distributed patches in order to increase the longevity of their user base.

This practice is creating a shift in the industry. More and more games are being developed not as finite pieces but as evolving ones. They are becoming digital "living" places of sorts. This is backed by economic models that see games as a service, rather than games as a product, and that benefit from retaining the attention of gamers as long as possible. For these models, the value of the game resides not only in its content but also in the community of players formed around it. In order to engage players for months or years, these games have to perform a continuous combination of new content release, dynamic programmatic events, and an established calendar of seasonal activities that gives them cadence and a sense of familiarity. More importantly, successful games have learned to establish constant feedback channels with their user base, allowing the users' input to become an element and guideline of design, in effect codesigning these worlds in the long run by fostering active and vocal communities. By forming communities, developers can increase the lifespan of games dramatically, with some of them, such as *World of Warcraft* (Blizzard, 2005), *Warframe* (Digital Extremes, 2014), and *Destiny 2* (Bungie, 2017), going live for years and even decades.

Toward a Future of Virtual Urban Possibilities

This follows a more recent phenomenon where a community of users employs digital platforms to collectively design a place. In this instance, the game developers do not create any digital worlds per se but instead release technologies that allow users to do it themselves. These technologies serve as digital building blocks that, when combined, can create vast digital landscapes. The potential of using virtual spaces, including video game environments, for collaborative design has been discussed for many years now (Maher et al, 2000; Hanzl, 2007). Indeed, the crowdsourcing approach to design has proved to be a powerful device of agency; communities of millions of users have in recent years flooded the virtual space, heralding exciting possibilities for participatory urban design.

Perhaps there is no better example at the moment than *Minecraft* (Mojang, 2009), an online platform developed by a single person, Markus "Notch" Persson, who released it initially free in 2009 (in unfinished alpha state). People use the commercial release—of which more than 100 million copies have been sold—to create, share, and modify spaces. *Minecraft* is essentially a social platform of programmable virtual Lego bricks that allows users to model environments and modify behaviors to essentially code their creations into a wide variety of scenarios. Many of these scenarios have become large-scale virtual cities that are community designed, negotiated, and built. These are used as a form of representation, for amusement, or simply as a vehicle for acquiring social recognition.

These processes of social construction have also been used to recreate existing places, including digital recreations of Paris, London, and New York. The *Minecraft* "Loop" project seeks to model thirty-five city blocks of the iconic Chicago Loop area, one of the densest neighborhoods in the city. The project is a collaboration between many *Minecraft* players who coordinate themselves using a variety of in-game and online tools. The team has already modeled more than twenty city blocks with a good degree of accuracy and representation, at both the hyperlocal and the urban scale (see figure 5.11).

The video game industry is currently going through a process similar to the shift from 2D to 3D graphics. Mixed reality technologies, discussed earlier, are gradually becoming available to the general public. Several systems and head-mounted displays (HMDs) from the likes of Oculus, Google, Microsoft, HTC, HP, Acer, and Valve, to name a few from a growing list of vendors, are commercially available at consumer prices. These systems are capable of projecting a virtual world that envelops the user with enough 3D depth and synchronization with our natural senses that a real feeling of presence is created. The original use of the term *presence* comes from a

Figure 5.11
A side-by-side comparison of the real Daley Plaza in Chicago (*left*) vs. a socially recreated version using the *Minecraft* (Mojang, 2009) video game (*right*).
Source: Image socially created on Mojang's platform.

seminal paper by Marvin Minsky (1980), who created the Laboratory of Artificial Intelligence at MIT. Minsky argued that a combination of new computational technologies, material sciences, control systems, psychology, and sensors would allow high-quality sensory feedback that would create a sense of "being there."

Current technology has partially achieved Minsky's vision, in which a sensorial stimulation leads the user's brain to achieve a state where it is momentarily convinced it is somewhere different from its actual physical reality. Video games are strategically poised to take advantage of VR systems, given that their central activity is to simulate synthetic worlds using transferable technologies and a methodological approach in creating spatial design. However, although it is technically possible to process and render current 3D games in VR, more often than not the experience leaves much to be desired, since they are designed to be consumed on 2D screens.

The biggest difference is that experiences are greatly intensified when consumed through HMDs and can become overwhelming to the user. Additionally, immersive stereoscopic images of synthetic realities displayed on VR systems at 1:1 scale and realistic 3D depth require a greater cognitive effort from users in order to absorb all the information transmitted. Current human-machine interface designs, such as joysticks, gamepads, mouse, and keyboard, have been optimized through the years to work with 2D displays and impose artificial barriers against more natural modes of interactivity. The challenge of solving the interface is not mere technical detail; rather, it entails our understanding of how humans relate to the world. As Brendan Keogh (2018) discusses by differentiating Maurice Merleau-Ponty's and Gregory Bateson's viewpoints on the example of a blind man with a stick, whereas the former saw two independent entities even though momentarily combined, the latter saw man and stick as a single system. This difference completely changes the worldview—and consequently the perception and the design of the world.

In order to achieve full presence, or in Minsky's (1980, p. 44) words, "the strength of a giant or the delicacy of a surgeon," VR technologies still need to become part of the player's body—which is not composed of two separate entities (the preexisting body before the person became a player, and peripheral tools), therefore in order for VR to fulfill its promise it must create a "cybernetic amalgam of material and virtual artifacts" (Keogh, 2018, p. 27) with the player's body.

Some video games built on VR technologies are moving into this direction. For example, while climbing has been an established activity in games for decades, to the point where it's hardly exciting, games in VR such as *The Climb* (Crytek, 2016), a rock-climbing simulator, are able to generate a larger emotional impact for the user due to the medium ability to instill a sense of presence in the user. After a certain time, the gadgets do not bother you as much, and your senses are fooled—as discussed before, we enjoy self-deception, where although fully aware you are standing in your living room, your brain responds to the perception that you are 50 meters above the ground. Other games, such as *The Lab* (Valve, 2016), create a series of short experiences aimed at showcasing VR's capabilities for spatial exploration, emotional manipulation, and narrative development. In a sense, the video game industry is right now in the process of creating a new language for the medium. The tools and methodologies of video game creation alongside the immersive quality of VR—which brings a greater sense of depth at both the micro and macro scales—and the interactivity and complexity of the environments brought by video games, increases their potential of being at the forefront of simulating spatial experiences and prototyping variations of designs.

Perhaps one of the best contemporary examples of this is a game called *Lone Echo* (Ready at Dawn, 2017), where the player assumes the persona of an android helping in a space station floating in orbit around the rings of Saturn. The game is initially devoid of any interfaces, preferring to bring a sense of embodiment and physicality to the way information is being conveyed to the player. The world is perceived as is, in all of its digital majesty amid the grandeur of space, along with the microdetail of the lived mundane environments of the station. Screens and computer terminals will give the user prompts, while holographic interfaces that emanate from the android's robotic limbs will provide additional information and action choices to the player. All actions are physical, however. The developers recreate the physicality of the station through the use of inverse-kinematics technology to animate the arms, hands, and even fingers of the players, cleverly contouring hands and fingers as they touch the surfaces of the walls, tables, handles, and computers in the station, bringing a performative sense to their behavior in place. Locomotion in the environment is done by pushing your body mass as astronauts do in microgravity.

The key to creation of such a compelling immersive experience is to be disciplined and aim to always keep the user immersed by removing everything that would seem out of place within the reality presented "in content," and to "embody" all informational analogies and points of interaction within the reality experienced by the player. This is the fundamental principle of language in a medium of total immersion. For example, motion is done through the physical movement of the arms and hands, as would happen in space; inertia is calculated and animated to increase spatial perception; and other artificial forms of locomotion, such as teleportation, are discarded as they tend to break reality. Information is given to the player through holographic displays that, although not in existence today, are believable within a sci-fi environment, and hence are coherent to the experience. Audio cues are simulated using 3D positional audio in relation to the player's head, but taking into account the acoustic properties of the environment, thus being of great guiding help when navigating with six degrees of freedom, but in the same instant providing the contextual audio to make the humming noises in a space station, the noiseless vacuum of space, and the chaotic reality of an emergency, eerily realistic.

Flexibility by Design

The purpose of this chapter is to give the reader a general overview of how the video game industry has learned to manipulate synthetic spaces across micro and macro scales in general and urban simulations in particular in order to create spaces that resonate and generate a wide spectrum of emotions in gamers, both as individuals and as part of larger communities of players. We also argue that spatial designers—including architects and urban planners—can benefit from the video game industry's knowledge regarding spatial legibility, place-anchored narrative design, the role of NPCs and elements of randomness needed to make the space alive, and forms of interaction alongside participatory and flexible design methodologies. Advances in computer science, and in particular in artificial intelligence, might bring deep changes in video game design, with neural networks taking playing styles and level design as parameters, for instance, to propose variations to the game, using AI agents to test and evaluate them, and eventually even proposing new games (Togelius, 2018).

All of these aspects have been gradually integrated into the processes and technologies available in the video game industry. As the complexity of the synthetic spatial simulations grew, so did the capabilities of the tools required to make them. Moving from the technological restrictions imposed by early computer systems, today's game developers use state-of-the-art design, modeling, programming, and simulation tools with fast prototyping environments and pipelines. Modular subsystems available to any video game studio range from realistic weather simulations to traffic management, from procedurally generated behavior of crowds and building typologies to real-time physics of material properties and light. These subsystems can be configured into a wide variety of experiences that portray cities at different scales and different purposes, oftentimes integrating them seamlessly, from the micro scale that focuses on recreating interactions on the ground to the macro scale that focuses on showcasing full urban dynamics at city scale, as utilized in games such as the Assassin's Creed series, *Grand Theft Auto V*, and *Cities XXL* (see figure 5.12).

Figure 5.12
A synthetically modeled city in *Cities XXL* (2015), a modern, larger, and more complex take on the city-building style of synthetic simulations originally pioneered by *SimCity*. *Source*: Focus Home Interactive, 2015.

In the end, it is clear to us that there exist many potential synergies between video game development and spatial design. As stated earlier in the chapter, this is an industry that has learned a great deal from the disciplines of architecture and urban planning, and that has created a parallel scaffolding of tools and methodologies that stem from advanced computer sciences and other disciplines. While some architecture studios do utilize video game engines to showcase their work in an interactive manner, designers and planners could also utilize them to improve communication of design choices, achieve greater social participation, simulate environmental conditions and effects of planning decisions, and ultimately bring a greater deal of flexibility to design practices.

6   Virtual Reality, Empathy, and Design

I'm hanging on the edge of a cliff over the Grand Canyon. I can hear a helicopter in the distance flying by; as I look around, it swoops nearby, toward the sunset. It's a beautiful sight. Unfortunately, I don't have time to savor it, since I'm only barely hanging on by a few fingers to a vertical wall of rock. My digital wristband tells me that my arm is getting tired; I need to reach a new grab point with my other arm, or I will fall to my death several hundred feet below. I see a ledge but it is out of my reach. At the last second, I decide to go for it. As I grab the sliver of rock, I get a rush of adrenaline. Success! Only a few more feet to go until I reach the top. I see the sunset over the horizon and the vastness of the Grand Canyon in front of me as I pull myself up. My prize: a combination of awe and dopamine. I close the session and see my score and time ledger hovering in front of me, and I note that I was a few seconds short of my personal record. . . . Guess I'll have to try harder next time. As I remove the head-mounted VR display, it takes a brief second to adjust to my surroundings. The pixels may have been fake, but the exhilaration and sweat are real. Welcome back.

What not long ago seemed some science fiction dream is today just a typical session of *The Climb*, a VR experience from the German developer Crytek GmbH (see figure 6.1). It is only one of the thousands currently available in digital stores. In an article for the *New Yorker*, Patricia Marx (2019) reports on her experience shopping around for VR applications, including applications that simulate visiting a space station and applications to create 3D paintings. The popularization of VR applications in recent years, although not pervasive as other technologies, shows that the technology is getting mature enough to attract an audience interested in the VR experiences rather than just the tech-savvy or people interested in

Figure 6.1
First-person perspective in VR in *The Climb*, an experience developed by Crytek for the
Oculus Rift system.
Source: Crytek GmBH, 2017.

the technology itself. Such immediate, accessible, and visceral experiences
are the best showcases for the latest generation of VR systems: the experience transcends the medium.

Many of these VR systems reached the market during the last few years
or so and have one key characteristic that sets them apart from other media:
they can hack our biology and force us to "rethink basic assumptions about
perception and the way we experience people, places, and things" (Greengard, 2019, p. 211). Unlike movies, video games, or television, VR can instill
a state of presence in the user, of being someplace else. While easy to grasp
as a concept, the feeling produced by VR is "hard to define because it has
to be experienced and requires a suspension of belief in order to remember
that the virtual isn't real" (Abrash & Katz, 2014).

The suspension of belief echoes a key concept behind the power of play:
self-deception. In its basic definition, self-deception is when I convince
myself (the deceived) to believe something is true though I (the deceiver)
know it is not. In virtual reality, we have an example of how self-deception
can be used as a creative artifice that alters the ways we engage with space:
our body engages simultaneously with the spatial features of the room
where we stand but also responds at a physiological level to the stimuli
provided by the VR environment. In VR, spatial perception is influenced

by the liminal characteristics that connect us to both real and imagined worlds. Scientific research has found that psychological and physiological responses in VR environments are similar to such responses in the physical world. Martens et al. (2019) compared the physiological responses (salivary cortisol and alpha-amylase, blood pressure, pulse, and skin conductance) of subjects using a stressor VR elevator (which simulated taking the participant up the outside of a tall building; once at the top, the participant was asked to step off the elevator platform) with a control elevator, and they found that both groups responded similarly at a physiological level. Psychological and physiological reactions to situations that are intrinsically spatial and that are difficult to reconstruct in a laboratory under realistic and yet safe conditions (such as fear of heights or fear of flying) have been receiving special attention from clinicians who have been using VR treatments (Wiederhold & Wiederhold, 2003; Freeman et al., 2018).

Artifices of self-deception should not be considered as tricks, but rather should be viewed as elaborate intellectual and technical devices conceived by humans to change the way we perceive the world, and that have intrinsic values as investigative tools. In the case of VR, it creates self-deception by synchronizing data inputs over our multiple sensors, including retinas and vestibulocochlear nerve (which conveys information related to sound and equilibrium to our inner brain). If the data processed by our brain meets certain parameters, our brain subconsciously fills in the blanks and creates a coherent model of the world, which is consequently perceived as real. In this sense, VR engages enough of our perceptual systems to create a feeling of presence on an instinctual, unconscious level.

Achieving a state of presence is no mere gimmick. It actually opens up the possibility of perceptually transcending barriers involving the physical aspects of time and space, as well as the psychological and social aspects of identity. Comparing the same video games in 2D, 3D, and VR environments, Roettl and Terlutter (2018) found that the distinctive feature of the VR version of the game among players is the sense of presence, which links perceptions, intentions, and actions within the video game environment.

Equally important to note is that in VR environments we can be anyone, go anywhere, at any time—and this is an exhilarating proposition. Humans are escapist creatures; we often derive pleasure and wonder from "elsewhere," wherever "there" is, a desire that historically has been reflected in art, philosophy, and literature. From the earliest cave paintings to Plato's

allegorical cave, we frequently use paintings, cinema, and literature to project ourselves into alternate worlds and out-of-body experiences, if only for
a fleeting moment. This state of transcendence characterizes play. It happens when players conceive imaginary worlds shared among them during
the play or the impersonation of different characters that inhibit this imaginary. It also happens in what Diane Ackerman (2000) calls "deep play," in
which the creation of alternative spatialities is a condition of play.

This state of transcendence is also at the core of the practice of design
and its fundamental goal of proposing possible spaces and times in order to
create multiple physical and psychological experiences—and good design
usually proposes experiences that allow people to engage with space outside
their ordinary habits. An engaging design creates surprises, breaks down the
direct correlation between function and form, and makes fruition part of
the spatial experience.

VR brings together the states of transcendence and presence. If the state
of transcendence refers to a movement toward the outside (being somebody
else, being somewhere else), achieving a state of presence is a powerful and
intimate experience that is capable of forging a greater empathic connection
between the person and his own self and his immediate surroundings. The
state of presence indicates the person is fully embodied in space, open to all
immediate sensory aspects of space, including other people sharing the same
space. Empathy might become a strong feeling among people sharing space.

Empathy here is understood as a sense of similarity between the subjective experience of one person and the experience of others, without losing the uniqueness of each one's personal experiences (Decety & Jackson,
2004). Psychologists and neuroscientists argue that empathy has given
humans crucial evolutionary advantages; these experts have been finding
the neural bases of human empathy, employing several techniques in fields
that include genetics, pharmacology, patient studies, and functional neuro-
imaging (Zaki & Ochsner, 2012).

It is in the power of creating empathic states that we find what may be
one of VR's most important contributions to design, since without empathy
design is meaningless, disconnected from needs and desires. As suggested
by architect Michael Sorkin (2013, p. 63), "the creation of artistic forms that
do not simply shock but satisfy—an architecture of empathy", in which
architecture enhance each person's experience in relation to others sharing
the same space. It is important to note that no particular aesthetic should

be linked to this state of empathy (as Sorkin seems to imply by criticizing modernism), since empathy involves the creation of a profound sense of being in a shared space.

Empathy is not something to be experienced passively through the medium of VR, but rather something that can be enhanced and engaged through good experience and application design. In this case, design takes advantage of the unique capabilities of the medium to the point where VR can become a critical component in the toolkits of designers, architects, and urbanists. VR is a unique tool to create a state of empathy between the self and the other, a total and physiological (although not bodily) immersion in space.

We propose to discuss how VR can be used as a richly informed digital environment where spatial design can fulfill some of its powers to creatively define how we experience concrete spaces. However, we must start taking a step back in order to understand the roots and technical characteristics of this relatively new domain.

The Modern Vision of VR

The modern vision of virtual reality systems—the one involving funky goggles and digital "rooms" that provide coordinated sensory deprivation and stimulation—was defined in science fiction literature in the first half of the twentieth century. One of the earliest descriptions appears in Stanley Weinbaum's "Pygmalion's Spectacles," a short story originally published in 1935, in which a professor named Albert Ludwig invents a pair of glasses that can show a movie while engaging other senses, such as hearing or smell. This was an interactive experience where the user could engage with other characters in the movie, already foreshadowing the dynamic interplay of contemporary applications. The ultimate goal was to transport users to the movie world and place them inside the screen. Weinbaum's vision of a VR system was quite prescient: it described not only many of the functional components (such as the goggles) but also the types of experiences that are not dissimilar from some real contemporary features, such as immersion and interactivity.

In 1950 Ray Bradbury wrote a short story titled "The Veldt," originally published in the *Saturday Evening Post* that year and later included in Bradbury's 1951 collection *The Illustrated Man*. The piece is a thinly veiled criticism of technological dependency in modern societies and the role it plays in our constant escapism and dehumanization. The tale describes a typical upper-middle-class family in a nondescript near future. Their home is highly automated, taking care of their needs, and called "the happy life house." The centerpiece of the story, however, is the children's nursery, a room where content is seamlessly projected onto all the walls and surfaces in order to create an enveloping simulated space: virtual reality in a room. The nursery can generate hyperrealistic scenarios such as an African savannah with hunting lions, where primal human fears manifest—featured in the 1969 film adaptation, directed by Jack Smight. The children's fascination with the room, and their parents' inability to cope with it, unfortunately, leads to a cryptic and gruesome finale.

While sci-fi writers dreamed, inventors were also proposing new types of audiovisual systems capable of engaging the senses more expansively than existing TV sets. In the mid-1950s Morton Heilig, a Hollywood cinematographer, proposed the first multisensory system, which he called the Sensorama. Heilig filed for a US patent in 1961 (US3050870A) and was able to produce a functional unit in 1962. It wasn't the most elegant of machines; users sat in a contraption with a moving seat while keeping their heads in front of a covered projector screen that showed three-dimensional images. The device generated stereo sound and even emitted different smells synchronized with the filmed content. As Heilig proposed in 1955, his machine was intended to be the cinema of the future: "Open your eyes, listen, smell, and feel—sense the world in all its magnificent colors, depth, sounds, odors, and texture—this is the cinema of the future!" (Heilig, 2001/1955, p. 246).

Years later, in 1965, Ivan Sutherland created the first functional head-mounted display (HMD), which he named "the Ultimate Display" (Sutherland, 1965). This headset was connected to a CCTV camera that followed users' head and body movements; it was mounted on a heavy structure that required the user to wear a harness over their back and shoulders (unsurprisingly, the system was soon nicknamed the "sword of Damocles"). As the user moved around the room, so did the camera, zooming over a physical model created with basic geometric figures. In a precursor to modern wireframes from contemporary 3D graphics, the geometric shapes had painted crossing lines, which enhanced their three-dimensional characteristics.

It was there, in what would now be described as a crude experience, that several of the early fundamentals of modern VR systems were established.

HMD, check. Emphasis on stereo vision and three-dimensional content, check. Real-time user feedback, check. Perhaps most important of all was philosophical intent. Sutherland intended his device to become a window to a transposed reality in the first person by stimulating the visual senses. His description explains how a larger dream was essentially trapped within the confines of 1960s analog technology. Sutherland was onto something when he coined the name of his contraption; his vision called for a new form of media that would make the other display systems of his time irrelevant and obsolete.

In the 1970s Andrew Lippman and his team at MIT's Architecture Machine Group ("Arch Mac") used funding from the American Federal Advanced Research Projects Agency and the Office of Naval Research to create the Aspen Movie Map (Naimark, 2006), the first virtual travel system, in what could be considered an early precursor of Google's Street View. The team created an orthogonal camera array paired with a gyroscopic sensor and used it to painstakingly photograph the entire town of Aspen, Colorado. They carefully drove along the center of each street and took a series of pictures every 10 meters or so, by hacking a bicycle wheel to measure the distance between shots. The images were then scanned into a laser disc and used as texture maps for basic polygonal 3D models. The data was also linked to the corresponding coordinates and used to create what at that time was labeled a hypermedia system, which, unlike the traditional passive noninteractive media of the time, allowed users to navigate the images within a visual display, performing frame-by-frame sequencing utilizing an on-screen map as a user interface.

Over the following decade more developed visions of virtual reality were embraced across mainstream media and captured the public's imagination. These visions were multicultural and appeared in a wide range of media, from literature and manga to animation and film. Seminal novels such as William Gibson's *Neuromancer* (1984) and Neal Stephenson's *Snow Crash* (1992) popularized the cyberpunk vision of fully interactive and immersive synthetic realities combined with our own. In Japan, Masamune Shirow created the manga series *Ghost in the Shell* (1989–90), and in the West movies such as *The Lawnmower Man* (1992) and *The Matrix* (1999) influenced the vision behind VR and popularized the medium while generating significant hype worldwide.

Research labs in universities around the world continued to create more complex headsets and large virtual environments, such as CAVE (Cave

Automatic Virtual Environment) systems, first developed in the early 1990s. These were still prohibitively expensive technologies, with headsets costing upward of $50,000, and were clunky, heavy to wear, and could only display low-quality graphics at very low frame rates. The gap between the attractiveness of the vision and the state of reality grew, and soon people lost patience, even challenging the feasibility of the vision. As Biocca et al. wrote in 1995, "The promise of VR has yet to be proven—it's still mostly a vision. . . . Most virtual reality technology still has the look and feel of a prototype . . . just a portal looking out on a more mature technology to come" (Biocca et al., 1995, p. 13).

Jason Lanier (2017, p. 03), one of the pioneers of VR for decades until the 1990s, wrote in his comprehensive history of the technology that "even though no one knows how expressive VR might eventually become, there is always that little core of thrill in the idea of VR," combining a "holistic form of expression . . . out of the dull persistence of physicality." By the turn of the century, however, the hype behind VR had fizzled, and the technology essentially disappeared from the consumer market, mostly remaining in the halls of a few sectors, such as academia, the military, and the health-care, aerospace, and manufacturing industries. Although neuroscientists kept exploring various applications of what today we would see as rudimentary VR—for instance, using VR to study human behavior in real-world activities, such as driving, or in the treatment of psychological and mental health disorders (Tarr & Warren, 2002)—these experiments have seldom left the laboratories, which led this phase to be known as "the VR winter." Research funding dried up, and VR generally became a poster child for hype. It would follow the famous hype cycle described by Gartner (2013, 2014) and go through a decade-and-a-half hiatus before reaching a level of sophistication that drew new interest from the public.

The Resurrection of a Vision

Fast-forward to 2012, when Palmer Luckey, who described himself as a VR-obsessed teenager, showed John Carmack (long considered one of the top technology developers in the video game industry and the closest one could get to a true rock star in the gaming world) a cheap VR head-mounted display (HMD) he had assembled using off-the-shelf parts scavenged from smartphones. He had integrated a smartphone LCD display with a gyroscope to achieve head tracking with three degrees of freedom and fairly low motion-to-photons latency (the delay between the user's movement and the corresponding rendered image on the display). Luckey created a solution that reduced the amount of optics needed for a high degree field-of-view by warping the video output from his graphics card. This had the additional advantage of reducing the HMD weight, which made it smaller and more comfortable to use for long periods of time. Carmack showed it to some of his game-developer friends during a popular industry conference. The press seized upon the story, reigniting interest in the video game and sci-fi communities.

Luckey used Kickstarter, a popular crowdfunding platform, to raise the financing needed to get the project from prototype to sale. Within a few weeks he reached thousands of backers, who collectively pledged over $2.3 million. He called his company Oculus VR; the HMD prototype won awards at many trade shows, including the Consumer Electronics Show, the largest of its kind in the world. Two years later Facebook bought his company for $2 billion. Facebook realized that VR experiences were fundamentally different than other media and invested in developing a series of software development kits (SDKs) that creators could use to experiment. Over the next few years, 150,000 SDKs were purchased at over $300 apiece by professional and enthusiast developers around the world, who used them to create thousands of VR-specific applications ranging from realistic universe simulators and accurate virtual depictions of public spaces (such as movie theaters, where one can share a movie screening with other users' avatars) to abstract and sometimes psychedelic environments. Interestingly, there were a large number of roller-coaster simulators, which for a time were all the rage among early adopters—and it actually makes sense and reinforces the sense of presence of VR, since a roller-coaster ride creates a visceral perception of space by stimulating our vestibular-related sensations.

Beyond the multiple games and entertainment applications, VR SDKs have been hacked to create a variety of art installations allowing multiple users to "switch" heads, document the plight of migrants around the world, or even faithfully recreate terrorist attacks. Other applications blended art with architecture, archaeology, and tourism. For instance, visitors to the ancient Roman ruins of Emperor Nero's palace can partake in the Domus Aurea experience, which virtually transports them to the original palace in all its glory at the height of imperial Rome, while dynamically blending the virtual experience with the actual ruins.

Many of these experiences have gone beyond simple entertainment to more profoundly explore the language of the medium in order to experiment with its capacity to generate new types of engagement with the audience. Laurie Anderson, a multimedia artist known for exploring and combining multiple technologies and artistic languages, from magnetic tapes in the 1970s to video art in the 1980s, became a pioneer of multimedia concerts in the 1980s and 1990s. Unexpectedly, Anderson became also quite popular—unexpectedly due the experimentation characteristics of her music, lyrics, and visuals. In 2017, in collaboration with Hsin-Chien Huang, she created her first VR artwork, *Chalkroom*, for the Massachusetts Museum of Contemporary Art. A year later, again in collaboration with Hsin-Chien Huang, Anderson created *To the Moon*,[1] a fifteen-minute journey in VR through constellations to celebrate the fiftieth anniversary of the Apollo 11 moon landing. Both works include shapes of ordinary objects, extinct life-forms made of chemical structures, and words in many languages, composing a distinctive landscape where realistic features have a secondary role. Exploring the language that would be appropriate for a medium that would go beyond mesmerizing images, they developed what Anderson (Anderson & Marranca, 2018, p. 38) calls a "very atmospheric visual language." Indeed, *Chalkroom* and *To the Moon* avoid the hyperrealism of many VR experiments and propose VR as a unique medium for creating a sense of presence that does not rely on mimetic representations of the physical world.

Pieces such as *Chalkroom* try to find an artistic language that explores what unique features the medium brings to art. The value of works such as *Chalkroom* is better assessed in contrast with what art venues have been doing around virtual reality. Museums such as the Louvre in Paris, the National Museum of Finland in Helsinki, and the Tate Modern in London have been adopting virtual reality as a medium to complement some of their shows. However, these tend to prove McLuhan's maxim: the first content of a new medium is the previous one. The content of all these experiences are either traditional artworks exhibited in a VR environment or the reconstruction of galleries, archaeological sites, or artist studios. Other artists who have been exploring VR include Jacolby Satterwhite, Rachel Rossin, and Lawrence Lek. More than breakthrough artworks, these artists' works show how difficult it is to face a new medium: although with distinctive qualities, in general they still feel like preliminary versions of VR experiments one can buy in commercial VR stores. Still, some of these artists, and a few art fairs, assume we are living in a time of exploration, of playing with an emergent technology, embracing its uncertainties and ephemerality. True, photography and cinema still produce breakthrough artworks, partially made possible by the digitalization of the technology, but none of these technologies face the fast and intrinsic technological obsolescence of virtual reality.

In part, this fast-paced obsolescence is fueled by technology giants investing substantial amounts of money in developing their own VR technologies in recent years, not wanting to be left behind in what could potentially be the next great human-machine interface. HTC partnered with game developer Valve to market the HTC Vive, a high-powered competitor to the Oculus Rift, and later went at it alone with the release of their Index HMD. Meanwhile, Google and Samsung released initial kits of their smartphone-powered HMDs. These used the flexibility of mobile devices to create and use both VR and AR functionalities, with data from onboard GPS sensors for locative media purposes (McCullogh, 2006), blending both AR and VR and becoming a version of mixed reality devices, capable of seamless transition between one and the other media forms available at the consumer level. Google's initial take on VR was actually an extreme example of how accessible these technologies were becoming; inspired by USC's Mixed Reality Lab FOV2GO project (which created a low-priced viewer using a smartphone holder made out of cardboard with cheap plastic lenses), Google released the Google Cardboard headset, alongside a suite of VR development tools for the company's Android smartphone ecosystem to kick-start the development community and increase public awareness of the technology, with artists again being early adopters, as seen in the work displayed in the HR Giger VR Gallery Cardboard.[2]

Conditions for Resurgence

So, what changed from the clunky and clumsy devices to the lightweight goggles competing in the market? Basically, Moore's Law manifested itself. Technology caught up while costs dropped, making the vision feasible. VR simply followed the long path of Gartner's famous hype cycle that shows the rate of expectations created by the adoption of new technologies. After the early research triggers in the 1960s, 1970s, and 1980s; the enormous hype accumulated in the early 1990s; and disillusionment at the turn of the millennium, simultaneous revolutions in hardware and software across a range of industries unexpectedly created the conditions required for change in the early 2010s.

On the hardware side, many of the biggest changes arrived on the coattails of technologies developed for one of the fastest-growing categories in consumer electronics: smartphones. As these devices gradually became the de facto personal interface with cyberspace in our wireless digital world, global consumption of smartphones skyrocketed from almost one billion handsets a year in 2013 (Gartner, 2014) to 2.4 billion in 2019 (McNair, 2017). Site-specific experiments such as the CAVE would not have any space in the era of mobile devices, in which mobility and wireless connectivity were quickly becoming the standard for most personal technological devices.

Major tech players such as Apple, Google, Microsoft, and Samsung invested heavily in the market, pouring billions of dollars into research and development and prompting a technology race pursuing higher-quality displays; high-performance, low-energy systems on a chip (SOCs) that integrate both the central and the graphic processing units (CPU-GPU); battery technologies; and miniaturization and increased accuracy of sensors (particularly microphones and cameras, embedded GPS sensors, gyroscopes, accelerometers, and magnetometers), which are used by the myriad of applications being developed today. As consumers broadly adopted the handsets, they demanded more complex applications within richer multimedia interfaces that used the embedded sensors in novel ways. This subsequently pushed developers to specialize in methods such as machine learning and sensor fusion. App by app, a broader range of automated interpretations of sensor data also brought greater flexibility of design in potential uses, to the tune of millions of different apps, which are available in today's digital marketplaces.

Meanwhile, the software tools needed to create high-quality virtual worlds became accessible outside the corporate world, academia, and research labs. These tools (primarily game engines and 3D-modeling software), which less than a decade earlier involved licensing costs of several hundred thousand dollars, became widely available for free or next to nothing. They fostered a thriving development community and have now shifted into full design tools working within fully immersive environments (see figure 6.2). This shift was not the result of altruism among software vendors but rather of internal pressures within the video game industry; this sector, which is

Figure 6.2
A full user interface (UI) editor in a VR environment integrated within Unreal Engine, which allows for the full creation and design of environments and interactive spaces within a VR HMD.

currently worth $116 billion a year, required greater flexibility of business models and talent training. The industry produces some of the most technologically advanced software in the world: as explained earlier, video games today are essentially shared interactive hyperrealistic synthetic worlds, played simultaneously across millions of computers and game consoles on every continent. Their development requires a high degree of software specialization in computer graphics, interaction design, artificial intelligence, simulation systems, and network optimization, among other skills.

The industry has its roots in work by computer scientists in the 1960s and 1970s, but video game development tools evolved dramatically in the following decades. First, as games required higher graphical fidelity, game developers employed a large number of artists and designers, shifting priorities in the production process to design functions. This caused a rift in the production methods and tools required, particularly over the last fifteen years. Many of the tools were redesigned to favor shared and streamlined design pipelines with popular design applications. Second, as games shifted from single-player experiences with closed and linear scripted levels offering a high degree of control to online multiplayer games in open worlds (often in simulated cities) that prioritize emergent gameplay, with greater emphasis on prototyping and testing, game makers accordingly introduced accessible interfaces for rapid prototyping and large-scale user testing. Third, the leap from 2D to 3D graphics as the de facto mode for contemporary video

gaming forced the industry to sharply increase technological sophistication, moving from crude 3D graphics with basic texture mapping at low
resolutions to many of the same graphic techniques and physical simulations (approximating visual quality) used by top visual effects companies
in the film industry. More important, however, is that this shift also forced
game designers to rethink the way they conceptualize and create their virtual worlds, from highly curated linear processes following the single vision
of a core team to open, iterative design processes intertwining the vision of
designers with that of the broader public through feedback loops integrated
within the pipeline.

Meanwhile, as video game software matured, there was also an aggres-
sive push for a cyclical technology race in hardware and semiconductors,
as related by video game historians Steven Kent (2001) and Tristan Donovan (2010). Development of dedicated graphics processing hardware (called
graphics processing units, or GPUs) evolved from a niche category of products in the late 1990s to what today is one of the most important semiconductor markets. For video games to have their intricate look, a GPU must
perform the mathematical processing needed to display millions of tex-
tured polygons as well as light and physics simulations on screen, at very
fast refresh rates in real time. This has led to a divergence in semiconductor
design, with GPU manufacturers favoring processors optimized for a high
degree of parallelization of simple mathematical functions over the high-
complexity processing capabilities in a few parallel cores used in modern
CPU design. This increased parallelization has also made GPUs the ideal
processor architecture for modern machine-learning and deep-learning
applications.

Beyond the technical side of computer graphics, the video game industry also learned from other industries, such as film and television, how to
design grounded and coherent worlds, believable characters, and complex
narratives. Through iteration, video game developers have learned how to
manipulate emotions, feverishly adding time-honored techniques from traditional media by creating their own language based on its unique advantage: interactivity. Moving from "seeing" to "playing" is powerful, and
the holistic experience that VR pioneers such as Lanier had aimed for was
becoming possible. The idea of well-defined authorship, still prevalent in
the arts and architecture, loses relevance in video games in which multiple
players collaborate to create the worlds they inhabit—creation that also

encompasses destruction, disruption, amendments, and abandonments. Video games seem to have grappled with the idea that play is a collaborative process that enhances creativity within basic rules and parameters, whereas most VR artworks still treat people as spectators.

As many gamers know, playing requires going beyond representation into direct engagement and participation, which is difficult to maintain over long periods of time. The industry gradually developed and evolved more sophisticated control systems, learned to convey information optimally in interfaces, and experimented with dynamic and responsive feedback loops, all of which are critical for maintaining the illusion of player agency in virtual worlds.

In short, the billions of dollars invested by two global industries made fully immersive VR technically feasible, while the economies of scale from these industries made the technology accessible to mass consumers. Moreover, the vision of VR has remained highly compelling to a large group of people, as seen in the interest among the developer community, which has created thousands of VR experiences and applications to date; among the financial backers who crowdfunded this development; and among the media (both mass and social), which has given it extensive coverage. Looking ahead, it is clear that many of the world's largest technology companies intend to enter this field; the major financial investments they have made in recent times indicate stabilizing conditions for the technology to mature.

Mixed Reality, Immersive Media, and the Future of Design

All of these technological developments are essentially meaningless without ad hoc experiences to drive them. As mentioned above, beyond the technical breakthroughs, the key challenge is creating the appropriate language for the medium. Marshall McLuhan and Quentin Fiore (1967, p. 5) once wrote that "all media work over us completely"; different media become extensions of our senses and modify our cognitive processes accordingly. From the Bronze Age onward, the written word moved us away from the auditory space, where all our senses were engaged simultaneously, and we increasingly relied on abstract sequential language and media that emphasized linear thinking. In the previous century, audiovisual and electronic media rekindled our senses, but immersive computing presents a much greater possibility of returning us to our natural selves in the acoustic space.

As a result, we must learn how to interact and create in immersive environments by eschewing many of the lessons from previous media that no longer apply.

If McLuhan pointed out that some technologies have narrowed our perception of the world to specific senses (radio relied only on audition, and the press only on vision), he pointed out that new media such as cinema and television required us to rely on multiple senses. Following this argument, VR is undoubtedly much more powerful as a comprehensive sensorial environment. Whether we are in a CAVE or moving in our living room with VR goggles, our senses are physiologically perceiving the world as relayed to us by the VR experience. VR becomes a powerful self-deception technology that simultaneously (and perhaps counterintuitively, if we think of its deceptive characteristics) impels us to engage with the world through multiple senses. It encompasses not just visual technologies but also sound, as well as haptic devices that suggest a realistic sense of touch, allowing users to feel a virtual material's texture, shape, weight, temperature, and motion within space. Such haptic devices range from gloves to full-body suits connected to VR head-mounted displays,[3] and they are used for sports performance, in simulating firefighter drills, and in training ground crew in airports or surgeons in delicate operations. Technological improvements are making the stimulation of electrotactile interfaces between humans and machines more reliable (body sweat and electrode peel-off have been barriers to achieving full-body immersion through devices) (Akhtar et al., 2018). Thus, the self-deception of VR is becoming complete, opening up doors for practical and creative experiences inside VR environments: if the physicality of objects is not there, our senses are equally stimulated by VR technology.

Design comes as a key driver of this technology. Here design is intended to reconnect our senses to a total perception of the world—even in imaginary worlds, our senses engage with them in full. Again relying on McLuhan, in VR research we are passing the time when, as with every new medium, it had initially used the medium it made obsolete as its initial content. The dozens of VR hackathons, commonly organized jointly by academia and industry, bring together companies, engineers, artists, technologists, and users pushing the boundaries of VR, avidly exploring a language that is unique to this technology.

At its core, the technology is a perfect fit for the iterative process of ideation, synthesis, and communication of novel, but still temporary, ideas needed for good design. Empathy is a critical function among designers, specifically the capacity to understand the user's desires and requirements to envision the possibilities of intervention. An extra challenge for spatial designers is to work on possible combinations that could turn technological breakthroughs into collective experiences. *Clouds over Sidra* (2015), created by Gabo Arora and Chris Milk, is a VR film that brings you to a Syrian refugee camp to follow Sidra, a twelve-year-old girl who has lived in the camp for eighteen months with thousands of other refugees. In a 2015 TED Talk about the project, Milk called VR "the ultimate empathy machine."[4]

In several industries, from architecture to the automotive industry, designers are using VR to communicate new ideas to a variety of industry specialists and to gather their feedback. VR becomes a creative space that combines product development with user experience evaluation, making the feedback loop more interactive between designers, technologies, and the user (see figure 6.3). Traditionally there has been a knowledge gap between design professionals, who understand the constraints and practices related to any technology, and the general public, whose imagination is not limited by these constraints and practices. While one might think that a collective process of curation would express the will of the public, this usually leads to bland design, and consequently guidance by the designer is key. The trick is to balance and modulate the simultaneity of opinions and intentions in the process, distilling those that strengthen the cohesiveness of design. Moreover, different from the consultation processes long established in design, with VR the creative technology is commercially accessible, so the public can effectively be a cocreator. This is a challenge to both language and design process.

Virtual reality holds the potential to help bridge this knowledge gap. Creating immersive experiences that avoid the limitations of two-dimensional surfaces and instead utilize the language of spatial computing puts users into a cognitive state of mind that relies less on abstraction and consequently becomes more effective in communicating ideas. In other words, don't overanalyze, experience it! Interpretation of mass and scale becomes irrelevant when perceived at a one-to-one scale in an immersive environment. Legibility and navigation in architectural spaces can be assessed directly through user testing before a brick is laid down. And design variations can be directly experienced by users under a multiplicity of conditions, including time of day, weather, and the passage of time.

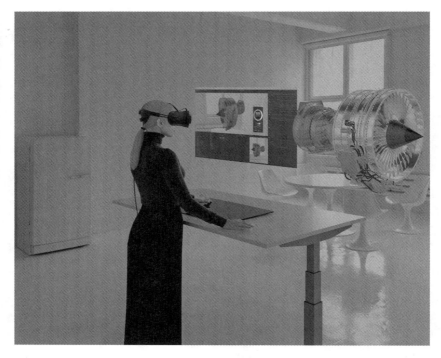

Figure 6.3
Overlay visualization of a virtual workspace concept designed by Varjo for its VR HMD
design environment.
Source: Varjo Technologies, 2019.

Perhaps more importantly, virtual reality allows users the freedom to
role-play; by recreating a variety of scenarios and contexts, one can experience designs from multiple viewpoints, stepping into someone else's shoes.
Here the notions of presence and empathy return from a complementary
perspective. In social neuroscience, shared presence is the subject's ability to identify another whose intentions are related to the subject's own
intentions. Creating shared perceptions is the path to forming collective
intentions, a form of cooperation that stems from a mutual understanding
of intentions and views. In fact, although in its infancy, social neuroscience
is using VR to study social cognition by creating what is called impossible
real-world interactions, when participants' embodiment is manipulated to
put them in situations they cannot experience through their own physical
bodies (Parsons et al., 2017).

Consider how a child would envision a plan for a public park. What seems like an attractive design for adults might not be so appealing to children, since the scale is different when you're under 3 feet tall. Exploration, risk, and rewards have complete different spatial meanings depending on who the user is. Opportunities for play can be found in every nook and cranny, often beyond the reach of adults. But hidden chances for potential accidents may also arise from spaces that designers, often adults, do not notice. Spaces that seem fully legible to an adult might seem confusing to children, especially when these areas are filled with taller people. Being in space as a child is a completely different experience, one that we almost forget as we get older. This has been recreated in other media, such as films and television, where the world is sometimes shown through the eyes of a child. The difference in VR is interactivity and immersion: observing someone is not the same as becoming them. Now we can be children again. And once both adult designers and children can share the same space from the same viewpoint, using VR body devices to even induce the same spatial physical experience, the final user of space (in this case, children), can become codesigners.

Role-playing for situational design and communication can be a good step toward making sure that a variety of perspectives from different stakeholders are represented. A collection of similarly relevant questions can be approached and considered in the design process. Is a planned space inviting for minority groups? Different scenarios can be created in the space, from racially segregated to socially diverse, recreating scripted procedural situations ranging from social inclusion to aggression to let users experience these events. Is a space safe enough for a firefighter? It is possible to simulate accidents and crises where they themselves can explore and navigate the space and perform their tasks, which has been done using a combination of VR headsets and full-body haptic suits. Is a proposed design sufficiently accessible for someone in a wheelchair? In a simulation, you can move about in a wheelchair and decide directly whether your experience navigating the space as a mobility-impaired person is acceptable or subpar.

These scenarios and many more can be experienced socially and shared across a community, and feedback methods can be used for collective thoughts and concerns to be documented and integrated. Actually, there is scientific evidence that VR has longer-lasting effects in participants in perspective-taking experiments than those exposed to traditional methods. Experiments showed that VR also elicited stronger empathy with social groups different from their own—from people with disabilities to the homeless—extending positive behaviors to real life, making participants advocates for the social changes in the real world (Herrera et al., 2018).

Design decisions affected by constraints such as the natural laws of physics, systemic restrictions, or regulatory restrictions can be better explained through simulation systems encoded in the behavior of synthetic worlds experienced firsthand. It is hard to explain to laypeople technicalities such as the structural performance of different materials in infrastructures, floor-to-area ratio, land-use distribution, and traffic flow density. Concepts and terms that are common among planners, architects, transportation experts, and civil engineers are frequently abstracted into incomprehensible numbers for the average person. And yet, these are often critical elements behind many design decisions that seem baffling to the larger community, which has little choice but to accept them within an unbalanced distribution of decision making through imposed technical expertise. Even within the same industry, specialists have a hard time understanding each other. The Finnish start-up Varjo, in collaboration with Volvo, has been developing a device that uses dual 12-megapixel cameras to collect images of the outside world and embed them into a VR environment. Thus, when test-drivers use VR headsets when driving, and virtual elements appear in the VR environment, drivers react according to what they perceive in this simulated environment. Using this mixed reality technology, engineers and designers incorporate driver's behavior data to enhance the design and safety features of cars.

Building on existing VR content-development platforms can allow people to participate in design exercises where they directly propose iterations through easy-to-use simplified WYSIWYP (What You See Is What You Play) tools. These can already be found in a new collection of resources developed for rapid prototyping of VR environments within existing game engines such as Unreal or Unity. However, VR does not achieve its full potential when used as an isolated platform. Rather, it must be fully integrated into the toolkit that planners use to analyze cities, design and communicate ideas, and interact with the public. The technical pipeline is already being integrated by software companies such as Autodesk, Unity, and Epic (among many others), by making existing CAD and building information modeling (BIM) design software compatible with 3D modelers, existing game engines such as Unigine, and VR rendering pipelines. These tools are being paired with urban simulation systems (such as ESRI's CityEngine, developed by the ETH Computer Vision Lab in Zurich), which permit large-scale procedurally generated urban typologies within game engines, as well as other systems, including UBEM (urban building energy models) for energy-consumption simulations, SUMO (Simulation of Urban MObility) for transportation, and color 3D printing technology, such as ZPrinter, among a range of other applications (Tato et al., 2012). These combinations of technologies allow designers to model directly in voxel-based 3D environments, creating virtual mock-ups of spaces they can immediately explore at 1:1 scale using VR technology (de Klerk et al., 2019)—sort of a *Minecraft* VR.

These technologies allow for a wide variety of applications in design. In many spatial design fields, such as architecture, landscape architecture, urban design, and environmental planning, simulating "inaccessible realities" is an essential playing field for testing new ideas (Portman et al., 2015, p. 376). Spatial designers propose realities that are inaccessible in space and time, and they have been using VR to assess a user's reaction to them. Based on presence and empathy, designers can amass data about the user's engagement with space and propose changes accordingly. VR can also foster participatory design with immediate effects. One can see new dynamics where participants engage directly with design proposals, mutate them, and see the consequences of their choices in real time. The multiplayer capacities of existing engines create a space for simultaneous multiuser sessions held across space. Content management systems that permit open publishing of design suggestions allow design intent to be curated socially over time. Both of these possibilities essentially amplify creativity and become an interface between professionals and nonprofessionals by performing interactions through a shared language of design. Gradually, these simulated, immersive, socially created virtual components represent the building blocks of an inclusive participatory and transparent design process.

The Road Ahead

Several challenges remain ahead in terms of adopting MR technologies, and more specifically VR, for general use and for spatial and urban design in particular. On the technical side, developers still must overcome biology. R&D has initially focused on the vestibular-ocular system, then on auditory systems, with the haptic system coming into play only recently, and still far behind—and there are no current digital technologies that can convincingly engage our senses of smell or taste. But it is clear that VR is on the path to becoming a full sensory experience.

Most important of all will be the design of the language of the medium. Media scholar Lev Manovich (2000, p. 195) emphasizes the power of what he calls "icons of mimesis" to legitimize each art language—the illusion of mimicking simulating the texture of fruits and human flesh in painting, and of authentically representing moving nature, as trees blowing in the wind in cinema. Content creators and experience designers have gradually discovered that they could not just port or treat VR experiences as extensions of photography, film, or video games. It took decades for these media forms to design their own language and communication techniques. It took frantic experimentation on the part of thousands of creators, each learning from their peers, to establish a successful cross-cultural code that allows a certain degree of individual expressiveness and uniqueness—a process that continues to this day.

Perhaps Sutherland (1965) was right to name VR "the Ultimate Display." It may be that VR, with all of its communication potential that taps directly into our biology, is the ultimate expression of McLuhan's ideas on media as an extension of the senses (see McLuhan & Fiore, 1967). Lanier's (2017) statement that VR is a postsymbolic medium expresses the true core of this idea, and this poses a challenge to designers, since we have become quite adept at inserting symbols as ways of encoding information into most of the systems we utilize in our daily lives. In a fully immersive environment, information will have to rely less on abstractions in order to utilize the medium's strengths; as a result, a new language will have to be created, one that both informs and engages. This is a fascinating challenge for designers, full of opportunities for expression.

A new generation of auteurs have embraced the medium, from experimental documentary creators like Nonny de la Pena and Asad Malik, who have been presenting in VR sessions at documentary film festivals, to established film directors like Alejandro González Iñárritu and game makers such as Ready at Dawn and Crytek. They've been asking some of the fundamental questions of the medium: How do we induce emotions without relying too much on gimmicks? How do we frame a narrative in a continuous world? How do we sustain presence in abstraction? How do we engage in immersive interaction? And perhaps the most important one: How do we use VR to create alternate identities, which can be embraced by users and help shift their perception of the world?

There's still a lot of work to be done; we are still in the very early days, with a flux of new experimental VR experiences proposing something new, many creating a true state of wonder or engaging our sense of empathy to help us understand the world. What is becoming clear is that in tandem with developments in the technology itself, there is a growing number of VR users (designers, technologists, artists, engineers, and the general public) trying many approaches in order to find the appropriate language that will make VR a fully distinctive medium, which might contain, but cannot be replaced by, its previous media. Photography replicated painting, cinema replicated a temporal sequence of photographs, and video replicated a low-resolution version of cinema—until the point at which they established themselves as a fully distinctive medium. It is time for virtual reality.

To achieve that, there is also the question of social acceptance of the medium. In the short term, the central goal of VR proponents is to bring an HMD of sufficient quality and integrated as seamlessly as possible into our daily relation with other media, and also to have a strong flow of high-quality and unique experiences commercially available—or else risk another public backlash. Additionally, as the sensor package required by these devices becomes more powerful and includes cameras, LIDAR and depth sensors, they may create privacy concerns among the public, creating an additional barrier to their adoption. Recent lessons from augmented reality devices showed that people close to users of AR glasses often felt uncomfortable being with a person wearing a device that could potentially invade their privacy, for example, when Google launched their AR platform Google Glass in 2013, they suffered a public relations backlash, when early adopters were using the devices in public spaces, making some nearby people feel unease, and even having some of its users labeled "glassholes" and banned from certain places.

The fact is that the technology still faces stigma as a socially isolating technology. This is partially because it is physically impossible to simultaneously share a headset, which creates the impression that the medium can only deliver lonely experiences. Indeed, when one sees images of players in one of the many VR playgrounds popping up around the world, the impression is of a bunch of people wearing headsets, handheld devices, gloves, or full-body VR devices who, although in the same physical space, are engaged in an isolated experience.

Actually, this couldn't be further from the truth. This is a pre-medium perspective, of trying to understand VR based on depictions of previous media (photographs or journalistic videos). Many of these experiences are dramatically social by design. It is very common for VR users to simultaneously share coherent online worlds, even within the same physical space (see figure 6.4); this isn't new per se, but simply a natural evolution of transporting massively multiplayer online (MMO) games to the new media. MMOs are widely accepted and have been among the most popular game types over the past decade. Video games—not photography, cinema, or computerized 3D models—seem to be the starting point for understanding how virtual reality can have social impacts.

Some will still reject VR as a dehumanizing, artificial mask that prevents true face-to-face interaction. As discussed in this chapter, scientific evidence

Figure 6.4
A group of people simultaneously playing in the "Arena Scale" virtual reality environment demonstration using a series of Oculus Quest headsets at the Oculus Connect 5 Developers Conference (2018). The digital objects in the virtual environment are physically mapped with real objects in the real world, creating a hybrid physical-virtual world to be experienced socially.
Source: UploadVR, 2018.

shows that this is far from the truth. In fact, people feel more empathetic to others who are different from themselves after experiencing the world through their eyes and bodies. Experience design will be key in demonstrating that VR is not a substitute for physical interaction but can enhance social interactions and permit new social experiences. Like all new media before it, it will take some time before society comes to grips with the role and place of VR in everyday life; it is clear, however, that beyond the foreseeable technical advances, we still have a long way to go before the technology becomes unobtrusive and pervasive enough to disappear into the background of our daily habits and create myriad mixed reality experiences. As the expression attributed to Roy Amara, known as Amara's law, states, "We tend to overestimate the effect of a technology in the short run and underestimate the effect in the long run"; however, the future will come faster than we think.

7   Learning to Play

Bauhaus, Media Lab, Fab Labs

All systematization seems to be the opposite of the primary characteristic of playfulness, which is to be free from established constraints. However, just as Magic Johnson played basketball at the highest level and within the strict rules of the game while still enchanting the public with his playfulness on court, so too must designers face the challenge of understanding the transformations triggered by technology, which will change several functional aspects of spaces, while still being creative.

Cedric Price was a visionary English architect practicing in the second half of the twentieth century who built very little but still had a remarkable influence on contemporary architecture. He combined sensing technologies, robotics, and artificial intelligence to propose responsive spaces with variable programs and forms, such as his Fun Palace. Archigram, also based in England, proposed buildings and urban infrastructures that combined technological advancements, from capsules to spacesuits, with open possibilities emerging from the interaction between users, infrastructures, media, and the environment. They often expressed their ideas in graphic novels and posters influenced by mass media and pop-culture graphics. The group was frequently considered futuristic and visionary but of little practical consequence. As David Greene, one of the five members of Archigram, said in an interview for the *Guardian*, "We were trying to bridge the gap between what was built and what might be built" (Moore, 2018).

There can be no doubt that Price and Archigram were provocative and inspirational and influenced generations of architects. However, even though Price and some members of Archigram taught in architecture schools, none of them intended to systemize their ideas and proposals into learning environments.

There are, however, some designers who embrace play and technology as the driving force of their endeavors to transform spatial design but who also work to establish a coherent conceptual and methodological framework that is intended to form new generations of designers. Three endeavors in the last hundred years have sought to organize learning environments around the idea that technological innovations would provoke profound changes in architectural and urban spaces. The Bauhaus was an arts school that operated in Germany between 1919 and 1933, when it was closed as a result of pressure from the Nazi government. As soon as it was established, the Bauhaus became the center of innovation in Europe and, soon afterward, the world, combining different art forms and technologies around the idea that industrialization could lead to new ways of life. Walter Gropius, its creator and most prominent director, had a clear vision of the powerful influence that modern technological innovations such as pervasive electricity, poured concrete, exposed steel, and, most importantly, the new industrial production methods (already in full force in the automotive industry) would exert on the building of houses and cities as well as the reshaping of society. Millions of people were moving to urban areas, and providing them with housing and other urban facilities would only be possible if engineers and designers adopted industrial approaches. The result, Gropius believed, should not be cities where workers were subjugated by the machinery and lived and worked in noxious environments, but rather a liberating life in which art and technology fed each other. Indeed, Gropius knew that these new technologies were transforming traditional arts, such as tapestry and glassware, and creating new ones, such as photography and filmmaking. Imbued with the notion that industrial technology was transforming every aspect of society, the Bauhaus brought different disciplines together in a single location where they could nurture each other without boundaries.

Fifty years later, a new technological transformation arguably as powerful as the Industrial Revolution was underway. This time, information and communication technologies powered by high-performance, interconnected personal computers were creating a networked society on a global scale. Changes were happening rapidly in the economy, labor market, and society. Likewise, the influence of information and communication technologies began to be felt in spatial design. At this time, the United States was the epicenter of several of these technological innovations, and

Nicholas Negroponte and William Mitchell became some of the most productive and vocal thinkers about the transformations that digital technologies would bring to the way we experience and design space. While at the School of Architecture and Planning at the Massachusetts Institute of Technology, they created the Media Lab, which was to become an innovative powerhouse responsible for various breakthroughs combining digital technologies and design. Over the years the Media Lab has attracted researchers from a wide range of specialties—from fashion to biology, from physics to music—to think about and make the future, and the multidisciplinarity that characterized the Bauhaus has become even more essential to the laboratory's work.

Within three decades of its creation, the Media Lab saw the emergence and expansion on a global scale of a movement known as Fab Labs. Although their origin can be traced in part to the Media Lab, Fab Labs neither share the same pedagogical ideals as the Bauhaus nor seek to be a center of innovation and exploration like the Media Lab. Among the characteristics that make the Fab Labs an example of a novel approach to learning about technologies that can reshape spatialities is their decentralized structure. Fab Labs are grounded on the idea that with digital tools—from open-source design software to cheap, small, and easily assembled computer boards, and from 3D printers to inexpensive wireless Internet—anyone anywhere can create, tweak, and build their own objects, tools, games, and devices. There is no unified pedagogy (Bauhaus) and no think-tank configuration (Media Lab); it is instead a collaborative global network of makers and learners.

None of these learning approaches is better than any other; they merely reflect their own times. Their common denominator is that they all embraced the fact that new technologies were reshaping society and design, that exploring technologies entails fostering imagination and playfulness, and that knowledge should be shared to benefit society as a whole.

It is not the function of play to teach anything—that would undermine the very sense of play. But we can learn with play. In this book we have tried to summarize what we have learned by talking with spatial-design practitioners, game designers, virtual reality developers, and students and researchers exploring these technologies; by reading authors who, even when critical, are enthusiastic about the changes that technology brings to society; and by bouncing ideas back and forth with so many other enthusiasts. It has been a playful intellectual journey that we hope readers can reflect upon and enjoy.

Acknowledgments

The idea for this book slowly took shape along a few years of informal discussions about how data science and digital technologies had been proposing novel models to understand cities, but this was happening at the cost of eliminating surprise from their analysis. As in play, the unexpected, the serendipitous moments, should be cherished, because they carry with them possibilities of innovation. We were lucky to mature the ideas of this book while working at the Senseable City Lab, at the Massachusetts Institute of Technology—and we'd like to thank all our colleagues who, for more than fifteen years, have been creating such an insightful and joyful lab.

During the research phase, we have discussed specific ideas and chapters with scholars, video game and mixed reality designers, architects, technologists, gamers, artists, and curators. Some of the conversations were more formal, as interviews, but many were open discussions, often split into several sessions. We'd like to particularly thank Will Jennings (Demiurge), Eric Klopfer, Scot Osterweil, Matt Adams (Blast Theory), Alexandria Heston (Magic Leap), Timmy Ghiurau (Volvo VR-AR Research), Amy Korte (Arrow Street), Hilary O'Shaughnessy (Watershed), Alisa Andrasek, Guto Requena, Carlo Ratti, and Dennis Frenchman.

Finally, writing this book was fun and challenging, and we could not have done it without the support of our families. Fábio Duarte thanks Vanessa Sevilhano and Valentina Duarte, and Ricardo Álvarez thanks Mona Perez, Emiliano Alvarez, Maria José Alvarez, Mateo Alvarez, Teodora Felix, and Guillermo Alvarez.

Notes

Introduction

1. Details of the Programmable City project can be found at https://progcity.may noothuniversity.ie/about/.

2. Details of the Playable City project can be found at https://www.playablecity.com.

3. Details of Shadowing can be found at https://www.playablecity.com/projects /shadowing/.

Chapter 1

1. The original Portuguese reads: "O poeta é um fingidor / Finge tão completamente / Que chega a fingir que é dor / A dor que deveras sente"; the English version given is a free translation.

Chapter 2

1. https://www.voanews.com/usa/still-most-visited-place-orlando-had-75-million -visitors-2018.

2. https://www.bizjournals.com/orlando/news/2018/06/14/orlandos-race-toward -100m-visitors-will-happen.html.

3. https://www.occompt.com/wordpress/wp-content/uploads/2020/11/TDT-Annual -Collection-Hist-by-FY-20.pdf.

4. https://www.thenational.ae/uae/burj-khalifa-dishes-out-gold-bars-1.405444.

5. https://www.thenational.ae/lifestyle/motoring/from-a-bugatti-to-lamborghinis -the-supercars-of-the-uae-police-in-pictures-1.738842.

6. United Nations: World Urbanization Prospects. The World's Cities in 2018 Report, page 22, https://www.un.org/en/events/citiesday/assets/pdf/the_worlds_cities_in_2018 _data_booklet.pdf

Chapter 3

1. Examples include the AI-enabled solutions developed by Xkool, the AI design software cloud-based platform developed by a company named Xiaoku Technology (https://www.xkool.ai/n/about), and Autodesk's Dreamcatcher (https://autodeskresearch.com/projects/dreamcatcher).

2. Flanagan (2009) lists several synonyms for *urban games*, including locative games, massive games, flashmob art, ubiquitous games, and pervasive games. We prefer the term *urban games* for the technologies used and questioned by players.

3. More on *Node Runner* is available at http://med44.com/v2/noderunner.php.

4. *Run an Empire* is available at http://www.runanempire.com.

5. More on the work of Blast Theory is available at https://www.blasttheory.co.uk.

6. Games for Cities is a rich database of games developed to engage multiple stakeholders in urban planning and design and can be accessed at http://gamesforcities.com/database/.

7. Details about the Hackable City initiative can be found at http://thehackablecity.nl.

8. Details about the Playable City program and selected projects can be found at https://www.playablecity.com.

9. Full disclosure: both authors have been working in the Senseable City Lab at MIT for many years.

10. The pavilion is a result of workshops at MIT, designed by Carlo Ratti Associati, engineered by Arup, and built by Siemens and Lumiartecnia.

11. More details on the 3D Water Matrix can be found at https://www.codaworx.com/project/water-matrix-science-and-industry-museum.

12. Information about the Mediated Matter group is available at https://www.media.mit.edu/groups/mediated-matter/overview/.

13. Information about the Silk Pavilion is available at https://www.media.mit.edu/projects/silk-pavilion/overview/.

14. Information about Living Mushtari is available at https://www.media.mit.edu/projects/living-mushtari/overview/.

15. The Self-Assembly Lab's projects can be seen at https://selfassemblylab.mit.edu.

16. Ubiquitous Energy (http://ubiquitous.energy/) is currently one of the front-runners in getting photovoltaic transparent glass to market.

17. Information about Warka Tower can be found at http://www.warkawater.org/warka-tower-copy/.

18. The catalog of microorganisms included in C-Mould is available at https://exploringtheinvisible.com/2018/05/03/c-mould-collection-of-microorganisms-of-use-in-living-design/.

Chapter 4

1. Although the markings on spring scales usually indicate mass (kilograms, for instance), mass and weight are not the same. Weight is a force and represents the force of gravity on a mass, which is why, when mass is represented as a weight, it implies the gravitational field of Earth.

2. *L'arrivée d'un train en gare de La Ciotat* can be watched at https://archive.org/details/youtube--e1u7Fgoocc.

Chapter 5

1. This is an expanded and revised version of an article first published as R. Álvarez & F. Duarte (2017), Spatial design and placemaking: learning from video games. *Space and Culture* 21(3), 208–232, doi:10.1177/1206331217736746.

2. MoMA, *Applied Design*, press material available at https://www.moma.org/documents/moma_press-release_386891.pdf.

3. Andrew Louis, *Evolution of Wolfenstein Games 1981–2017*, at https://www.youtube.com/watch?v=50smRp6SPxM.

Chapter 6

1. A short video of the work can be seen at https://www.designboom.com/technology/laurie-anderson-to-the-moon-virtual-reality-installation-vive-07-16-2019/.

2. HR Giger VR Gallery Cardboard is available on the Google Play store.

3. For an example of a full-body suit, see https://teslasuit.io; for examples of haptic gloves, see https://haptx.com.

4. Both *Clouds of Sidra* and Chris Milk's TED Talk are available online.

Bibliography

Abrash, M., & Katz, D. (2014, May 2). *Why virtual reality isn't (just) the next big platform*. [Lecture conducted from Carnegie Mellon University, Pittsburgh, PA]. https://www.youtube.com/watch?v=dxbh-TM5yNc

Ackerman, D. (2000). *Deep play*. Random House International.

Akhtar, A., Sombeck, J., Boyce, B., & Bretl, T. (2018). Controlling sensation intensity for electrotactile stimulation in human-machine interfaces. *Science Robotics*, *3*(17). doi:10.1126/scirobotics.aap9770

Al, S. (2017). *The strip: Las Vegas and the architecture of the American dream*. MIT Press.

Alhabash, S., & Wise, K. (2014). Playing their game: Changing stereotypes of Palestinians and Israelis through videogame play. *New Media & Society*, *17*(8), 1358–1376. doi:10.1177/1461444814525010

Ali, S. (2010). *Dubai: Gilded cage*. Yale University Press.

Anderson, L., & Marranca, B. (2018). Laurie Anderson: Telling stories in virtual reality. *PAJ: A Journal of Performance and Art*, *40*(3), 37–44. doi:10.1162/pajj_a_00432

Andrasek, A. (2015). Indeterminacy & contingency: The Seroussi Pavilion and Bloom by Alisa Andrasek. *Architectural Design*, *85*(3), 106–111. doi:10.1002/ad.1908

Andrasek, A. (2016). Xenocells: In the mood for the unseen. *Architectural Design*, *86*(6), 90–95. doi:10.1002/ad.2116

Andrasek, A. (2019). In search of the unseen: Towards superhuman intuition. *Architectural Design*, *89*(5), 112–119. doi:10.1002/ad.2487

Anholt, S. (2006). *Competitive identity: The new brand management for nations, cities, and regions*. Palgrave Macmillan.

Armstrong, R. (2020). *Experimental architecture: Designing the unknown*. Routledge.

Arnheim, R. (1974). *Art and visual perception: A psychology of the creative eye*. University of California Press.

Ash, J. (2013). Technologies of captivation. *Body & Society, 19*(1), 27–51.

Augé, M. (2008). *Non-Places: An introduction to supermodernity* (J. Howe, Trans.). Verso.

Aumont, J. (1996). Lumière revisited. *Film History, 8*(4), 416–430.

Bader, C., Patrick, W. G., Kolb, D., Hays, S. G., Keating, S., Sharma, S., . . . Oxman, N. (2016). Grown, printed, and biologically augmented: An additively manufactured microfluidic wearable, functionally templated for synthetic microbes. *3D Printing and Additive Manufacturing, 3*(2), 79–89. doi:10.1089/3dp.2016.0027

Bateson, P. (2014). Play, playfulness, creativity and innovation. *Animal Behavior and Cognition, 1*(2), 99–112. doi:10.12966/abc.05.02.2014

Baudrillard, J. (2000). *The vital illusion.* Columbia University Press.

Baudrillard, J. (2006). *Simulacra and simulation.* The University of Michigan Press.

Biocca, F., Kim, T., & Levy, M. R. (1995). The vision of virtual reality. In F. Biocca & M. R. Levy (Eds.), *Communication in the Age of Virtual Reality* (pp. 3–14). Lawrence Erlbaum Associates.

Borden, I. (2001). *Skateboarding, space and the city: Architecture, the body and performative critique.* Berg.

Borges, J. L. (1962). *Labyrinths: Selected stories & other writings.* New Directions.

Bradbury, R. (1951). *The illustrated man.* Doubleday & Company.

Brents, B. G., Jackson, C. A., & Hausbeck, K. (2009). *The state of sex: Tourism, sex and sin in the new American heartland.* Routledge.

Briceño, H., Chao, W., Glenn, A., Hu, S., Krishnamurthy, A., & Tsuchida, B. (2000). *Down from the top of its game: The story of Infocom, Inc.* http://web.mit.edu/6.933/www/Fall2000/infocom/

Bromber, K., Krawietz, B., Steiner, C., & Wippel, S. (2016). The Arab(ian) Gulf: Urban development in the making. In S. Wippel, K. Bromber, C. Steiner, & B. Krawietz (Eds.), *Under construction: Logics of urbanism in the Gulf region* (pp. 25–38). Routledge.

Brooks, D. (2013). *A history of future cities.* W. W. Norton.

Butt, T. (2014). *Surf science: An introduction to waves for surfing.* Alison Hodge.

Caillois, R. (1961). *Man, play and games.* Free Press of Glencoe.

Calleja, G. (2011). *In-game: From immersion to incorporation.* MIT Press.

Calvino, I. (1978). *Invisible cities.* Harcourt, Brace & Co.

Chase, L. (2009). *Picturing Las Vegas.* Gibbs Smith.

Chin, J., & Vasarhelyi, E. (Directors). (2015). *Meru* [Film]. Music Box Films.

Chiu, C. (2009). Contestation and conformity. *Space and Culture, 12*(1), 25–42. doi:10.1177/1206331208325598

Chomko, J. (2014, September 6). *Interview with Shadowing creator Jonathan Chomko*. Playable City. https://www.playablecity.com/news/2014/09/06/interview-with-shadowing -creator-jonathan-chomko/

Chouard, T. (2016). The Go Files: AI computer wraps up 4–1 victory against human champion. *Nature News & Comments*, March 15. https://www.nature.com/news /the-go-files-ai-computer-wraps-up-4-1-victory-against-human-champion-1.19575 [DOI:10.1038/nature.2016.19575]

Coombe, W., & Melki, J. (2012). Global media and brand Dubai. *Place Branding and Public Diplomacy, 8*(1), 58–71.

Damisch, H. (2000). *The origin of perspective*. MIT Press.

Davidson, C. M. (2008). *Dubai: The vulnerability of success*. Columbia University Press.

Dawson, W. (1978). *Indirections: Shakespeare and the art of illusion*. University of Toronto Press.

Debord, G. (2007a). Introduction to a critique of urban geography. In K. Knabb (Ed.), *Situationist International anthology* (pp. 8–11). Bureau of Public Secrets. (Original work published 1955)

Debord, G. (2007b). Theory of the dérive. In K. Knabb (Ed.), *Situationist International anthology* (pp. 62–66). Bureau of Public Secrets. (Original work published 1958)

Decety, J., & Jackson, P. L. (2004). The functional architecture of human empathy. *Behavioral and Cognitive Neuroscience Reviews, 3*(2), 71–100. doi:10.1177/1534582304267187

de Klerk, R., Duarte, A. M., Medeiros, D. P., Duarte, J. P., Jorge, J., & Lopes, D. S. (2019). Usability studies on building early stage architectural models in virtual reality. *Automation in Construction, 103*, 104–116. doi:10.1016/j.autcon.2019.03.009

Deleuze, G. (1988). *Bergsonism*. Zone Books.

Demastes, W. (2005). Hamlet in his world: Shakespeare anticipates/assaults Cartesian dualism. *Journal of Dramatic Theory and Criticism, 20*(1), 27–39.

de Waal, M., & de Lange, M. (2019). Introduction—The hacker, the city and their institutions: From grassroots urbanism to systemic change. In M. de Lange & M. de Waal (Eds.), *The hackable city* (pp. 1–22). Springer.

Donovan, T. (2010). *Replay: The history of video games*. Yellow Ant.

Duarte, F., & Firmino, R. J. (2009). Infiltrated city, augmented space: Information and communication technologies, and representations of contemporary spatialities. *The Journal of Architecture, 14*(5), 545–565. doi:10.1080/13602360903187493

Duarte, F., & Firmino, R. J. (2018). *Unplugging the city: The urban phenomenon and its sociotechnical controversies*. Routledge.

Duggan, E. (2017). Squaring the (magic) circle: A brief definition and history of pervasive games. In A. Nijholt (Ed.), *Playable cities: The city as a digital playground* (pp. 111–135). Springer.

Duncombe, S. (2007). *Dream: Re-imagining progressive politics in an age of fantasy*. The New Press.

Elsheshtawy, Y. (2009). *Dubai: Behind an urban spectacle*. Routledge.

Escher, M. C. (2007). *The graphic work*. Taschen.

Fishman, R. (1982). *Urban utopias in the twentieth century: Ebenezer Howard, Frank Lloyd Wright and Le Corbusier*. MIT Press.

Flanagan, M. (2009). *Critical play: Radical game design*. MIT Press.

Florida, R. (2002). *The rise of the creative class: And how it's transforming work, leisure, community and everyday life*. Basic Books.

Flusser, V. (1995). On the word design: An etymological essay. *Design Issues, 11*(3), 50–53.

Foucault, M. (2004). Des espaces autres. *Empan, 2*(54), 12–19.

Fox, W. L. (2007). *In the desert of desire: Las Vegas and the culture of spectacle*. University of Nevada Press.

Freeman, D., Haselton, P., Freeman, J., Spanlang, B., Kishore, S., Albery, E., Denne, M., Brown, P., Slater, M., & Nickless, A. (2018). Automated psychological therapy using immersive virtual reality for treatment of fear of heights: A single-blind, parallel-group, randomised controlled trial. *The Lancet Psychiatry, 5*(8), 625–632. doi:10.1016/s2215-0366(18)30226-8

Friedberg, A. (2006). *The virtual window: From Alberti to Microsoft*. MIT Press.

Gaber, J. (2007). Simulating planning: SimCity as a pedagogical tool. *Journal of Planning Education and Research, 27*(2), 113–121. doi:10.1177/0739456X07305791

Gartner Inc. (2013). *Gartner says worldwide video game market to total $93 billion in 2013* [Press release]. http://www.gartner.com/newsroom/id/2614915

Gartner Inc. (2014). *Gartner says annual smartphone sales surpassed sales of feature phones for the first time in 2013* [Press release]. https://www.gartner.com/en/newsroom/press-releases/2014-02-13-gartner-says-annual-smartphone-sales-surpassed-sales-of-feature-phones-for-the-first-time-in-2013

Gell, A. (1998). *Art and agency: An anthropological theory*. Clarendon Press.

Giannetti, E. (2000). *Lies we live by: The art of self-seduction*. Bloomsbury.

Gibney, E. (2016). Google AI algorithm masters ancient game of Go. *Nature, 529*(7587), 445–446. doi:10.1038/529445a

Gil, J., & Duarte, J. (2008). Towards an urban design evaluation framework: Integrating spatial analysis techniques in the parametric urban design process. *eCAADe 26,* 257–264. http://papers.cumincad.org/data/works/att/ecaade2008_147.content.pdf

Goldberger, P. (1972, October 22). Mickey Mouse teaches the architects. *New York Times,* SM40.

Golding, D. (2013). Putting the player back in their place: Spatial analysis from below. *Journal of Gaming & Virtual Worlds, 5*(2), 117–130. doi:10.1386/jgvw.5.2.117_1

Goldschmidt, J. C. (2018). From window to solar cell and back. *Nature Materials, 17*(3), 218–219. doi:10.1038/s41563-018-0017-5

Gordon, E., & de Souza e Silva, A. (2011). *Net locality: Why location matters in a networked world.* Wiley-Blackwell.

Govers, R. (2012). Brand Dubai and its competitors in the Middle East: An image and reputation analysis. *Place Branding and Public Diplomacy, 8*(1), 48–57.

Greengard, S. (2019). *Virtual reality.* MIT Press.

Guattari, F. (1995) *Chaosmosis: An ethico-aesthetic paradigm.* Indiana University Press.

Habraken, N. J., & Gross, M. (1988). Concept design games. *Design Studies, 9*(3), 150–158. doi: 10.1016/0142-694X(88)90044-0

Hafeez, K., Foroudi, P., Dinnie, K., Nguyen, B., & Parahoo, S. K. (2016). The role of place branding and image in the development of sectoral clusters: The case of Dubai. *Journal of Brand Management, 23*(4), 383–402.

Hanzl, M. (2007). Information technology as a tool for public participation in urban planning: A review of experiments and potentials. *Design Studies, 28*(3), 289–307. doi:10.1016/j.destud.2007.02.003

Hassabis, D. (2017). Artificial intelligence: Chess match of the century. *Nature, 544*(7651), 413–414. doi:10.1038/544413a

Heilig, M. (2001). The cinema of the future. In R. Packer & K. Jordan (Eds.), *Multimedia: From Wagner to virtual reality* (pp. 219–231). W. W. Norton and Company. (Original work published 1955)

Hench, J. (2009). *Designing Disney.* Disney Editions.

Herrera, F., Bailenson, J., Weisz, E., Ogle, E., & Zaki, J. (2018). Building long-term empathy: A large-scale comparison of traditional and virtual reality perspective-taking. *PLOS One, 13*(10). doi:10.1371/journal.pone.0204494

Houlgate, S. (2016). Hegel's aesthetics. In E. N. Zalta (Ed.), *The Stanford encyclopedia of philosophy.* https://plato.stanford.edu/archives/spr2016/entries/hegel-aesthetics/

Huizinga, J. (1950). *Homo ludens: A study of the play-element in culture*. Roy Publishers. (Original work published 1938)

Imagineers Group (1996). *Walt Disney Imagineering: A behind the dreams look at making the magic real*. Disney Editions.

Is virtual reality real? (1993, October 28). *Nature, 365*(6449), 772. doi:10.1038/365772a0

Jaschke, K., & Ötsch, S. (Eds.). (2003). *Stripping Las Vegas: A contextual review of casino resort architecture*. Verl. d. Bauhaus-Universität.

Jenkins, H. (2001, June). Convergence? I diverge. *MIT Technology Review*, 93. http://web.mit.edu/~21fms/People/henry3/converge.pdf

Jenkins, H. (2003, January 15). Transmedia storytelling. *MIT Technology Review*. https://www.technologyreview.com/s/401760/transmedia-storytelling/

Jenkins, H. (2007). Narrative spaces. In F. von Borries, S. P. Walz, & M. Böttger (Eds.), *Space time play: Computer games, architecture and urbanism: The next level* (pp. 56–60). Birkhauser.

Jensen, B. (2013). Learning from Dubai: Is it possible? In A. Kanna (Ed.), *The superlative city: Dubai and the urban condition in the early twenty-first century* (pp. 60–73). Harvard University Graduate School of Design, Aga Khan Program.

Juul, J. (2013). *The art of failure: An essay on the pain of playing video games*. MIT Press.

Juul, J. (2019). *Handmade pixels: Independent video games and the quest for authenticity*. MIT Press.

Kanna, A. (2010). Flexible citizenship in Dubai: Neoliberal subjectivity in the emerging city-corporation. *Cultural Anthropology, 25*(1), 100–129.

Kanna, A. (2011). *Dubai, the city as a corporation*. University of Minnesota Press.

Kent, S. (2001). *The ultimate history of video games: From Pong to Pokemon and beyond*. Random House.

Keogh, B. (2018). *A play of bodies: How we perceive video games*. MIT Press.

Kim, H., Yang, S., Rao, S. R., Narayanan, S., Kapustin, E. A., Furukawa, H., Umans, A. S., Yaghi, O., & Wang, E. N. (2017). Water harvesting from air with metal-organic frameworks powered by natural sunlight. *Science, 356*(6336), 430–434. doi:10.1126/science.aam8743

King, M. (1981). Disneyland and Walt Disney World: Traditional values in futuristic form. *Journal of Popular Culture, 15*(1), 116–140.

Kitchin, R. (2011). The programmable city. *Environment and Planning B: Planning and Design, 38*(6), 945–951.

Kitchin, R., & Dodge, M. (2011). *Code/space: Software and everyday life*. MIT Press.

Klopfer, E., Haas, J., Osterweil, S., & Rosenheck, L. (2018). *Resonant games: Design principles for learning games that connect hearts, minds, and the everyday.* MIT Press.

Knight, W. (2019). Can machines be truly creative?—An interview with David Silver. *MIT Technology Review, 122*(2), 66.

Kohs, G. (Director). (2017). *AlphaGo* [Film]. Moxie Pictures.

Koutsabasis, P. (2012). On the value of virtual worlds for collaborative design. *Design Studies, 33*(4), 356–390. doi:10.1016/j.destud.2011.11.004

Kubovy, M. (1986). *The psychology of perspective and Renaissance art.* Cambridge University Press.

Laderman, S. (2014). *Empire in waves: A political history of surfing.* University of California Press.

Lanier, J. (2017). *Dawn of the new everything: A journey through virtual reality.* Henry Holt and Company.

Latour, B. (1996). *Aramis, or the love of technology.* Harvard University Press.

Leach, N. (2019). Do robots dream of digital sheep? *ACADIA 2019: Ubiquity and autonomy.* http://papers.cumincad.org/data/works/att/acadia19_298.pdf

Le Corbusier. (1987). *The city of to-morrow and its planning.* Dover Publications.

Lee, K. (2018). *AI superpowers: China, Silicon Valley, and the new world order.* Houghton Mifflin Harcourt.

Lemke, J. (2009). Multimodality, identity, and time. In C. Jewitt (Ed.), *The Routledge Handbook of Multimodal Analysis* (pp. 140–150). Routledge.

Lévy, P. (1997). Welcome to virtuality. *Digital Creativity, 8*(1), 3–10. doi:10.1080 /09579139708567068

Lévy, P. (1998). *Becoming virtual: Reality in the digital age.* Plenum Trade.

Levy-Warren, M. H. (2008). Computer games. In S. Turkle (Ed.), *The inner history of devices* (pp. 77–85). MIT Press.

Lewis, M. (2003). *Moneyball: The art of winning an unfair game.* W. W. Norton.

Loiperdinger, M., & Elzer, B. (2004). Lumiere's *Arrival of the Train*: Cinema's founding myth. *The Moving Image, 4*(1), 89–118. doi:10.1353/mov.2004.0014

Lynch, K. (1960). *Image of the city.* MIT Press.

Maher, J. (2013, March 20). The top of its game. *The Digital Antiquarian.* http://www .filfre.net/2013/03/the-top-of-its-game

Maher, M. L., Simoff, S., & Gabriel, G. (2000). Participatory design and communication in virtual environments. In *Proceedings of the Participatory Design Conference*

(New York, November 28–December 1). http://rossy.ruc.dk/ojs/index.php/pdc/article /viewFile/200/192

Manovich, L. (2000). *The language of new media*. MIT Press.

Martens, M. A., Antley, A., Freeman, D., Slater, M., Harrison, P. J., & Tunbridge, E. M. (2019). It feels real: Physiological responses to a stressful virtual reality environment and its impact on working memory. *Journal of Psychopharmacology*, *33*(10), 1264–1273. doi:10.1177/0269881119860156

Marx, P. (2019, December 9). The realer real. *The New Yorker*, 22–28.

Matthews, D. (2018). Virtual-reality applications give science a new dimension. *Nature*, *557*(7703), 127–28. doi:10.1038/d41586-018-04997-2

Maturana, H., & Varela, F. (1980). *Autopoiesis and cognition: The realisation of the living*. D. Reidel.

McCullough, M. (2006). On the urbanism of locative media. *Places*, *18*(2), 26–29.

McLuhan, M. (1962). *The Gutenberg galaxy*. University of Toronto Press.

McLuhan, M., & Fiore, Q. (1967). *The medium is the massage*. Bantam Books.

McNair, C. (2017). Worldwide internet and mobile users. eMarketer [Press Release]. https://www.emarketer.com/content/emarketer-updates-worldwide-internet-and -mobile-user-figures

Mead, S., & Black, K. (2001). Predicting the breaking intensity of surfing waves. *Journal of Coastal Research*, Special Issue 29, 51–65.

Meagher, M. (2015). Designing for change: The poetic potential of responsive architecture. Frontiers of Architectural Research, 4(2), 159–165. doi:10.1016/j.foar.2015.03.002

Meinardi, F., Mcdaniel, H., Carulli, F., Colombo, A., Velizhanin, K. A., Makarov, N. S., . . . Brovelli, S. (2015). Highly efficient large-area colourless luminescent solar concentrators using heavy-metal-free colloidal quantum dots. *Nature Nanotechnology*, *10*(10), 878–885. doi:10.1038/nnano.2015.178

Mele, A. R. (1997). Understanding and explaining real self-deception. *Behavioral and Brain Sciences*, *20*(1), 127–134. doi:10.1017/s0140525x9751003x

Miller, M. (2017). *An exploration of sherpas' narratives of living and dying in mountaineering*. [PhD thesis, University of Waterloo]. https://uwspace.uwaterloo.ca/bitstream /handle/10012/11895/Miller_Maggie.pdf?sequence=3&isAllowed=yDOI

Minnery, J. & Searle, G. (2014). Toying with the city? Using the computer game SimCity™4 in planning education. *Planning Practice & Research*, *29*(1), 41–55. doi:10 .1080/02697459.2013.829335

Minsky, M. (1980, June). Telepresence. *Omni Magazine*, 44–52. https://web.media .mit.edu/~minsky/papers/Telepresence.html

Mitchell, W. (1996). *City of bits*. MIT Press.

Mitchell, W. (1999). *E-topia*. MIT Press.

Moore, R. (2018, Nov 18). The world according to Archigram. *The Guardian*. https://www.theguardian.com/artanddesign/2018/nov/18/archigram-60s-architects-vision-urban-living-the-book

Moseley, G. L., Gallace, A., & Spence, C. (2012). Bodily illusions in health and disease: Physiological and clinical perspectives and the concept of a cortical "body matrix." *Neuroscience & Biobehavioral Reviews, 36*(1), 34–46. doi:10.1016/j.neubiorev.2011.03.013

Mugar, G., & Gordon, E. (2020). *Meaningful inefficiencies: Civic design in an age of digital expediency*. Oxford University Press.

Naimark, M. (2006). Aspen the verb: Musings on heritage and virtuality. *Presence: Teleoperators and Virtual Environments, 15*(3), 330–335.

Negroponte, N. (1969). Toward a theory of architecture machines. *Journal of Architectural Education, 23*(2), 9–12. doi:10.2307/1423828

Negroponte, N. (1970). *The architecture machine: Toward a more human environment*. MIT Press.

Negroponte, N. (1995). *Being digital*. Vintage.

Nichols, T. (2011). *The city as an entertainment machine*. Lexington Books.

Nijholt, A. (2017). Towards playful and playable cities. In A. Nijholt (Ed.), *Playable cities: The city as a digital playground* (pp. 1–20). Springer.

Nitsche, M. (2008). *Video game spaces. Image, play, and structure in 3D game worlds*. MIT Press.

Oxman, N., Laucks, J., Kayser, M. A., Uribe, C. D., & Duro-Royo, J. (2013). Biological computation for digital design and fabrication: A biologically-informed finite element approach to structural performance and material optimization of robotically deposited fibre structures. In R. Stouffs & S. Sariyildiz (Eds.), *Computation and performance: Proceedings of the 31st eCAADe Conference*. https://dam-prod.media.mit.edu/x/files/assets/pdf/278_%281%29.pdf

Panofsky, E. (1961). *La prospettiva come "forma simbolica" e altri scritti*. G. Feltrinelli.

Parsons, T., Gaggioli, A. & Riva, G. (2017). Virtual reality for research in social neuroscience. *Brain Sciences, 7*(12), 42. doi:10.3390/brainsci7040042

Pearson, L. C. (2019). System cities: Building a "quantitative utopia." *Architectural Design, 89*(4), 70–77. doi:10.1002/ad.2459

Pereira, A. L. (2009). Sport and risk: The case of high-altitude climbing. *European Journal for Sport and Society, 6*(2), 163–178. doi:10.1080/16138171.2009.11687836

Picard, M. (2014). Levels. In M. Wolf & B. Perron (Eds.), *The Routledge companion to video games studies* (pp. 99–106). Routledge.

Poole, S. (2000). *Trigger happy: Video games and the entertainment revolution.* Arcade.

Portman, M. E., Natapov, A., & Fisher-Gewirtzman, D. (2015). To go where no man has gone before: Virtual reality in architecture, landscape architecture and environmental planning. *Computers, Environment and Urban Systems, 54,* 376–384. doi:10.1016/j.compenvurbsys.2015.05.001

Rahwan, I., Cebrian, M., Obradovich, N., Bongard, J., Bonnefon, J.-F., Breazeal, C., Crandall, J. W., Christakis, N. A., Couzin, I. D., Jackson, M. O., Jennings, N. R., Kamar, E., Kloumann, I. M., Larochelle, H., Lazer, D., McElreath, R., Mislove, A., Parkes, D. C., Pentland, A., . . . Roberts, M. E. (2019). Machine behaviour. *Nature, 568,* 477–486. doi:10.1038/s41586-019-1138-y

Rapaille, C. (2007). *The culture code: An ingenious way to understand why people around the world live and buy as they do.* Broadway Books.

Ratti, C., & Claudel, M. (2015). *Open source architecture.* Thames & Hudson.

Riva, G., Wiederhold, B. K., & Mantovani, F. (2019). Neuroscience of virtual reality: From virtual exposure to embodied medicine. *Cyberpsychology, Behavior, and Social Networking, 22*(1), 82–96. doi:10.1089/cyber.2017.29099.gri

Roettl, J., & Terlutter, R. (2018). The same video game in 2D, 3D or virtual reality—How does technology impact game evaluation and brand placements?" *PLOS One,* 13(7). doi:10.1371/journal.pone.0200724

Rothman, H. (2015). *Neon metropolis: How Las Vegas started the twenty-first century.* Routledge.

Schindhelm, M. (2017). *Dubai high: A culture trip.* Arabian Publishing.

Schrijver, L. (2011). Utopia and/or spectacle? Rethinking urban interventions through the legacy of modernism and the situationist city. *Architectural Theory Review, 16*(3), 245–258. doi:10.1080/13264826.2011.621545

Schwartz, D. G. (2013). *Roll the bones: The history of gambling.* Winchester Books.

Sharp, J. (2015). *Works of game: On the aesthetics of games and art.* MIT Press.

Sheller, M. (2014). *Aluminum dreams: The making of light modernity.* MIT Press.

Shepard, M. (2011). *Sentient city: Ubiquitous computing, architecture, and the future of urban space.* MIT Press.

Sicart, M. (2014). *Play matters.* MIT Press.

Silver, D., Huang, A., Maddison, C. J., Guez, A., Sifre, L., van den Driessche, G., Schrittwieser, J., Antonoglou, I., Panneershelvam, V., Lanctot, M., Dieleman, S.,

Grewe, D., Nham, J., Kalchbrenner, N., Sutskever, I., Lillicrap, T., Leach, M., Kavukcuoglu, K., Graepel, T., & Hassabis, D. (2016). Mastering the game of Go with deep neural networks and tree search. *Nature, 529*(7587), 484–489. doi:10.1038/nature16961

Singer, D. G., & Singer, J. L. (2005). *Imagination and play in the electronic age.* Harvard University Press.

Skibba, R. (2018). Virtual reality comes of age. *Nature, 553*(7689), 402–403. doi:10.1038/d41586-018-00894-w

Sklar, M. (2015). *One little spark!: Mickey's Ten Commandments and the road to Imagineering.* Disney Electronic Content.

Solomon, R. C. (2009). Self, deception, and self-deception in philosophy. In C. Martin (Ed.), *The Philosophy of Deception* (pp. 15–36). Oxford University Press. doi:10.1093/acprof:oso/9780195327939.003.0002

Sommerlad, F. (2016). Promise and reality in Dubai's architectural design. In S. Wippel, K. Bromber, C. Steiner, & B. Krawietz (Eds.), *Under construction: Logics of urbanism in the Gulf region* (pp. 115–124). Routledge.

Song, Y., Chang, S., Gradecak, S., & Kong, J. (2016). Visibly-transparent organic solar cells on flexible substrates with all-graphene electrodes. *Advanced Energy Materials, 6*(20), 1600847. doi:10.1002/aenm.201600847

Sorkin, M. (2013). Origin of species. *Architectural Design, 83*(3), 60–67. doi:10.1002/ad.1591

Sutherland, I. E. (1965). The ultimate display. *Multimedia: From Wagner to virtual reality.* Retrieved from: http://www.w2vr.com/Book.html

Sutherland, I. E. (1968, December). A head-mounted three-dimensional display. In *Proceedings of the December 9–11, fall joint computer conference, part I* (pp. 757–764). ACM.

Sutton-Smith, B. (1997). *The ambiguity of play.* Harvard University Press.

Tarr, M. J. & Warren, W. H. (2002). Virtual reality in behavioral neuroscience and beyond. *Nature Neuroscience, 5*(S11), 1089–1092. doi:10.1038/nn948

Tassi, P. (2016, July 8). Here are the five best-selling video games of all time. *Forbes.* http://www.forbes.com/sites/insertcoin/2016/07/08/here-are-the-five-best-selling-video-games-of-all-time/#75ebe13d2dee

Tato, M., Papanikolaou, P., & Papagiannakis, G. (2012). From real to virtual rapid architectural prototyping. In M. Ioannides, D. Fritsch, J. Leissner, R. Davies, F. Remondino, & R. Caffo (Eds.), *Progress in Cultural Heritage: Preservation Lecture Notes in Computer Science* (pp. 505–512). Springer. doi:10.1007/978-3-642-34234-9_52

Themed Entertainment Association and AECOM. (2019). *TEA/AECOM 2018 Theme Index and Museum Index: Global attractions attendance report.* Themed Entertainment

Association. https://www.aecom.com/wp-content/uploads/2019/05/Theme-Index -2018-4.pdf

Thomas, B. (1994). *Walt Disney: An American original.* Hyperion.

Thompson, J. B. (1984). *Studies in the theory of ideology.* University of California Press.

Tibbits, S. (2017a). An introduction to active matter. In S. Tibbts (Ed.), *Active matter (pp. 11–17).* MIT Press.

Tibbits, S. (2017b). *Self-Assembly Lab: Experiments in programming matter.* Routledge.

Tibbits, S. (2017c). Conclusion: Active matter and beyond. In S. Tibbts (Ed.), *Active matter (pp. 339–343).* MIT Press.

Togelius, J. (2018). *Playing smart: On games, intelligence, and artificial intelligence.* MIT Press.

Townsend, A. (2006). Locative-media artists in the contested-aware city. *Leonardo, 39*(4), 345–347. doi:10.1162/leon.2006.39.4.345

Traverse, C. J., Pandey, R., Barr, M. C., & Lunt, R. R. (2017). Emergence of highly transparent photovoltaics for distributed applications. *Nature Energy, 2*(11), 849–860. doi:10.1038/s41560-017-0016-9

Tuters, M. (2012). From mannerist situationism to situated media. *Convergence: The International Journal of Research into New Media Technologies, 18*(3), 267–282. doi:10.1177/1354856512441149

Tuters, M., & Varnelis, K. (2006). Beyond locative media: Giving shape to the Internet of Things. *Leonardo, 39*(4), 357–363. doi:10.1162/leon.2006.39.4.357

Vale, L. (2014). *Architecture, power and national identity.* Routledge.

Venturi, R., Scott Brown, D., & Izenour, S. (1977). *Learning from Las Vegas: The forgotten symbolism of architectural form.* MIT Press.

Vilvestre, J. (2016, October 13). Future cities could be powered by windows that absorb sunlight. *Futurism.* https://futurism.com/future-cities-could-be-powered-by-windows -that-absorb-sunlight

von Borries, F., Walz, S. P., & Böttger, M. (Eds.). (2007). *Space time play: Computer games, architecture and urbanism: The next level.* Birkhauser.

Warner, M. (2004). Camera ludica. In L. Mannoni, W. Nekes, & M. Warner, *Eyes, lies and illusions: The art of deception (pp.13–23).* Hayward Gallery.

Weinstock, M., & Stathopoulos, N. (2006). Advanced simulation in design. *Architectural Design, 76*(2), 54–59. doi:10.1002/ad.240

White, H. (2009). *The content of the form: Narrative discourse and historical representation.* Johns Hopkins University Press.

Whitebread, D. (2018). Play: The new renaissance. *International Journal of Play*, *7*(3), 237–243. doi:10.1080/21594937.2018.1532952

Wiederhold, B. K., & Wiederhold, M. D. (2003). Three-year follow-up for virtual reality exposure for fear of flying. *CyberPsychology & Behavior*, *6*(4): 441–445. doi:10.1089/109493103322278844

Wieser, M. (1991, September). The computer for the 21st century. *Scientific American*, 94–104.

Williams, K., & Mascioni, M. (2017). *The out-of-home immersive entertainment frontier: Expanding interactive boundaries in leisure facilities*. Routledge.

Winnicott, D. W. (2005). *Playing and reality*. Routledge. (Original work published 1971)

Wright, F. L. (1935). *Broadacre City: A new community plan*. Architectural Record Publishing Company.

Zaki, J., & Ochsner, K. (2012). The neuroscience of empathy: Progress, pitfalls and promise. *Nature Neuroscience*, *15*(5), 675–680. doi:10.1038/nn.3085

Zenger, T. (2013, May 28). The Disney recipe. Harvard Business Review. https://hbr.org/2013/05/what-makes-a-good-corporate-st

Zosh, J. M., Hirsh-Pasek, K., Hopkins, E. J., Jensen, H., Liu, C., Neale, D., Solis, S. L., & Whitebread, D. (2018). Accessing the inaccessible: Redefining play as a spectrum. *Frontiers in Psychology*, *9*. doi:10.3389/fpsyg.2018.01124

Zukin, S. (1990). Socio-spatial prototypes of a new organization of consumption: The role of real cultural capital. Sociology, 24(1), 37–56.

Zukin, S. (2005). "Whose culture? Whose city?" In J. Lin & C. Mele (Eds.), *The urban sociology reader* (pp. 281–289). Routledge. (Original work published 1995)

Index